FROM VICTIMS OF CHANGE TO AGENTS OF CHANGE

The future of the teaching profession

edited by
Martin Johnson and
Joe Hallgarten

30-32 Southampton St
London WC2E 7RA
Tel: 020 7470 6100
Fax: 020 7470 6111
postmaster@ippr.org.uk
www.ippr.org
Registered charity 800065

The Institute for Public Policy Research is an independent charity whose purpose is to contribute to public understanding of social, economic and political questions through research, discussion and publication. It was established in 1988 by leading figures in the academic, business and trade-union communities to provide an alternative to the free market think tanks.

IPPR's research agenda reflects the challenges facing Britain and Europe. Current programmes cover the areas of economic and industrial policy, Europe, governmental reform, human rights, defence, social policy, the environment and media issues.

Besides its programme of research and publication, IPPR also provides a forum for political and trade union leaders, academic experts and those from business, finance, government and the media, to meet and discuss issues of common concern.

Production & design by **EMPHASIS**
ISBN 1 86030 197 5
© IPPR 2002

Contents

Preface

This publication is the result of a project undertaken by ippr between April 2001 and May 2002. Many conclusions are provisional and have been put forward to stimulate further discussion and research. The publication aims to be accessible to as wide an audience as possible, including teachers and parents. It is hoped that this publication will contribute to a process of wider, deeper thinking about the future of the teaching profession.

The book's first chapter summarises the editors' central conclusions from the project. Its subsequent chapters contain edited versions of most of the project papers. Other project papers are available on our website at www.ippr.org.

Acknowledgements

The editors would like to thank all those who have contributed to the ideas contained in this book, through seminars and informal discussions. As well as all the authors, we would particularly like to thank Sheila Dainton (ATL), John Howson (Education Data Services), Howard Kennedy (London Leadership Centre), Sandra Leaton Gray, Stephen Kershaw (DfES), Kathryn Riley (University of Roehampton) Ralph Tabberer (TTA) and Emma Westcott (GTCE) who gave valuable advice and support. We would also like to thank the following staff at ippr for their contribution to this publication: Laura Edwards, Peter Robinson, Jodie Reed, and Helena Scott. Naturally, none of the above carries any responsibility for the final version, which rests with the editors alone.

IPPR gratefully acknowledges financial support for this research project from The Esmée Fairbairn Foundation, the Paul Hamlyn Foundation and Protocol Teachers.

About the authors

Dara Barlin recently completed her MSc in Social Policy and Planning at the LSE. Prior to her research experience she held the postitions of labor relations specialist and political consultant with the American Federation of Teachers in Los Angeles. Dara is now a freelance researcher in the United States.

Tony Breslin taught and held senior and middle management positions at comprehensive schools in Haringey and Hertfordshire. Until August 2001 he was General Adviser (14-19 Education) in the London Borough of Enfield, and is now Chief Executive of the Citizenship Foundation.

Steve Haines is a freelance education researcher. He is graduate of York University and the Institute of Education, University of London where he specialised in Philosophy and Education. He has worked as a lecturer in special needs and currently works at the Qualifications and Curriculum Authority developing policy on national curriculum assessment.

Joe Hallgarten is a Senior Research Fellow in Education at the Institute for Public Policy Research. Prior to this, he was a primary school teacher in London and Manchester and a researcher at the National Union of Teachers' Education Action Zone Unit. Joe is currently leading a project on Local Exchange Trading Systems (LETS) in schools.

David Haselkorn is President of Recruiting New Teachers Inc, a US non-profit organisation dedicated to strengthening the teaching profession. He is the co-author of RNT's widely acclaimed *Careers in Teaching Handbook* and *How to Become a Teacher: A Complete Guide*. Mr Haselkorn was also a Senior Policy Advisor to the National Commission on Teaching and America's Future.

Merryn Hutchings is Reader in Education and Deputy Director of the Institute for Policy Studies in Education (IPSE) at the University of North London. Recent research projects focus on teacher supply and retention, social class and widening participation in HE, career and educational aspirations of young people, and the perspectives of girls in single-sex schools.

Martin Johnson is Education Researcher at the IPPR. He has over thirty years experience as a teacher, mainly in inner London, specialising in working with secondary pupils with behaviour difficulties. He is the author of *Failing School, Failing City*, an account of teaching in the most difficult secondary schools. He is currently working on a project on education in London.

Gill Penlington is a political analyst at the BBC. She was previously an education researcher at the Social Market Foundation, where her research interests included preschool learning, vocational education, and the role of the private and voluntary sectors in education.

Jodie Reed is a Consultant Research Assistant in Education at the IPPR and a graduate in Politics and Modern History from the University of Manchester.

Alistair Ross is Professor of Education and Director of the Institute of Policy Studies in Education at the University of North London (UK). He is International Coordinator of the Children's Identity and Citizenship in Europe Thematic Network, that links universities with interests in civic and social learning in 30 states. As well as a long-standing interest in children's political and social understanding, he has interests in social class and participation in higher education and in teachers' careers and teacher supply.

Elle Rustique-Forrester is a policy advisor with the General Teaching Council. Prior to this, she was a senior research fellow at the Centre for Educational Management, University of Surrey Roehampton, and was policy co-ordinator for the National Commission on Teaching & America's Future. She is a former high school teacher. Elle can be contacted at elle@merf.demon.co.uk.

Chris Yapp is a client principal at Compaq Global services. He has been involved in ICT aspects of education and training since 1994, including numerous policy groups in the UK and the EU. He is a Fellow of the Royal Society of Arts, a member of the RIIA, Chatham House, the Strategic Planning Society, and a Director of the Internet Society of England. Chris can be contacted at chris.yapp@compaq.com.

Foreword

If we are to meet the challenge of educating the next generation in a way that equips them for the future, then what is needed is nothing less than transformation of the teaching profession. We are in an era of profound change – a raft of government initiatives and the accumulated wisdom of the profession and research community on cognition, learning and pedagogy have all meant that classrooms and teaching are moving rapidly away from the familiar and traditional model of instruction. More momentum for change in professional practice comes from the increasingly swift application of advanced technologies in the service of learning and teaching. IPPR's informative and provocative contribution to the debate about the future of teaching comes at a critical and potentially transformational time for the teaching profession, with attrition from the profession causing considerable concern and recruitment into posts at its most testing. One of the most important messages in the book is a shared vision of the future of education that the teaching profession can own and shape – teachers as agents of change.

There exists a highly committed teacher workforce that has already demonstrated its capacity to raise standards. It is vital that the message of trust, so cogently called for in this publication, is expressed in a tone that recognises the need for teachers to own and engage with the Government's reform agenda, in order for it to be effective in the long term. The Government must demonstrate to teachers and to the public at large that it recognises and appreciates the fact that teachers are working harder and for longer hours, are raising standards, are improving teaching and at the same time taking on board a host of other responsibilities. There needs to be a massive boost to the morale of teachers, recognising that a high self-esteem, high trust profession is essential in order to build the capacity and enthusiasm for further improvement. At the moment, the sense of extreme overload among teachers is a cause for concern and must be addressed to avoid long term recruitment and retention problems. In order for schools to change significantly and for the profession to own the change, teachers will need to have the energy and positive motivation to innovate and develop practice that improves learning.

The General Teaching Council will take this debate forward through its work with teachers on the ground throughout the country, shaping education policy from within the ambit of the profession. The Council acts as a conduit for teachers to exert influence and to develop an authoritative professionalism, fit to meet the challenges of the future. The Council also has responsibility for demonstrating and maintaining the high standards which teachers set for themselves. The challenge for all of us, as set out so provocatively in the last section of this book, is how to orchestrate a movement for high quality teacher professionalism that will meet the needs of learners, parents, the community and the government.

Carol Adams
Chief Executive Officer, The General Teaching Council

1. The future of the teaching profession

Martin Johnson and Joe Hallgarten

IPPR's project, The Future of the Teaching Profession, was undertaken between March 2001 and April 2002. During that time, the future started to become the present. The period saw a huge transformation in the policy climate around teaching. One after the other, recommendations which might have been made at the end of the project were overtaken by announcements and action.

The speed and scale of change, together with the continuing high salience of the profession, presented both a boost and a challenge to us, the principal project staff. At the same time the project's key question remains as challenging now as it did then: 'How can the teaching profession be transformed to improve recruitment, retention and morale?' We hope this book, which brings together papers produced during the course of the project, both reflects upon some of the current issues and also looks towards a revitalised teaching force for the future. The analysis does not proceed from the point of view of the teacher: it derives from the needs of the pupil, the parent, the community, and the state in respect of schooling. It is assumed that all these interests require a teaching force which is sufficiently able and stable to induct the nation's young into society. It is also assumed that recent policies have created schools which are not addressing that task with sufficient breadth, so that schools must change, and with them the role of the teacher.

The future of the teaching profession is an issue not just for Britain, or Europe, but across the world. One factor facing many societies is the approaching bulge of retirement which makes the future supply of teachers problematic. In Chapter 5 Rustique-Forrester and Haselkorn provide some particularly illuminating insights into the experience of the United States. Many states are looking to replicate the English model of school improvement, with its heavy central demands on teachers, but others are looking beyond such approaches towards forms of schooling appropriate not just for an age of new technologies, but for an age in which philosophy must catch up with technology.

In this chapter we present an overview of our conclusions. Firstly, we argue that the government is right to concentrate on workload as the most unattractive feature of the profession. Questions about satisfying and dissatisfying features of the job, and their effect on teacher supply, are explored further in Chapter 2. It makes clear that the problem is not just the quantity but the nature of the work. Teachers resent work both when it is imposed and when it is not valued because it seems unnecessary or pointless. This represents a deprivation of professional autonomy, a characteristic of work expected by graduate employees and now demanded by teachers. The difficulty is that the government deliberately sought to impose work on teachers in support of its pupil standards agenda, and it must now find ways to maintain the momentum of that agenda while decentralising decision making about its delivery.

Secondly, we suggest that further increases in school funding are required in order to enhance staffing levels, of teaching staff in some cases and support staff everywhere. Schools as organisations are characterised by an absence of slack in staffing, so that every illness or vacancy is a crisis, and flexibility in deployment is impossible, but the future teacher will demand more flexible working patterns, and more time allocated to professional development.

Thirdly, we examine the Government's supposition that the job can be remodelled in such a way as to reduce demand for teachers by substituting other types of staff, or perhaps machines. There is no doubt that a radical reappraisal of current job content is needed, but its outcome ought to be a reduction in job size rather than a reduction in the numbers of teachers.

Lastly, we visualise a new direction for schools, and a new enhanced role for teachers. As world-class attainment in basic academic skills becomes embedded within schools, the excessively replicated central accountabilities and controls can be rationalised. With brave government, a large measure of accountability could be transferred to the local community served by the school. Teachers would become central to a negotiation between the school and the community on issues of curriculum, standards, culture and values. This, indeed, is a solution to the dilemma posed earlier: professional autonomy restored, but in a context of accountability which adds both status and challenge to the role.

At the end of its tether

At the project's inception, teaching appeared to be a profession at the end of its tether. Ever since the 1987 Teachers' Pay and Conditions Act and the 1988 Education Reform Act, teachers had felt themselves under a government cosh whose blows became progressively heavier. They believed they suffered an imposed and outdated curriculum, with frequent changes, a punitive inspection system, worsening staffing levels and tightening budgets, continually worsening pay levels in relation to other graduate occupations, ever-increasing bureaucratic demands, and continual attacks on the profession by the government, which together produced low morale, below-target recruitment to training, and the beginnings of staffing shortages.

The nadir was reached at the end of the nineties. Teachers had greeted the election of the Labour Government, confident of relief. Instead, the 'naming and shaming' episode, the re-appointment of the Chief Inspector, and the continuation of the spending squeeze plunged the profession into further depression. To this day, Labour is suffering from the credibility gap it established then. In 2002, teachers complain about government attacks on the profession though they ceased some years ago.

Do teachers and their representatives sound defensive and limited in vision? Perhaps that is the result of years of attack. The substantive change of attitude from the Government, which reached a first climax with the Secretary of State's speech to the Social Market Foundation in November 2001, will be regarded with scepticism and cynicism until teachers experience change in their working lives. Sadly, for this reason most of the debate on the future of the profession is taking place outside the profession. The apparent upsurge of militancy in Spring 2002 is a clear signal that the Government must not neglect the lag between a change in discourse at the top and a change in schools' experience. The Government has taken action on recruitment; many schools continue to suffer chronic staff turnover and shortage. The Government has taken action on workload; it has had no effect on teachers yet, and school managers resist it.

'Autonomy' is a key word in this debate. Job satisfaction for teachers is intimately connected with rights of decision in specific spheres of activity. Traditionally, these have centred on curriculum and pedagogy, with a freedom from detailed scrutiny of performance. Autonomy has been removed in every significant part of the job.

Research conducted by IPPR (Edwards 2002) confirmed the widespread negative feelings this generates. 'The teachers involved in the research, while on the whole enthusiastic about their work, felt downtrodden, stressed, overworked and undervalued…Linked to all of the negative factors of the job that have already been mentioned was a concern from both teachers and non-teachers that autonomy in the classroom is being undermined. A common complaint from both primary and secondary schoolteachers was that the curriculum was becoming increasingly restricted and allowed less room for teachers to make their own mark. Teachers described the pressure of covering every learning goal included in the literacy hour for example and often felt that there was not enough time to cover everything adequately. This was felt to lead to low morale. The primary school teachers in particular wanted more room to manoeuvre and make their own mark on their lessons.

> I thought you'd have time to get round creative ideas but the curriculum's so tight and you've only got one lesson to cover a particular thing. You're clock watching all the time in order to be able to cover everything
> *Primary school teacher*

The *principle* of a national curriculum was widely accepted at the time of its introduction, and has been hardly questioned since. Yet its detailed prescription of a subject-based model largely dating from 1902 has de-skilled teachers in the sense that they have been discouraged from both questioning the curriculum needs of their pupils and also developing innovative programmes. It has been taken for granted that the state has the duty to ensure a standard entitlement, but the appropriate contributions of teachers and parents and the community have been discarded. Whilst the 2002 Education Act and the Green Paper *14-19: Extending Opportunities, Raising Standards* start to restore some curriculum flexibility to secondary schools, the Government's desire for a teacher-led debate must continue to be signalled.

Simultaneously, the development of the interrelated structures of marketisation, inspection, and then target-setting produced very effective central government levers on teacher behaviour. The combination of an inspection system which emphasised records of policies and practices, and management newly devolved to school level but lacking training, confidence and competence led to paperwork overload. Teachers were required to write down everything they planned and did. What they did, particularly in primary schools, was to focus single-mindedly on the government-set targets.

Finally, the introduction of the literacy, numeracy, and then key stage three initiatives embedded central determination of pedagogy. After an initial recoil, the profession accepted this imposition because the imposed model seemed a good one – in many circumstances. Yet the concentration on the now very specific and narrow targets led to increased teaching to the test, a reduction in the range of pupil experience, and further reduced morale.

Box 1.1

NLS and NNS are having an impresssive degree of success, especially given the magnitude of the change envisaged (p77), *but*

- While focusing on targets may represent a useful starting point for large-scale reform, it may not be the best approach for continued success. (p82)
- A preoccupation with single achievement scores can have negative side effects, such as narrowing the curriculum that is taught or wearing people out as they focus on the targets. (*ibid*)
- We heard over and over in LEAs and schools that considerable time and energy are focused on test preparation. (*ibid*)
- ...[the Literacy and Numeracy Strategies] have added to teacher workload – particularly through time needed for planning, assessment, and documentation. (p83)
- ...it may be time for a shift in the balance of responsibility for the Strategies. (p85)
- The next stage of the literacy/numeracy reform may well be to strengthen efforts already underway and encouraged by DfES and the Strategies to build professional community both within and across schools. (p86)
- ...we suggest that national leaders re-engage in the kind of broader enquiry that led to the Strategies...it would be valuable for the system to engage in an investigation of the kinds of teachers and learners needed for the knowledge society, and then juxtapose these images against the kinds of teachers and learners being produced by implementation of the Literacy and Numeracy Strategies. (p89)

Watching & Learning 2, OISE/UT Evaluation of the Implementation of the National Literacy and National Numeracy Strategies Earl *et al* University of Toronto 2001

The literacy and numeracy strategies are described in Whitehall as models of public service reform. Independent evaluations (OISE 2001, see Box 1.1) are more balanced, and the government must avoid the temptation to seek to replicate their approach in dissimilar situations, or without noting their negative features. The cumulative weight of open admissions and pupil-led funding, league tables, and Ofsted is normally underestimated as the major driver of schools' responses to central initiatives. In particular, far from being a disinterested evaluator of school performance, Ofsted has operated as the Department's police, checking on whether the initiatives have been implemented as instructed.

The resulting workload is unacceptable to the profession. According to the most authoritative recent study (PwC 2001), for primary teachers it equates to over 47 hours per week over a 46 week working year. Both the total time, and the unwelcome nature of much of the work, contribute to demoralisation.

The essential paradox is that during this period of demoralisation due to workload and loss of autonomy, teachers, particularly primary, have improved their skills and transformed their performance. Very detailed planning of every lesson, and execution with absolute concentration on the individual attainment of those central targets, has led to continuous improvement in pupil attainment in the areas tested. The Chief Inspector has confirmed that the quality of teaching is better than ever (Ofsted 2002).

The problem for the Government, then, is how to maintain the drive for pupil attainment, how to ensure central leverage over decentralised delivery, while reducing the alienating effects of this pressure on the workforce. Indeed, this was an explicit theme within the SMF speech. The Government's own Performance and Innovation Unit has also recognised this issue. In its report on 'better policy delivery and design' the PIU argued: 'Excessive directive methods of government that appear to treat front-line deliverers as unable to think for themselves, untrustworthy or incompetent, undermine the very motivations and adaptability on which real-world success depends… Driving through policies with an implicit assumption that the main players are the problem, rather than part of the solution, is usually a recipe for failure' (Performance and Innovation Unit 2001).

Despite the success of some of the recent centralised interventions, it seems likely that such central prescription will begin to have diminishing returns.

Supporting teachers

The Government's intention to act on workload has become increasingly explicit, from the retention of PwC to conduct a thorough review, through a reference to the STRB, to the establishment of the Remodelling the Profession group. Some of its prescriptions, such as the transfer to other staff of peripheral duties, and the more widespread use of IT, command general support and merely await the injection of the necessary resources. However, these are longer term solutions. As yet, the Government continues to repeat the arguments of the headteachers that contractual limits on working hours are 'unprofessional' (a concept considered by Tony Breslin in Chapter 11) or would unreasonably confine management flexibility.

However, as Chapter 2 shows, headteachers have not learnt to prioritise, that is to manage, the work of their staffs. The Government must find a tool to produce a rapid cultural change in headteachers' offices; exhortation, even expressed in DfEE circulars, has been ineffective, and a revised contract remains the most powerful. As a matter of social policy, the government should also introduce a contract which is family friendly and supports a work-life balance. Johnson (2001) argues that a reasonable working year would be around 37.5 hours per week over a 46 week year, an annual total of 1,725 hours. This compares with current actual hours in excess of 2,100, and the trades unions' current implied claim of 1,460 hours.

The contract should also be revised in line with the Government's view of how the profession needs to be transformed. If admin is to be transferred, it should no longer be a duty; if the key tasks are the preparation and execution of lessons, realistic time allocations should be made. Johnson suggests that high quality lessons demand a 1:1 correspondence between preparation and execution, and calculates a contractual allowance of 19.3 hours per week for each.

At the same time, the Government should audit its own policies for their teacher workload content, in relation to the value of the output. In particular, it must enforce a rationalisation of the multiple and overlapping accountabilities on teachers, which include not only performance management, but also pupil target setting, management requirements on recording of lesson plans and other activity, and duplicate inspection by local authority and Ofsted.

Give us some slack

Many of the dissatisfiers in teaching could be removed by further increases in staffing. This is dependent on further funding increases arising from the Public Spending Review. The Secretary of State has noted the increased number of teaching posts created as a result of the funding improvements of 1999-2001, and exhorts schools to think twice about the kinds of extra staff required. However, secondary schools in particular are aware that pupil teacher ratios remain higher than a decade ago; this translates into larger classes, a higher contact ratio, and extra work. Considerable reduction in pupil teacher ratio will be necessary before schools are likely to conclude that they have sufficient teachers – and this is unlikely to occur until produced by reductions in pupil numbers, in primary from 2000 and secondary from 2005.

The Secretary of State frankly states that it will not be possible to find the additional teachers required. We believe it essential to transform the job to make it sufficiently attractive to do so. Taking together the small potential increase in 'standard' graduate entry, the much greater potential in locally recruiting underqualified groups, in career development for support staff, in encouraging career changers, and particularly in encouraging the return of inactive teachers, a group studied by Gill Penlington in Chapter 3, recruitment numbers could add up, particularly if the transformation also encourages retention. These issues are considered in more detail in the following four chapters.

The gain from increased staffing levels can be summarised as improved flexibility. As compared with most organisations, schools are currently characterised by a lack of slack in staffing, so that any absence or vacancy creates a crisis. More flexible deployment would allow better ways of dealing with absence, would enable staff training, give time for staff liaison. It would also ease flexible employment patterns. Staff would be attracted by part-time, job-share and other family friendly employment practices.

Who does what?

Remodelling the profession is a process which also depends on continuing increased resources for schools. Some accounts of remodelling school staffing assume a reduction in demand for teachers as other staff substitute for them. Predictions of the trend depend on the future of the one teacher, one class form of organisation which has persisted since the introduction of mass education. Some visions depend on independent individual learners sitting at individual monitors as an alternative, but they may be based on a partial analysis of the sociology of schooling. Pupils, particularly from disadvantaged backgrounds, often give bleak accounts of their school experience, but that may be a reflection of the culture they bring into school. If so, models of teaching must contend with the pupil as unwilling learner, a phenomenon of all state education systems highlighted by the PISA report (OECD 2001).

Further, state schooling is inevitably concerned with more than pedagogy. It has socialisation and social control functions. Indeed, one of the fascinations of teaching is the tension between the vision of opening out young minds to a world of possibilities on the one hand, and on the other the routine of requiring discipline and conformity. Forms of organisation in school are determined at least as much by the latter as the former. Traditionally, much of this learning has been in what was called the 'hidden curriculum', unplanned practices connected with classroom and school organisation and routines.

For these reasons, teaching and learning in state schools will remain a social activity. Neither the machine aided auto-didacticism idealised by the IT dreamer, nor that plus the one-to-one tutorial, can provide the motivation for the reluctant, or experience and learning about group behaviour. Chris Yapp gives further thought to this issue in

Chapter 11. No doubt pedagogies and organisation will become more flexible when IT is fully integrated into schools, and staffing increases will allow more one-to-one support for those who need it, but the basic unit of school organisation will continue to be the class – a group of pupils with a small group of staff. If resources allow, perhaps the normal size of the group will decline, towards 25, but schools will have classes.

This is the background for consideration of the development of new staffing structures. One model has a smaller number of teachers acting as learning managers, and leading teams of other staff. Teachers would form an elite, highly paid cadre. This model is flawed for one simple reason. Analysis of the variety of tasks undertaken by teachers, with a view to transferring some of them to other kinds of staff, reveals that the most highly-skilled, difficult, and exhausting task is to teach a lesson to a class. It requires a different order of skill, and therefore training, than activities such as ordering stock, compiling data, or even designing curriculum. It also requires a different order of skill than working with an individual or small group on one specific learning task which has been organised by another member of staff; this is typically the work now undertaken by classroom assistants. With schools remaining organised in classes, teachers will remain the largest group of staff.

The outcome of the remodelling exercise will be the recognition of the lesson as the central and overwhelming focus of the work of teachers, and a further increase in expectations of the quality of lessons. In a sense, the teacher's role will be reduced in scope, in order to concentrate on pedagogy. The transfer of other duties will not reduce the demand for teachers: it will reduce their workload and enhance their ability to deliver those expectations.

Some of the transfer, such as clerical and administrative work, is unproblematic, given the funding to employ additional staff. The issues arise with work involving greater pupil contact, such as supervision. Currently, supervisors are likely to be responsible for order in the playground at lunchtime, and are likely to be low-paid and low-trained. Their effectiveness is mixed, but in many secondary schools they are unsuccessful, with senior members of teaching staff required to resolve the incidents which supervisors encounter. Being of the same community as the pupils is an insufficient basis for an adult to achieve compliance from a group of young people; supervision requires a high level of interpersonal skills.

At the moment, most supervision of the classes of absent teachers is carried out by supply teachers. As Barlin and Hallgarten show in Chapter 4, this is now a business turning over £600 million, and there are increasing concerns about cost and quality control, as well as the effects of the casualisation of the profession on the stability of children's educational experience. The Secondary of State wondered aloud whether there is a case for expert supervisors to cover the classes of absent teachers, but the case depends on the development of a job with training, qualification and pay levels far higher than current.

The future school staff, then, will have a larger range of jobs, and of potential roles within each job (see Box 1.2). There will be a restoration of the classroom assistant to perform routine tasks such as the legendary (but infrequent in practice, except in early years) cleaning the paint pots, but also wiping up the sick, mounting displays, maintaining equipment. There will be an increase in clerical, administrative, technical and learning resources staff. Support for individual pupils will develop, requiring more mentors and counsellors, as well as home and community liaison staff. These will relieve teachers of much of the 'pastoral work' which is currently so time-consuming. The range of jobs needs a standard ladder of entry qualifications, varying from levels two to five, pay and conditions, and training. It will become much more common for people from unskilled backgrounds to work their way to become qualified teachers in their local schools, and there are a number of social policy benefits to this development.

Box 1.2 A staffing typology for the future school

pupil related
  individual support
    teaching assistant
    special needs assistant
    nursery nurse
    counsellor
    mentor
    home liaison worker
  group work
    supervisor
    main scale teacher
    upper scale teacher
    advanced skills teacher
    community liaison worker
back-up
  clerical/admin (for all pupil related staff)
  classroom assistant
  lab/workshop technician
  IT manager
  learning resources manager
  catering
  cleaning
  maintenance

One implication of the increase in number and variety of jobs is the more complex management task. Staff communication will become even more important. To counter the possibility of demarcation problems, team-building, co-ordination, and flexible staff deployment must be developed. In the light of the current quality of management, there are considerable implications for training.

Any such remodelling must aim to make every job within a school attractive. If teachers merely pass the least attractive elements of their job down the line, we may merely pass shortage problems in a similar direction. Career progression in these professions is an obvious factor, but the pay issue cannot be ignored. The welcome increases in national expenditure in education must benefit all those in education, from learners to teachers, cleaners to Heads.

A learning profession

The much more specific role of teachers will be associated with more stress on professional development, continuous updating of skills by reference to research findings and best practice. The Government's aspirations with regard to the continuing professional development of teachers are sound. They require contractual changes, now under consideration, cultural change, and significant further increases in funding. Few schools devote much management time to staff training and development, and the introduction of a compulsory performance management system has had little impact on this as yet. Part of the problem is the simple practicality: training outside the pupil day is unpopular and may be unproductive if the participants are exhausted, but training within the pupil day is disruptive. This difficulty will be resolved when levels of teaching and supervisory staff are improved so that satisfactory arrangements for covering for absent staff become possible.

A feature of the literacy and numeracy strategies was a central judgement on good pedagogical practice followed by a rigidly prescriptive universal dissemination. As it turned out, the judgement was accepted by the generality of primary teachers. This could be effective where the aims related to a finite and comparatively easily measurable set of skills and knowledge. Such a method will be more difficult where the aims relate to social skills and process. Systematic networks of communication about good practice must allow upward as well as downward flows.

All teachers should have an individual professional development programme, self-generated as much as management determined. Training costs must be met and time provided as a sign of the value attached. The contract should recognise professional development as both a right and a duty. The current duty is to work for five days a year under the direction of the head, but not specifically for training. This should be abolished, and replaced by a duty on the teacher to engage in professional development for 70 hours a year, and a duty on the employer to provide appropriate development opportunities and an agreed individual programme. Further, as part of a radical revision of pay structure, access to and advance along the top pay scale should be by further qualification (Johnson 2001).

Training activity will vary between observation and reflection of other teachers' good practice, through subject refresher courses, to academic study and research.

Presently, training has a poor image because of quality issues. In some cases, such as the New Opportunities Fund IT training, a cheap product is a poor product; in others, the free market in whole-school training days lacks quality control. Schools need an external support to help regulate their development programme. Appropriately sized local education authorities seem the obvious location.

Another substantial training challenge, mentioned above, is in management. The coincidence of the introduction of local management and mechanisms of intense national pressure has resulted in negative styles of management in schools, which are a major source of dissatisfaction within the profession. School managers must be trained to view staff as the overwhelmingly important resource in schools, the role of management as supporting and enabling staff to be effective, and to devote a substantial proportion of budget to staff development.

Relaxation lessons?

If teachers are to focus on the lesson, what constraints will there be? How can the Government resolve the dilemma between central prescription and professional dissatisfaction?

An essential prerequisite for this resolution is that the Government must relax a bit. It must reassess the evidence about both the performance of schools and their popularity. It must believe that a state service which is preferred to private alternatives (affordable to an increasing number of parents) by a consistent 93 per cent of parents must be doing something right. It must accept that the service is being delivered by public servants with commitment and honest endeavour. It must appreciate the continual improvement in pupil performance revealed by formal assessments.

This is not to advocate a washing of hands. It is to advocate policies which seek to encourage bottom up continuous improvement, with a limited central identification of weaknesses which need particular efforts. In order to rejuvenate the teaching profession, government must accept that ten speeches by ministers praising it are counter-productive if they are followed by one initiative which displays a lack of trust. These things are generally believed, accepted, and appreciated. It is unfortunate that policy is being unduly influenced by a small group of people on the basis of their superficial knowledge of a small and untypical group of schools. In particular, the goal for all public services to 'be designed around the needs of the user', and to allow 'greater choice for the consumer', as the prime minister has asserted, is unachievable unless the centre learns to let go.

There is no doubt that national targets for pupil attainment have been an effective lever on school behaviour. They performed the service of reminding us all of the prime importance of basic literacy and numeracy skills. That has been thoroughly absorbed in primary schools, although monitoring is required to ensure that there is no draining away of that perspective.

However, they have two kinds of drawbacks. Firstly, national curriculum test results have been used in a variety of ways which cannot be sustained by the data. Most obviously, their widespread use as an indicator of the quality of the school is quite clearly unsupportable, and damaging to schools with disadvantaged intakes.

Secondly, the problems of disciplining teachers by undue attention to a narrow range of pupil outcomes are becoming clear. For both teachers and pupils, the test result is the object, and learning becomes secondary. It is very like the driving test; we adopt behaviours necessary to pass, such as driving at less than 30 miles per hour when necessary, but forget or discard them as soon as we gain the certificate.

As the importance of lifelong learning continues to grow, so does the inculcation at school of commitment to learning. Further significant improvements in pupil outcomes will depend on motivating the demotivated. Indeed, motivation is increasingly seen to be at least as important as 'ability' in achievement for all pupils. Instrumental attitudes to certification are barriers; instead, we must return attention to the processes of education, to curricula and pedagogies which engage.

The end of credentialism?

As argued above, the national curriculum and associated testing have ossified the curriculum. The Government has recognised this, but its version of flexibility is to introduce additional vocational choices into key stage four. Vocationalism at compulsory school age profoundly misreads the workforce needs of employers and the economy, quite apart from any inappropriate weighting of those needs as against society's requirements of education.

Both employers and society need young people not with more knowledge, but with improved social skills, defined widely. We need oral communication skills. We need interpersonal skills and teamwork. We need better understanding of self, community, and society. We need young people who have self-esteem because they have discovered their own creativity and imagination. We need young people who are disciplined and self-disciplined, who can promote the social above the personal.

For some older pupils, workplace related learning may be a means to some of those ends. This analysis argues for a much more radical revision of curriculum and pedagogy, with a reassertion of creative and expressive arts and crafts and social studies, including, of course, citizenship.

However, such a curriculum would not be amenable to the comparatively simple assessment procedures of the national tests. Instead, teachers must be empowered once again to design such curricula and pedagogies, because they are in the best position to judge how to engage young people. If process is to be valued again, then teachers must be empowered to assess pupil performance directly. This raises issues of standardisation and quality control, but the profession's assessment skills have been transformed in the last decade, as a result of the introduction of national curriculum levels.

We conclude, then, that professional autonomy in the core activities of curriculum and pedagogy should be restored, not only to make the job more attractive, but to improve the educational experience of young learners. But this should not be an entirely unco-ordinated autonomy.

Central control...?

It is inconceivable to return to teachers all decisions on what is taught in schools. As the main funder, Whitehall must retain rights. As a key public service, education must remain subject to central democratic control. The judgement to be made is about subsidiarity, the principle that different kinds of decision should be made at different levels. We argue that teaching will be made more attractive, and indeed that the service to pupils will be enhanced, if detailed decisions about curriculum and pedagogy are made locally by teachers, at the centre of the community. However, these decisions must be made within two contexts.

The first is the overall strategic aims and priorities set by government. The Department for Education and Skills Strategic plan for the period to 2006 lists 32 targets, a dozen of which relate to schools (see Box 1.3). Many are structural, but others depend on work by teachers in schools. The strategic plan could be developed into an significant policy instrument, perhaps agreed after explicit public and political consultation and debate, and written in a way which would give a clear steer to other players, including schools, as to the foci for their activity.

Indeed, there is a case for the profession itself to lead such a process. In partnership with pupils, parents, and the wider community, teachers could devise their own preferred priorities and targets, and seek to negotiate with the Government (and in particular the Treasury) on their adoption as public service agreement targets. There are some difficulties about how the process could be organised and led, but the period up to 2004, when the next spending review will take place, is sufficiently long to devise a procedure and conduct a full debate on what areas of learning should be the focus for the next set of PSAs. It may even be possible to debate the assessment methods to be used. Teachers could be the first to develop a new model for giving public servants and service users ownership of the success criteria by which they are judged.

Box 1.3 Targets for schools

- Increase the percentage of 11-year-olds who achieve Level 4 in each of the Key Stage 2 English and maths tests to 85 per cent, by 2004.
- Narrow the attainment gap, by ensuring that there are no Local Education Authorities where less than 78 per cent of pupils achieve these standards.
- Increase the percentage of 11-year-olds who achieve Level 5 in each of the Key Stage 2 English and maths tests to 35 per cent, by 2004 (additional target announced on 13 March 02).
- Ensure that by 2007, 85 per cent of 14-year-olds achieve Level 5 or above in each of the key stage 3 tests in English, maths and ICT and 80 per cent in science:
  - as milestones towards these targets, 75 per cent to achieve Level 5 in English, maths and ICT, and 70 per cent in science by 2004;
  - for 2004, as a minimum performance target at least 65 per cent to achieve Level 5 and above in English and maths, and 60 per cent in science in each LEA and
  - reduce from the current 25 per cent to 15 per cent by 2004 the proportion of pupils who do not achieve at least one Level 5 at Key Stage 3 in English, maths or science, thereby narrowing the attainment gap.
- Increase the percentage of pupils obtaining 5 or more GCSEs at Grades A* to C (or equivalent) by four percentage points between 2002 and 2004 with at least 38 per cent achieving this standard in every LEA by 2004.
- Increase the percentage of pupils obtaining 5 or more GCSEs at Grades A* to G (or equivalent) including English and maths so that by 2004, 92 per cent of 16-year-olds reach this standard.
- Increase the number of specialist schools to at least 1,500 by 2005 and raise the number of Beacon Schools and City Academies year on year.
- Reduce year on year the number of secondary schools classed as failing.
- Ensure that by 2006 no school has fewer than 25 per cent of pupils achieving 5 higher grades at GCSE.
- Ensure that all pupils who are permanently excluded obtain an appropriate full-time education.
- Reduce unauthorised absence from schools by 10 per cent between 2002 and 2004.
- Increase by 3 percentage points the numbers of 19-year-olds achieving a qualification equivalent to NVQ level 2, compared to 2002, by 2004.
- Increase the proportion of 19 year olds achieving a level 3 qualification from 51 per cent in 2000 to 55 per cent in 2004.

Education and Skills, Delivering Results: A Strategy to 2006 at www.dfes.gov.uk./delivering-results/contents.shtml

---

...or community influence?

The second context is the needs and aspirations of the communities served by the school. Theoretically, these were expressed through the mechanisms of the local education authority, but their recent marginalisation has left a gap. An expansion of staffing to include specialised home and community liaison workers would permit a range of important developments.

Firstly, there could be a more effective articulation of the specific curriculum needs of local children and young people. Within the overall principles laid down by government, the curriculum offer of a school or group of schools would be determined by negotiation between the community and the staff. This would be the means of producing a proper diversity between schools, as opposed to the artificial marketised creation currently touted by Downing Street. Secondly, it would allow a coherent reformulation of the school's role to transmit culture. Effective community involvement would reinvigorate the reflection of the range of local cultures which has been under pressure since the introduction of the national curriculum.

However, this does raise the issue of conflict between local cultures, and between them and the culture of the school. A teacher confronted with a GCSE student who is being forced into an unwanted marriage is at the centre of a complex ethical problem. The introduction of citizenship into the curriculum already makes it more difficult to sidestep such problems. The outcome must be that school staff, including teachers, must work with their communities to build shared values and shared views on acceptable behaviour.

This will be much easier if school staff, particularly teachers, become more representative of their communities. Chapters 6 and 7 explore the ethnic and gender makeup of the teaching force. Ross argues that it is important for all schools to have teachers from ethnic minorities, because it is white pupils who need to confront society's racism, but also that far more ethnic minority teachers are needed in areas of ethnic minority population concentration. Hutchings reveals the complexities of gender issues in teaching, pointing out that we need more men in some areas of the profession, and more women in others, if schools are to become appropriate models of gender and power relations. Class is also a factor, because that fraction of the middle class which dominates our 'elite' universities rarely enters the profession. Hallgarten examines this phenomenon in Chapter 8.

If we are correct in believing that social education will become a higher priority, then a local input into such questions is vital if the school's teaching is to have legitimacy. As society increasingly deplores social disorder and simultaneously feels powerless to impose order, a school-community axis may be the only site for positive intervention.

We argue, then, for the development of institutions and processes at local level which would enable the local community to replace Whitehall as the main agent of accountability for schools. Prescriptive central targets would be replaced by more general principles and frameworks; it would be for the community to establish precise targets for its schools, related to the curriculum it had selected. National inspection would continue to provide data and alert government where action was required, perhaps on non-compliance with national frameworks, or on excessive inequality.

In such a system, teachers would be central to designing and negotiating both curriculum and pedagogy. With plenty of off-the-shelf models and ample research time and support available, this would not be the onerous task feared by some, but would promote their status as pivotal professionals for national social development. This may seem like an excessively grand vision for the future role of the teacher. In reality, teachers have always dealt in these matters, but the recent impositions have made it difficult to devote the necessary time to them. An explicit recognition of this role of schools, and a grant to teachers of the autonomy to develop it within a national strategic framework and supported by sufficient training, would not only revitalise the profession but support other important social policy objectives.

Agents of change

The idea that teachers should be agents of change is not a new one, yet its practice would be. As Tony Breslin's chapter explains, we should not wish to 'restore' the standing and role of teachers to any misinformed golden age. Even when they were relatively autonomous, teachers retained control mainly of their own 'secret gardens' – these may not have been penetrated, but rarely did they penetrate other schools, localities, or national policies. For the last two decades, teachers have been the victims of change. Government viewed them as an obstruction to be overcome in the implementation of the Education Reform Act. A different government viewed them as passive tools to be used in its centralised push on standards. It is time once again to see teachers for what they are: a highly skilled workforce, committed to public service and the betterment of the nation's children and young people, an important resource in the grass roots implementation of social policy objectives. With a mixture of appropriate support and benign neglect from government, and renewed engagement of parents and the wider community, teachers can finally become genuine agents of change.

References

Edwards L (2002) *Only If...* at www.ippr.org.uk/research

OECD (2001) *Knowledge and Skills for Life* Paris: OECD

OISE (2001) Earl L, Levin B, Leithwood K, Fullan M and Watson N *Watching and Learning 2, OISE/UT Evaluation of the Implementation of the National Literacy and National Numeracy Strategies* London: DfES

PricewaterhouseCoopers (2001) *PricewaterhouseCoopers Teacher Workload Study, Interim Report* at www.dfes.gov.uk

Johnson M (2001) *A 21st Century Contract* at www.ippr.org.uk/research

Ofsted (2002) *Standards and Quality in Education 2000/01: The Annual Report of HMCI* London: HMSO

Performance and Innovation Unit (2001) *Better Policy Delivery and Design* London: The Cabinet Office

2. Making teacher supply boom-proof

Martin Johnson

The aim of this chapter is to investigate the truth about the supply of and demand for teachers, in both short and longer terms. It also attempts to suggest some ways in which supply may be maximised. Teacher shortages are not a new phenomenon, particularly in London and the South-East. When the economy is booming, some schools are struggling. In the late 1980s, vacancy levels in London were higher than current levels, and the Inner London Education Authority trawled Europe and further afield to attract staff. Is teaching always to be unattractive when a range of alternative graduate opportunities abounds?

We begin by looking at the facts of current supply of and demand for teachers, before moving on to projections of future supply and demand. We then turn to some policy implications for the situation we find. Notwithstanding some trends within society generally towards greater career mobility, it will be essential in the short term to maximise retention if the supply of teachers is to be adequate. Research findings on the sources of job satisfaction and dissatisfaction for teachers indicate that intrinsic features of the job are undoubtedly the most important. Hence, if more people are to be retained in the profession, or to be encouraged to return, deeper thinking is required about teacher roles and job content.

Supply

The supply of teachers may be defined as that number of adults of working age who are qualified, and either in employment or prepared to be in employment as teachers. The bulk of teacher supply consists of those in service. Historically, the largest number of primary teachers ever employed was just under 200,000 (full-time equivalents, England only), in 1976, with the peak for secondary teachers being 232,000 in 1980. After a reduction in numbers by almost 10 per cent in the first half of the eighties, during a period of falling pupil numbers, there was a more gradual decline, which continued until the mid-nineties. In 1998, there was another slight fall. Only in 1999 did rapid and significant increases begin. In January 1998 there were 397,700 teachers in service, but within three years the number had risen to 410,300, the highest since the late eighties. Of these, 206,500 were primary, if the 11,600 occasional teachers are included, so that the employment of primary teachers is at an all-time high.

Two trends are worth noting. One is a long-term trend of increasing numbers of

Table 2.1 Teachers in service in England (FTE), thousands, by year									
	1985	*1990*	*1995*	*1996*	*1997*	*1998*	*1999*	*2000*	*2001*
Number of teachers	414.9	405.1	399.6	399.8	399.2	397.7	401.2	404.6	410.3

Sources: DfEE 2000a Table 14 and DfEE SFR 16/2001

part-time teachers, rising from under 36,000 in 1985 to 52,000 in 1990 and almost 69,000 in 2000 (almost 66,000 of whom are in England). The other is the growth of occasional, or supply teachers, who numbered 16,600 in 2000 and 19,000 in 2001. There is a close correspondence between the increase in supply teachers and the increase in vacancies, and this is examined further in Chapter 4.

The PIT contained 289,000 teachers in March 1999 (England), of whom 71,200 were aged under fifty and had taught some time within the previous 6 years. 33,000 of these were secondary teachers (DfEE 2000a). A survey in 1991 found that 17 per cent them intended to return in the future, with 42 per cent undecided. On the assumption that intentions are unchanged, 5,610 secondary teachers who have taught recently and are under fifty intend to return. A further 13,860 are undecided, on the same assumption. In current circumstances, it would be beneficial to discover whether this pool exists, and if so, how to entice it back into service.

Demand

Demand for teachers may be measured by the number of teachers in service plus the number of vacancies. The former is described above.

Vacancies

The DfES defines a vacancy as 'a full-time permanent appointment (or an appointment of at least one term's duration) that was advertised but not filled.'

The vacancy figures certainly do not tell the whole story about staffing difficulty, particularly in relation to quality issues, but there are two ways in which they are valuable. Firstly, the definition provides a good indicator of the excess of demand over supply, in the sense that no suitable teacher is both willing and able to take up that number of posts. The work is being done by people who are not prepared to undertake the whole responsibility of the job on a permanent basis. While the number of vacancies increased by 2,020 between January 2000 and January 2001, the number of supply teachers increased by 2,400.

Secondly, the DfES statistics are collected on the basis of a stable and precise definition, and thus have the benefit of reliability, critically enabling a long-term analysis of vacancy trends.

Table 2.2 Teacher vacancies in primary and secondary schools, England, 1989-2001

	Secondary		Primary	
	Number	%	Number	%
1989	2424	1.3	3116	1.8
1990	2778	1.5	3716	2.1
1991	1977	1.1	3245	1.9
1992	824	0.5	1074	0.6
1993	550	0.3	793	0.5
1994	624	0.4	762	0.4
1995	517	0.3	793	0.5
1996	587	0.3	861	0.5
1997	726	0.4	1088	0.6
1998	968	0.6	1391	0.8
1999	939	0.5	1376	0.8
2000	1246	0.7	1420	0.8
2001	2580	1.4	2110	1.3

Sources: STRB Reports, DfEE SFR/16/2001

Table 2.2 shows a cyclical pattern which relates closely to the economic cycle, and in particular the market for graduate employment. 1989-90 was a particularly difficult period, and in percentage terms more difficult than present. We must also notice the unparalleled jump between 2000 and 2001, of some 70 per cent, which led DfEE to question whether headteachers had completed the form accurately.

The series of surveys of vacancies in secondary schools, carried out by the Times Educational Supplement in conjunction with the Secondary Heads Association, consistently gives higher figures than the official statistics. Its figure for September 2001, 5,000, should be compared with the 4,600 reported in January 2001. As yet, there is no explanation for the discrepancy, but the series is beginning to have utility as another indicator of trend. Taking both sets of data, it is reasonable to believe that the number of vacancies in secondary schools increased during 2001, and that the situation is now as serious as in the previous peak in 1990. In primary schools, vacancy levels have not reached those of 1990.

In comparison with other occupations, vacancy rates of around 1 per cent may seem very low. For schools, however, a single unfilled vacancy presents significant organisational difficulty and threatens pupil performance. Work can only be shared amongst other staff by means of increasing class size and reducing the number of classes, but this may be impossible for accommodation reasons, let alone undesirable for educational reasons. In primary schools, it is likely to produce mixed-age classes, in which the organisation of learning is more difficult. In secondary schools, it increases the likelihood of teaching a subject by a non-specialist. The other solution is for the class to be taught by a succession of supply teachers, with all the problems of discontinuity.

The current national rate of 1.3 per cent hides very significant variations, with two main variables. The more important is geographical. As an approximation, difficulties are in inverse proportion to distance from London and the Thames corridor. The rate for inner London is 4.3 per cent, for the North West 0.5 per cent. Superimposed on that, for secondary schools difficulty relates to the position of the school within the local hierarchy of popularity. A third factor applies particularly, but not only, to primary schools: local reputation amongst the teacher community with regard to the quality of the management. It is a reasonable assumption that when the national rate exceeds one per cent, many schools will have great staffing difficulty.

To summarise, the DfES definition of vacancies is such that it is a good measure of excess demand. It bears repetition that the bulk of schools in England are fully staffed. Many headteachers might feel that they have made appointments from smaller fields than previously; many secondary heads will be uneasy at deploying non-specialist staff, or teachers from abroad with no knowledge of the National Curriculum; yet the large majority of schools will have a full complement of teachers. On the other hand, current levels are such that the most affected schools face severe organisational difficulties. The most affected schools are the least attractive, in that they are the most challenging. Their pupils are the most needy. Equity in social policy demands that these difficulties are reduced.

Is demand pupil-driven?

We now turn to the determinants of demand. According to the DfES, demand for teachers is determined primarily by pupil numbers. The trend in pupil numbers is as follows: a period of year on year reduction bottomed out in 1990, at 7.225 million, and was followed by a year on year increase predicted to peak at 8.097 million in 2002. Numbers are predicted to fall to 7.771 million in 2009.

However, Figure 2.1 shows that over the last ten years the number of teachers has not moved in step. Continuing increases in pupil numbers were not reflected in extra teachers. Only in 1999 did significant increases begin. In 1991, 7.276 million pupils were taught by 442,094 teachers, in 1998 7.984 million pupils were taught by 437,980 teachers.

The relationship is shown clearly by the pupil-teacher ratio. For primary schools in England, the PTR was lowest in 1987 (21.9), and increased each year until 1998, when it was 23.7. The figure for 2000, 23.3, shows only a slight reduction, despite the significant movement towards the Government's target with regard to infant class size. For secondary schools in England, the PTR has continued to increase, from 15.3 in 1990 to 16.9 in 1998, and 17.2 in 2000. This is the highest secondary PTR for 25 years. While the academic debate continues about the importance of class size, schools almost always aim for the smallest classes they can achieve, and regard an increase in PTR as a worsening of their circumstances.

Table 2.3 Pupil numbers, by phase, England and Wales
Actual figures 1986–2001. Projections, 2002-2009

	Primary 000s	Secondary 000s	Total 000s		Primary 000s	Secondary 000s	Total 000s
1990	4159	2970	7225	2000	4579	3394	8068
1991	4216	2957	7276	2001	4545	3450	8090
1992	4253	3005	7353	2002	4507	3496	8097
1993	4328	3059	7481	2003	4445	3542	8081
1994	4402	3128	7626	2004	4387	3568	8048
1995	4471	3191	7756	2005	4356	3559	8008
1996	4547	3209	7851	2006	4326	3546	7963
1997	4584	3242	7921	2007	4305	3507	7903
1998	4614	3275	7984	2008	4292	3457	7838
1999	4611	3326	8032	2009	4469	3414	7771

Source: STRB 2001

Figure 2.1 Pupil and teacher numbers 1990-2000, England and Wales

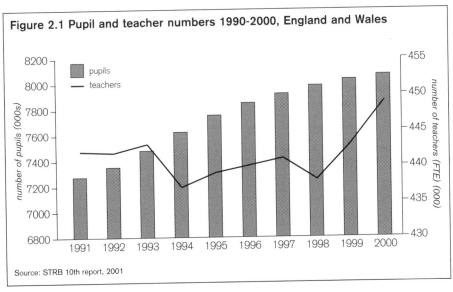

Source: STRB 10th report, 2001

Or money driven?

These figures do not support the Government's view that the demand for teachers depends primarily on pupil numbers. A more likely connection is with the perceived ability to pay. As a generalisation, schools will employ as many teachers as they can afford, given their availability. Additional teachers permit smaller classes, and more flexibility to deploy teachers for both pupil contact and non-contact tasks. Of course, the budget is allocated according to a formula at least 80 per cent of which is based on pupil numbers, so that there is a strong indirect link between pupil numbers and

Table 2.4 Pupil-teacher ratio 1990-2001 (England)

	Primary	Secondary	Overall		Primary	Secondary	Overall
1990	22.0	15.3	16.9	1996	23.2	16.6	18.5
1991	22.2	15.5	17.2	1997	23.4	16.7	18.6
1992	22.2	15.8	17.4	1998	23.7	16.9	18.9
1993	22.4	16.2	17.8	1999	23.5	17.0	18.8
1994	22.7	16.4	18.1	2000	23.3	17.2	18.6
1995	22.9	16.5	18.3	2001	22.9	17.1	18.3

Sources: STRB 2001; for 2001, DfEE SFR 16/2001

teacher numbers. However, in the nineties a large proportion of the schools forced to reduce staffing were not subject to falling rolls.

The increasing substitution of teachers by support staff and voluntary workers, particularly in the primary phase reduces the direct connection between school budgets and demand for teachers, but this remains a more satisfactory causal link than pupil numbers directly.

Figure 2.2 shows a close relationship between schools' funding and number of teachers employed. As real terms funding declined in the mid-nineties, so did teacher numbers.

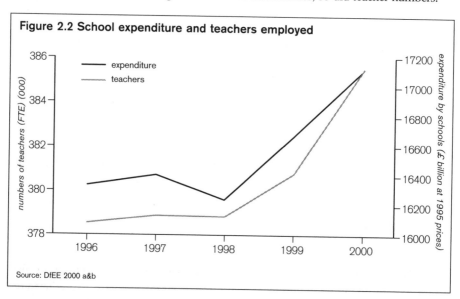

Figure 2.2 School expenditure and teachers employed

Source: DfEE 2000 a&b

Projection of future demand

The conclusion to be drawn is that the future demand for teachers depends overwhelmingly on the resources made available to schools. The Government plans to increase spending on education by 5.4 per cent a year in real terms between 2001 and 2004. The Treasury projects Education Standard Spending to rise from £38,787 million in 2000-01 to £49,189 million in 03-04, implying similar real terms increases for schools. This commitment cannot readily be translated into teacher demand, but there is no reason to believe that there will be a radical shift in the proportion of school revenue budgets being spent on staffing. The tendency to increase support staff spending within that category is likely to continue, but is difficult to quantify.

Any increase in real terms earnings for teachers would reduce demand. However, a year on year increase of 5.4 per cent spending on teachers with no real terms increase in school funded teacher pay, would increase demand by some 22,150 in 01-02, a further 23,350 in 02-03, and a further 24,620 to a total of 480,420 in 03-04, as against 410,300 employed in January 01. Even if only five per cent a year additional posts were created, this would increase demand to some 475,000.

In contrast, the Government made a manifesto commitment to increase the number of teachers by 10,000 during the next Parliament. It thus seems that between 10,000 and 70,000 additional teachers will be required in the period to 2004.

However, it is important to differentiate within the overall market. With primary pupil numbers projected to continue to fall by 158,000 between 2001 and 2004 and for this trend to continue, total primary funding is almost certain to reduce. At current staffing standards, this implies a reduction in demand of about 6,900 teachers. However, pupil numbers in the secondary phase are projected to rise by 118,000 between 2001 and 2004, when they will peak. Assuming constant per pupil funding, this would generate demand for an additional 6,900 teachers.

The number of school age children will decline after 2004, with projections to 2009 currently available. They suggest a reduction of 277,000 within that period. At current staffing standards, this would imply a reduction in demand of about 15,400 teachers. The number of births is projected to continue to decline to 2011.

Projected supply

Changes in the supply of teachers depend on the flows into and out of the profession. There are three groups inflowing: newly qualified, those new to the maintained sector, and those returning to the maintained sector after a break. The latter group includes teachers who have been teaching elsewhere than maintained schools, for example independent schools or further education, as well as those taking a career break, and is examined in detail in Chapter 3.

Recruitment to training

The Government sets targets for training based on its projections of future supply and demand. It could be argued that the present situation is rooted in the excessive cutbacks in targets during the 1980s. For a number of years, there has been under-recruitment as against these targets. Proportionately, the most serious shortfalls have been in the subjects of maths, science, modern languages, design technology and, more recently, IT. Targets were met in the early nineties, a period of recession and relatively high graduate unemployment. As the economy recovered, the targets receded. The peak year for recruitment to training was 1993, when over 33,000 students started either the four-year BEd. or the one-year PGCE. A feature of the last decade has been the decline of BEd.

Table 2.5 Recruitment to training, 1990-2001

	Primary		Secondary		Total		Total
	BEd.	PGCE	BEd.	PGCE	BEd.	PGCE	
1990	9524	4806	2314	7150	11838	11956	23794
1991	10726	5537	3003	9526	13729	15063	28792
1992	12109	6255	3380	10236	15489	16491	31980
1993	11487	6501	3158	12080	14645	18581	33226
1994	9450	5640	2970	13440	12420	19080	31500
1995	9240	5700	2460	13630	11700	19330	31030
1996	8360	5450	2580	14260	10940	19710	30650
1997	7800	5220	2650	14260	10450	19480	29930
1998	7430	5640	2200	13140	9630	18780	28410
1999	7380	6000	1960	12880	9340	18880	28220
2000	7330	7090	1630	14060	8960	21150	30100
2001	7110	7170	1560	15540	8660	22710	31370

Sources: STRB reports

The most recent assessment of graduate employment reports continuing competition, with real increases in starting pay and recruitment incentives. In response, the Government has introduced incentives, notably the training grant of £6,000 to all PGCE students from September 2000, and the golden hello of £4,000, payable after a successful induction year, for new teachers of shortage subjects. The outcome has been increased entry to PGCE, although BEd. continues to decline.

However, figures for entry to training must be regarded with great caution. In recent years, there has been a dramatic drop-out between entry to training and taking up employment in teaching. Of the cohort who completed training in 1998, 12,430 started BEd. courses in 1994, and 19,480 started PGCE in 1997. However, only 9,640 students completed the BEd. in 1998, a drop-out rate of 22 per cent. 17,090

PGCE students completed, giving a total of 26,730 newly qualified teachers in 1998. Yet in March 1999, only 19,120 of these NQTs were employed as teachers, at a time of increasing vacancies. Thus, of the 31,910 who started training, exactly 40 per cent did not become teachers. Indeed, in modelling supply and demand, the DfES assumes a wastage rate in training of 25 per cent from BEd. and 11 per cent from PGCE, with a further wastage of ITT completers ranging from 16 per cent of primary women to 30 per cent of secondary men (DfEE 1998).

We do not know how many of the 7,610 who qualified but did not take jobs within the first year have done subsequently, or may do in the future. We do know that there is a surge of drop-out after students experience teaching practice. This loss is excessive, not in comparison with other occupational training, but because of the costs involved, and because of the urgent need to maximise supply. One effect of the introduction of financial incentives to train may be a further increase in this wastage, if it attracts students with a lower level of commitment. The Teacher Training Agency is conscious of the need to improve the matching of entrants to training to the demands of the course and the profession, but the problem may be related more to the content of the job and morale in staffrooms than to the weaknesses of trainees.

Outflows

Turning to outflows from the profession, in 1999 these totalled 29,800, of whom only 5,800 retired. Another 10,400 moved to part-time or occasional work, or to another education sector, but 12,800 left the service. This movement is discussed in detail below. Thus, despite the recruitment of new teachers exceeding retirements by 14,300, there was a net increase of only 2,800 teachers in 1999, at a time when demand began to outstrip supply. The DfES calculates that currently, the net inflow to the profession is 5,100, 1.2 per cent per annum (DfES 2001). With excess demand at the current level, and growing rapidly, this is very inadequate in the short term.

Outflow through retirement will increase dramatically in the medium term. Between 3,000 and 3,500 teachers retired each year on age grounds in the 1990s, but the bulk of retirements were premature, or on the grounds of ill health. Changes in regulations had the effect of reducing loss by these means. However, of teachers in service in 1999, some 62,100 will reach the retirement age of 60 between 2005 and 2009. Even on the unlikely assumption that none leave service before age 60, some 12,400 teachers a year will retire during that period. Between 2010 and 2014, this figure would rise to 17,300 a year. Of course, any tendency of these 148,500 teachers (36 per cent of the workforce) to leave teaching before the age of 60 would transfer the replacement need earlier. Compared with the current net inflow of 5,100, these figures look very challenging.

To summarise, the supply of teachers (which is not meeting current demand) is tending to grow at a rate of about 1 per cent per annum. It is too early to say whether recruitment incentives are having any significant effect. In the medium term, historically very large numbers of teachers will retire, and on current trends recruitment will be insufficient to replace them.

Finding enough teachers in a buoyant economy

From the Secretary of State outwards, there is an understanding that recruitment, retention, and morale of teachers are key issues for the continued progression of the standards agenda. Some measures to address these issues are in place, others are in development, and many more are being floated in the education world. However, there is inevitably a time-lag between central decision, implementation, and local effect on mood. Staff-room morale remains low, and dissatisfaction high.

Short-term: retention, retention, retention

During the period to 2004, with increasing demand in the secondary sector, changes to recruitment to training can have only a marginal effect on supply. There are two significant sources for the number of additional secondary teachers required. The first is a reduction of the wastage of teachers other than by retirement. The second is an increase in recruitment from the pool of inactive teachers.

In 1999, 1,900 men and 7,000 women in the 25-35 age group left teacher employment in maintained schools, joining a pool which contained 71,200 aged under 50 and with recent teaching experience. Insufficient is known about this pool, but it is quite clear that in the short term demand for secondary teachers cannot be met unless both a substantial proportion of leavers can be persuaded to return, and also fewer teachers leave other than for retirement. This theme is pursued later.

National interventions are required. Maximising retention and recruitment from the PIT by making the job of teaching less unattractive is absolutely essential. Research into teacher job satisfaction and the attractions of the profession is very consistent. It shows that intrinsic characteristics of the job make it attractive. Working with children, working with colleagues, and opportunities for creativity and autonomy are highly rated. Extrinsic factors such as pay and conditions, including holidays, are far less important for teachers, but rated more highly by those not attracted. Major factors producing dissatisfaction are workload, pupil behaviour, poor management, particularly amongst primary teachers, and public criticism which is perceived to be unjustified. It is necessary for this evidence to be the basis for policy to ameliorate the short-term predicament. These factors are discussed below in reverse order.

Public criticism

The Government changed its stance on public criticism after a very short period in office. It seems to have adopted the traditional teaching tip, offer praise at least three times as often as complaint. However, four years later, there remains a widespread belief amongst teachers that they are constantly under attack. This may indicate two problems. The first is the very great lag between policy decision in government and culture change in over 20,000 institutions, many of which have become increasingly atomised. The second is the very low state of morale within the profession. This in itself is a recruitment issue, as trainees are deterred from entering the profession by the entreaties of staff in schools where they train.

Management

One recent study (Hutchings *et al* 2000) found that almost four in ten of teachers leaving the profession cited poor management as central to their decision. This indictment must be set within the context of radical changes in the demands on school management over the last decade, arising from two sources.

The first is the pressure arising from the multiple accountabilities written into the 1988 Education Reform Act. The Better Regulation Task Force (2000:9) concluded 'we believe that this number of layers [of accountability] and reporting lines undermines rather than strengthens real accountability.' In a study of headteachers, the Task Force identified governors, the local authority, the DfEE, and Ofsted as together producing this overload. Teachers feel under excessive scrutiny, but the buck, and the scrutiny, stops in the headteacher's office. Both pupil outcomes and Ofsted inspections focus attention on the quality of management, which indeed is a common factor in sending a school into Special Measures.

The second is the substantial expansion of the school management role with the introduction of local management. A range of legal, financial, premises, and personnel functions have been transferred from local authority to school level. Given inadequate training in these areas, it is unsurprising that some headteachers had neither the time nor the skills to be successful. Two long-term issues arise. Local management imposes proportionately very large additional demands on primary schools, and there is an obvious diseconomy of scale in devolving specialist responsibilities. A major evaluation of the benefits of local management is needed. An alternative more limited approach being adopted is to investigate the transfer of such responsibilities back to non-teaching staff.

In general, headteachers have transmitted these pressures down to their staffs. Demands from the centre have been interpreted bureaucratically. Heads, especially in primary schools, have required detailed evidence of teacher performance, largely under the impression that Ofsted in turn requires it. In its interim report on teacher workload, PricewaterhouseCoopers (2001:35) found 'primary teachers who showed us very detailed, usually hand written, plans for each lesson, and who said the headteacher required them to submit a copy of their complete set of each week's lesson plans in advance at the start of the week. It was not clear to us ... for whose benefit this enhanced level of activity was taking place nor whether anyone, other than the teachers themselves, were likely to need to refer to such detailed accounts of individual lessons. We have concluded that in a significant number of primary schools, the workload created by such school level requirements may be disproportionate to the value it adds.'

It is suggested that bullying by management is particularly widespread in teaching, compared with other occupations. Under local management, there is no effective check on headteacher behaviour. It would be particularly unfortunate if today's young teachers were to imbibe autocratic management styles on the way to becoming tomorrow's headteachers.

The weakness of management has been recognised by the Government, with additional training for serving and aspiring heads, and the establishment of the National College for School Leadership. Although the issue is more salient in the primary phase, more needs to be done in the short-term if wastage is to be reduced. One measure which would help is to reduce pressure of central prescription on heads. Another would be to rationalise the overlapping patterns of accountability.

Pupil behaviour

There is a strong consensus amongst experts that frustration over pupil behaviour is becoming an increasingly strong cause of dissatisfaction, but there is little research evidence. This may be due to issues of research instruments, but it has long been recognised in connection with the attractiveness of the profession to school-leavers and undergraduates (Smithers and Hill 1989, Spear et al 1999). Although attention is often focussed on the most extreme and dramatic examples of violence and vandalism, only a few schools are dominated by that level of tension. Dissatisfaction arises from the more general reluctance on the part of children of all ages and backgrounds to accept the authority of the teacher. Control becomes more difficult, more time-consuming, and more stressful.

Orthodox prescriptions for dealing with this issue are of two main kinds. The first is to concentrate on issues of pedagogy and school organisation. The rationale is that children will be engaged and positive if the school experience is good enough. The second is to criticise the lack of sanctions available to teachers, and to seek to exclude badly behaved pupils and provide alternative education.

The Government is working on both strategies. The highly under-trumpeted

SureStart programme is attempting to work with parents and children to produce pupils who are more school-ready, in terms not only of skills but also of attitudes. One outcome of the primary Literacy Strategy may be that more literate pupils find it easier to engage with the secondary curriculum. On the other side, there is investment in units for troublesome pupils, both on and off site. In Excellence in Cities areas, the mentor programme is already helping. There has been progressive re-interpretation of the regulations on exclusion from school, with the overall effect of putting the rights of the school community in balance with the rights of the disruptive pupil.

Unfortunately, these policies impinge only tangentially on the perceived general reduction, on the part of all pupils, of respect for the authority of the teacher. Improvement in pupil behaviour is not likely in the short term. This is because it is closely connected with very deep social issues regarding the nature of authority within all our institutions, the development of mores and values, the structure of the contemporary family, and so on. The long-term application of joined up policies is necessary.

In the short term, further measures in schools would require additional staffing. Although smaller classes would make class control less problematic, the employment of more support staff to support, advise and mentor pupils might be more practicable than additional teachers.

Workload

Chapter 1 suggested that the Government is right to prioritise teacher workload, following research by PricewaterhouseCoopers (2001), which showed that the average working time during term is 54.5 and 55.3 hours per week for primary and secondary teachers respectively, although the working year, 2122 and 2174 hours for secondary and primary teachers, was in line with other managers and professionals. Headteachers, however, were found to work for 2397 (primary) and 2567 (secondary) hours a year.

Working hours have been increasing for many years (STRB 2001). There has been little increase in contact time. Currently, teachers spend just 40 per cent of their working hours teaching and covering classes, counselling pupils and running visits (PricewaterhouseCoopers 2001). Most of the extra hours are spent in non-contact activities. It is sometimes alleged that overall pupil contact has reduced, because teachers now spend hours on paperwork that they used to spend in extra-curricular activities with pupils. Two basic causes underlie this trend.

Since its introduction the National Curriculum has been subject to frequent top-down change. The National Literacy Strategy then introduced centrally determined pedagogy. Thus much additional work has been produced by continual changes to content, and latterly method. They are made more onerous by being imposed.

Secondly, the demands of multiple accountabilities have increased radically the recording of teacher activity. This includes the setting of targets for individual pupils, recording their performance, detailed plans of lessons, and detailed evaluations of lessons. Much of the workload is contained not in the activity itself, but in the requirement for standardised and detailed written accounts of it. Whilst this has facilitated more systematic monitoring of teacher performance, much of the pile of paper generated is never read by anyone. It provides evidence for management that it has managed. PricewaterhouseCoopers found that only 12 per cent of schools think strategically about workload issues; 'Many headteachers appeared never to have considered their staff's workload as an issue for them to be concerned with.' (PricewaterhouseCoopers 2001:17) PwC point out that managements regard teacher time as a 'free good', because there is no cost to additional hours.

Workload is the most important dissatisfier for both trainees (Sands 1993, Chambers and Roper 2000) and teachers (Barnard 1998, Scott 1999, Spear *et al* 1999). However, the dissatisfaction lies not in the number of hours per se, but in two related factors. Many hours are spent in work which is imposed, rather than self-generated. Much of this work is also judged as being unnecessary and unproductive, in terms of pupil performance.

If working hours during term time could be greatly reduced, and spent on activities valued by teachers, a major cause of wastage and disincentive to return to the profession would be removed. Effective action on workload is possible within the short-term, although achieving consensus will not be easy.

Recommendation

Action on workload must be based on the following principles:

- All sides must recognise that the Government has a duty to continue action on levels of attainment for all learners, which requires continuous change on the part of producers. However, the Government must implement the IPPR proposal on workload impact statements (IPPR 2001). Whenever an initiative is launched, it must contain a precise assessment of time required, and the resource to be made available, for its implementation. This would enable schools to assign an appropriate level of staff time.

- There is continuous pressure on teachers to improve the quality of their teaching at the level of the individual pupil. Whilst centrally provided lesson plans can assist, preparing work for individuals is necessarily time-consuming. Preparation of lessons already takes almost as long as teaching them, 16.3 hours and 18.2 hours per week for secondary and primary teachers respectively (PricewaterhouseCoopers 2001). The contractual or other arrangements by which teacher hours are determined must recognise the key importance of lesson preparation. It is often said that this is impossible because of individual differences in time needed, but negotiations should centre around the above figures.

- There must be a mechanism through which school managements are disciplined to regard teacher time as a scarce resource, to be allocated with care in accordance with a school's planned priorities. This would constitute another radical culture change, so soon after the change from a self-determined workload to one externally imposed. The unions insist that a limited hours contract is the only effective mechanism. The Government finds such a proposal unprofessional. Whatever solutions are found, they must be realistic in relation to the skill level of management in schools, previously discussed.

- As between the current working week of 55 hours in term time and the union claim for 35 hours, the Government must make a judgement about reasonable working time. This may have not been necessary when teachers were self-directed, but is appropriate in a period of central direction. Given the unusual working and holiday pattern of teachers, it may be better to express this in annual terms. These patterns themselves need challenging, since it may be workflow as much as workload which is a cause of teacher stress.

Almost any outcome which effectively reduces teachers' hours will tend to increase the supply of teachers, because workload is the key dissatisfier. However, its effect will only be fully felt if the elements of imposed work perceived to be unproductive are removed (see below). At the same time, this development will also increase demand for teachers.

What about pay?

There is no evidence that pay is a major factor in terms of the attractiveness of the profession (Reid and Caulwell 1997, Scott 1999, Varlaam et al 1992). It seems that male secondary teachers might tend to be more concerned, and particularly those of the traditional shortage subjects (Hillman 1994, Smithers and Hill 1989). In London, specific pay factors apply. Nevertheless, a recent study showed that half of London teachers leaving the profession for other employment were taking a pay cut (Hutchings et al 2000), and recent industrial action may be as much connected with underlying causes such as the other dissatisfiers discussed here as with the very real cost of living difficulties.

Of course, labour market theory suggests that increasing reward will tend to increase the supply. However, the teacher wage bill, at over £15 billion (not including supply teachers), is a sufficiently large proportion of public expenditure to warrant particularly close scrutiny and parsimony by the Treasury. It will note that undergraduates underestimate teacher salary levels (Teacher Training Agency 2001), and suggest that improving their perceptions might be more cost-effective than raising pay.

An obvious test for the market mechanism would be to increase pay for secondary teachers of maths and science, in terms both of entry and progression. Physics teachers are known to be more salary conscious than teachers generally (Stewart and Perrin 1989). There is already some local pay drift for these groups, by schools using the flexibility available to them within the national scales.

Recommendation

●   Pay incentives for teachers of maths and science should be explored.

The disadvantage of this test would be the possible effect on morale amongst secondary teachers generally. Designers of pay systems for teachers in England and Wales must contend with the strong collective culture within the profession. Indeed, the Green Paper on reform of the profession explicitly set out to change the culture, and to gain acceptability for a more individualised pay structure. The result was the subversion of an attempt to impose performance related pay. However, if the Government could persuade interested parties that an experiment to target longstanding shortage subject teachers was reasonable, it could be very instructive.

Intrinsic satisfiers: creativity and autonomy

Turning from negative features which need to be reduced, wastage can also be reduced by enhancing the positive features of the job, currently under some pressure. Teachers consistently report that they enjoy the core work of classroom contact with pupils, and this was confirmed by IPPR's own research (Edwards 2002). A major component of satisfaction is the responsibility and freedom to determine the course of events in the classroom. Another is the opportunity to apply initiative and creative skills to both content and pedagogy (Bloomfield and Selinger 1994, Fraser et al 1998, Heafford and Jennison 1998, Spear et al 1999).

Many of the teachers who report that currently there is insufficient autonomy and opportunity for creativity are too young to have known the uncontrolled atmosphere before 1988. Nevertheless, they are dissatisfied by the total weight of central prescription. The interplay of accountability mechanisms produces the total effect. This is compounded, in primary schools particularly, by a deep lack of confidence after more than decade of top-down prescription, and changing impositions.

Secondary schools are somewhat different; they are used to the discipline of external examination syllabuses, if at least equally unhappy with the recent frequency of imposed changes to them.

Whether or not any centrally developed policy is given statutory force, it becomes compulsory in effect when Ofsted is asked to inspect its implementation. The National Literacy Strategy has no regulatory backing, but very few schools had the confidence to face an inspection without it. Further, the influence of Ofsted is such that most schools which have learned to tweak the NLS return to a by-the-book approach for an inspection.

Government agencies claim that these consequences are unintended, and cannot understand why their frequent calls for teachers to regard such innovations as supports rather than chains appear to be disregarded. The simple reason is that the paralysis of judgement has been created by its own network of controls and demands.

As discussed in Chapter 1, the policy debate within Government on the tension between centralisation and devolution, particularly within public services, is crucial to this issue. Yet over the next three years, the standards agenda in secondary schools is under threat from a shortage of teachers to implement it. If teaching is to be sufficiently attractive to overcome the shortage, it must regain greater scope for creativity and professional autonomy.

Medium term: recruiting whom?

In the medium term, measures taken to improve recruitment to the profession can come into effect. Given the increasing loss from retirement, there will be a continuing need to maximise recruitment, from both graduates and mature entrants.

New thinking on subject qualifications

The Secretary of State requires training institutions to be satisfied that secondary trainees' previous education equips them to teach the subject for which they train. As presently interpreted, this is a barrier for a very large number of graduates. For example, in 1999 over 33,000 students started Business Studies courses, and the same number started Social Studies. The demand for teaching these subjects is limited in comparison with the numbers of graduates, and there is little encouragement for them to consider secondary teaching.

The key lies in the further growth of the Government's policy on continuing professional development. It has to find mechanisms by which teachers have much more access to self-motivated development. If beginning teachers had access to further subject study, their degree subject would be much less important. The Primary Numeracy Strategy included five day intensive courses in maths for school co-ordinators. One outcome has been an enhanced confidence in teaching the subject in primary schools. It would make sense to concentrate on shortage subjects, and the deployment of such staff to teach maths might help to resolve the academic dispute.

One method would be to qualify fully to teach only at Key Stage 3, with full qualification to Key Stage 4 to be confirmed after suitable professional development in the subject. The Key Stage 3 Strategy should enhance the ability of staff to teach a range of subjects.

Recommendation

- There should be easier access to teacher training for graduates in non-National Curriculum subjects.

Attracting the mature

Whatever the trends within society generally with respect to the notion of career, demand for teachers will only be met in the medium term by an increase in the entry of the so-called mature student. Whilst the Teacher Training Agency is working to ease career change, far more needs to be done.

Given that the main attraction of the job is working with children in a creative environment, publicity should concentrate on this. It is essential to appeal to the altruistic sentiments of people who may doubt the value to society of the work they have been doing for perhaps ten to fifteen years. Those who express an interest must be facilitated in tasting the job, again concentrating on classrooms. This is dependent on the assumption that the reality of the job has been made more attractive by the means described earlier. At the moment, potential applicants must cold-contact a school, which may be unable to prioritise the task of providing a suitable experience.

Many potential mature entrants may be geographically immobile. This increases the need for a range of training opportunities, including the further marketing of distance learning packages. At the moment, the number of part-time and otherwise flexible courses is restricted, and availability depends on location.

Mature trainees need financial packages of a different kind from postgraduates. Their commitment is less in doubt, but their needs for earnings and security whilst in training are greater. At the moment, all trainees are entitled to a bursary. The argument for a training salary is strong, but strongest for mature entrants. They need a monthly payment, continuity of National Insurance contributions, and pension entitlement.

Is it a career break – or an end?

In 1999, there were 33,000 women in their twenties and thirties who were not working as teachers, but had done so within the previous six years (DfEE 2000a). Chapter 3 discusses how they could be attracted to return. Some ideas are hardly new. The STRB reported in 1993: 'means are needed to keep in touch with potential returners, to offer them refresher courses, and to support re-entrants.' But with changing working patterns and expectations, such initiatives have gained currency and urgency. Instead of the current patchy shoestring good practice, we need properly resourced measures applied everywhere, with the recognition that the local education authority is in the best position to implement them, or enable others to do so.

Paraprofessional progression

Another pool of recruits whose potential is only starting to be developed is classroom support workers. The numbers of support staff employed have increased by a third in the past five years, to some 157,000 (including librarians and technicians, but excluding admin, catering and cleaning staff). A large number of these staff work directly with pupils, but many have very little training, and almost all are low paid. On the other hand, some are qualified teachers who have chosen a less arduous means of working with children.

There are a few schemes for staff who wish to progress from classroom assistant to qualified teacher. However, many have few educational qualifications, and the road from access courses to Qualified Teacher Status is long and difficult. Only a minority of them claim an interest in becoming teachers. Nevertheless, an expansion of these schemes would serve a number of purposes. Most classroom assistants are members of the same social groups as the pupils with whom they work, and live locally. Concentrating these schemes in the cities would develop a prospect of secure, relatively well-paid work for relatively disadvantaged groups, increase the supply of teachers in those areas most likely to be under pressure, and improve the social identity between teachers and taught. These gains would outweigh the high costs of recruiting from such a pool. Other children's professionals, from learning mentors to youth workers, should be offered similarly tailored pathways to qualified teacher status.

A more representative profession

Recruiting from the paraprofessionals may address the important requirement to make the profession more representative of the whole society, but much more needs to be done. There is a need for far more teachers from minority ethnic groups, largely but not only in schools whose pupils are from those groups. This is discussed in detail in Chapter 6. To summarise, there are a number of measures which could be taken to improve recruitment. Currently isolated examples of good practice in identifying target groups and investing in them must be spread far more rapidly. In two ways, new initiatives must aim at non-traditional entrants. Firstly, local interventions must be made with those whose occupational, class, or ethnic backgrounds are different from the typical graduate. Secondly, there must be more systematic targeting of people in mid-career who are looking for a more socially useful job.

Recommendation

- Medium term measures to increase recruitment should target mature entrants, teachers in career breaks, career progression for paraprofessionals, and minority ethnic entrants.

However, it is vital to keep in mind that none of these measures will be effective unless the experience of teaching is more positive than at present. The changes to the job described as essential in the short-term are the only basis of an attractive profession in the longer term. Only if potential teachers find high morale in staff rooms will their tasting or training encourage them to go further.

More important, from the point of view of numbers, there is no point in turning on full the tap of recruitment unless the plug is preventing wastage. Of course, in principle, flows in and out of the profession are both inevitable and necessary. As has been shown, however, the current and future imbalance of supply and demand requires both the maximisation of inflow and the minimisation of outflow. As medium term becomes long term, the huge outflow through age retirement only reinforces the requirement.

There is no reason to presume that in the medium term the factors which make the job attractive, or unattractive, will change fundamentally. The key to adequate supply in this period will remain the balance of intrinsic satisfaction as against extrinsic dissatisfiers. If that balance is right, it will be possible to attract entrants from the target groups described above and produce the numbers of teachers society needs.

Long-term: dipping in and out?

What will be the need for teachers in the second and succeeding decades of the century? The further ahead the view, the more uncertain the clarity. Most radical views about changes to teaching and schools are centred around the potential of new technologies. As was mentioned in the previous chapter, whilst it is important not to underestimate their effects, neither should they be overestimated. This is discussed further in Chapter 10.

It is common to make a contrast between schools and hospitals. A doctor transported from the hospital of a hundred years ago would recognise neither the equipment nor the practice. The teacher similarly transported would be perfectly at home. It is not the validity of the contrast which is in question here, but the inference to be drawn from it. Should we conclude that teachers are essentially conservative, if not luddite? Or might we conclude that there is something about teaching and learning which is essentially timeless, because it crucially involves human interaction between teacher and learner?

It is certain, however, that turnover will be at a high level, at least at the start of this period. The 86,400 teachers who will reach retirement age between 2010 and 2015 (DfEE 2000a), if they have not previously left the profession, will need to be replaced. In comparison with approximately 8,000 who are retiring annually at the moment (apart from ill-health retirements), this is what Government agencies are entitled to describe as a challenging target.

A complication to the calculations on demand is the possible trend towards redefinition of the concept of career. It is now commonly said that the notion of a career for life is outdated, that we can expect the worker of the future to change occupation a number of times during a working life. If this is to be true for teaching, it has huge implications for training targets.

This argument may be underpinned by some loose thinking. It seems to be based on the argument that many jobs are disappearing, as new technologies make them redundant. Workers need to be flexible, to train and retrain, as the job market is said to change ever more rapidly. However, Meadows (2000) shows that people aged over 25 are not changing their jobs any more frequently than in the past. Many jobs are changing in character, rather than disappearing, as they use new kinds of tools. We suggest above that teaching will be like that. People leaving school within the next five years can have every confidence that in fifty years time, society will need teachers.

Employers also are increasingly concerned by excessive staff turnover. Recent research (Hay 2001) suggests a rapid worldwide increase in turnover in the last five years, perhaps in line with the economic cycle, with significant cost implications. These arise not only from the relative cost-effectiveness of training, a highly significant factor for Government in the case of teachers, but the high costs associated with recruitment. It is not unlikely that employers will begin to use contractual and financial disincentives to discourage job-flitting.

Another trend which may contribute to the suggestion of a more mobile workforce is the restlessness of youth. The 'gap year' has not only become ubiquitous, but is becoming serial. More and more graduates in their twenties intersperse employment with world travel. The assumption is that this generation will continue this attitude throughout its working lives. If it does, it will be the first in history to overcome the nesting instinct. It seems more plausible to regard twenties mobility as an affluence-induced postponement of settling down. For the purposes of teacher retention, it is the quality of previous teaching experience which will determine the readiness of the returning traveller to resume (or begin) a career in classrooms.

Recent ministerial interviews suggest that we must prepare for a more transient teaching force, as workers dip into the profession and dip out again. This idea correctly identifies the importance of two aspects of the recruitment of career changers. Firstly, as previously discussed, conditions must be created to assist the transition. Secondly, potential entrants must not be deterred by the fear of being trapped in the job.

This makes the 'dipping' idea half-correct. Dipping-in is necessary. From the point of view of the demand for teachers, dipping-out as a more widespread phenomenon could be disastrous. Supply will be insufficient in the long-term if wastage rates are not kept to a minimum.

There is another problem for the teaching profession in the concept of transience. Like many other jobs, it will continue to contain a large element of craft skills. They are advanced interpersonal skills, largely but not only exhibited in direct pedagogic relationships. Like all craft skills, despite the importance of training, they develop largely through experience and reflection upon experience. New, young teachers are a great asset to a school, often bringing vitality and innovative drive. A school needs a blend of assets, and it would be a mistake to discount the importance of experience.

Lastly, teaching is different from other occupations in the importance of stability to the clients. As consumers, we like to see the same face serving us, but it is infrequently central to our satisfaction with the service. As hospital patients, we want to be treated by the same staff throughout our stay; but that is likely to be a matter of weeks at most. As pupils, we need to be taught by the same person for the school year at least, and longer in many cases. We may well be clients of one school for five years or more, and a rapid turnover of staff demoralises us. Pupil performance depends so much on the teacher-pupil relationship that schools cannot be successful without relatively stable staffing.

None of this rules out more flexible approaches to teaching as a career. Of course there is room for those who want to specialise in one aspect of the teacher's role, those who want to teach part-time while pursuing another career, those who want to combine teaching with world travel, or those who want to take periodic breaks from its rigours. Yet it must never be forgotten that a major factor associated with failing schools is instability of staffing. Over the next decade, the dimensions of the challenge to find sufficient teachers are such that we need as many as possible who dip in to stay in.

Conclusion

After years of decline, in which schools employed fewer teachers relative to the number of pupils, the Labour Government has initiated a period of real expansion. Although more people are employed as teachers than for many years, the effect has been that demand cannot be met. As further increases in funding take effect, demand will grow further, possibly to unprecedented levels. By 2014, over 40 per cent of the workforce will have retired.

With rising rolls in secondary schools to 2004, their staffing difficulties will be particularly acute. As always, these difficulties will be experienced differentially according to geography and status. They cannot be resolved in the short-term by expansion of training. Instead, national action must be taken to reduce wastage from the profession and to maximise the return of those out of service.

This can be done only by improvements to the job itself, currently unattractive because of excessive unnecessary workload, poor pupil behaviour, poor management, and overarchingly the loss of opportunities for creativity and professional autonomy which offer job satisfaction. If these improvements are made, they will form the basis of improved recruitment into the profession of mature entrants, support staff, and minority ethnic groups.

There are real difficulties over the next three years. They are capable of resolution. They can be resolved within the Government's spending plans. They cannot be resolved unless the Government concludes its internal debate over centralist policies in the public services, and allows teachers, schools, and local authorities to deliver the targets it rightly wants to set.

References

Barnard N (1998) 'Status Worries New Teachers' *Times Educational Supplement* 4 December 1998

Better Regulation Task Force (2000) *Red Tape Affecting Head Teachers* London: Cabinet Office

Bloomfield A and Selinger M (1994) 'Magic Moments in Mathematics Teaching' *Mathematics Teaching* 20.3

Performance and Innovation Unit (2001) *Better Policy Delivery and Design: A Discussion Paper* London: Cabinet Office

Chambers G and Roper T (2000) 'Why Students Withdraw from ITT' *Journal of Eduation for Teaching* 26.1

Cockburn A, Hadyn T and Oliver A (2000) *Why Not Teaching?* University of East Anglia School of Education and Professional Development

DfEE (1998) *Teacher Supply and Demand Modelling: a Technical Description* London: HMSO

DfEE (2000a) *Statistics of Education: Teachers* London: HMSO

DfEE (2000b) *Statistics of Education: Schools* London: HMSO

DfEE (2000c) *Press Release 2000/0247* 1 June 2000

DfEE (2001) *Statistical First Release 16/2001* London: HMSO

Edwards L (2002) *Only If...* at www.ippr.org.uk/research

Fraser H, Draper J and Taylor W (1998) 'The Quality of Teachers' Lives: Teachers and Job Satisfaction in the Primary School' *Evaluation and Research in Education* 12.2

Hay (2001) *The Retention Dilemma* London: Hay Group Working Paper

Heafford M and Jennsion B (1998) 'Destined to Teach: A Case Study of a PGCE Cohort Over Sixteen Years' *Journal of Education for Teaching* 24.2

Hillman J (1994) *National Undergraduate Perceptions of Teaching as a Career* Commission for Education Insights into Education and Training

Hutchings M, Menter I, Ross A and Thomson D (2000) *Teacher Supply and Retention in London, 1998-99* University of North London School of Education

IPPR (2001) *Press Release* 30 April 2001 *Workload Impact Statements*

Meadows P (2000) 'Pensions and the Labour Market' in IPPR (2000) *New Economy* 7.4

PricewaterhouseCoopers (2001) *Teacher Workload Study – Interim Report* Available at www.dfes.gov.uk

Reid I and Caudwell J (1997) 'Why Did Secondary PGCE Students Choose Teaching as a Career?' *Research in Education* 58

Sands M (1993) 'Student Withdrawals from Teacher Training' *New Era in Education* 74.2

Scott C (1999) *Teachers 2000 Project in England: A Study of Teacher Satisfaction, Motivation and Health* Nottingham Trent University

Smithers A and Hill S (1989) 'Recruitment to Physics and Mathematics Teaching: A Personality Problem?' *Research Papers in Education* 4.1

Spear M, Gould K and Lee B (1999) *Who Would Be a Teacher? A Review of Factors Motivating and Demotivating Prospective and Practising Teachers* NFER

Stewart M and Perrin R (1989) 'A Comparison of Physics Graduates and PGCE Students' Attitudes to a Career in Teaching' *Physics Education* 24.5

School Teachers' Review Body (1992) *School Teachers' Review Body First Report* London: HMSO

STRB (1993) *School Teachers' Review Body Second Report* London: HMSO

STRB (2001) *School Teachers' Review Body Tenth Report* London: HMSO

Teacher Training Agency (2001) *Press Release 06/01* 27April 2001

Varlaam A, Nuttall D and Walker A (1992) *What Makes Teachers Tick? A Survey of Teacher Morale and Motivation* London: LSE Centre for Educational Research

3. Who returns to teaching? The profile and motivation of teacher returners

Gill Penlington

Very little is known about people who take a career break from teaching. Beyond the raw statistics detailing age and gender, there is no official information at all about the profile of the eleven thousand former teachers who return each year to the classroom.

Identifying who these returners are, and developing strategies to attract more of them back to the classroom is an important strand of the Government's recruitment and retention policy. If teaching is to become a world-class profession, attracting the brightest and best recruits, it needs to encourage movements of staff. Teachers should be encouraged to take career breaks and develop their talents in other professions but should also be given a clear route back into the classroom should they wish to return.

As figures for recruitment to Initial Teacher Training improve, attention has turned to retention. The fact that 40 per cent of teachers leave the profession within the first three years is often highlighted. In fact, the attrition rate for teachers compares favourably with many other professions. The fact that many teachers are leaving is only a problem if few of them are returning. At present, there are estimated to be almost 300,000 qualified teachers of working age who are not employed in schools (DfEE 2000). We predicted in Chapter 2 that 5,610 former secondary teachers in the PIT are intending to return to the profession, and a further 13,860 are undecided about whether to return.

How can more of these undecided former teachers be encouraged back into the classroom? What inducements do they need to persuade them to return? One way of finding out is to look at the characteristics of those people who do decide to return to teaching after a break, and see whether any lessons can be learnt from their experiences.

Our research presents a profile of the eleven thousand teachers who will return to the classroom this year. Based upon questionnaire responses gathered from over 20 centres across Britain running refresher courses for returners, and supplemented by primary data collected by Goldsmiths College over the last four years, we hope to provide a picture of the type of people who are going back to teaching. Who are they? What motivates them? And what can policymakers and practitioners learn from their experiences?

What is known already

At present, there is only a limited amount of information about teacher returners in England. In 1998-9, the most recent year for which data is available, a total of 10,700 former teachers entered full-time teaching[1] (DfEE 2000). This represents 39 per cent of the total teaching intake for the year, compared with over 50 per cent at the peak. The numbers of re-entrants are skewed towards primary teaching: 6,000 former teachers re-entered the nursery and primary sector, with 4,700 going back to teach in a secondary school.

Two things are notable about these figures. Firstly, there is a striking gender imbalance. Women returning to teaching outnumber men by more than 8 to 1, and this phenomenon is especially pronounced within the primary sector, where the ratio is more like 11 female returners for every one male. A quick look at the age profile of returners explains why this is the case.

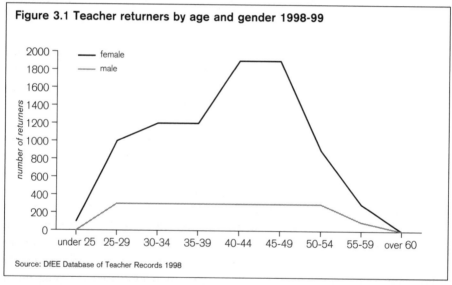

Figure 3.1 Teacher returners by age and gender 1998-99

Source: DfEE Database of Teacher Records 1998

The vast majority of female re-entrants are aged between 40 to 49, suggesting that they are parents re-entering the job market after a period out to care for children. The age profile of men, by contrast, is more evenly spread, suggesting that their decision to return to teaching was less influenced by family decisions.

Secondly, the percentage of teacher returners as a proportion of the total entrants to the teaching profession has fallen steadily since 1991. At its peak they accounted for over half the total intake. By 1998 only 38 per cent of entrants had taught before. Although there has been a slight upturn in the proportion of re-entrants in 1999, it is not big enough to suggest that the trend is being reversed.

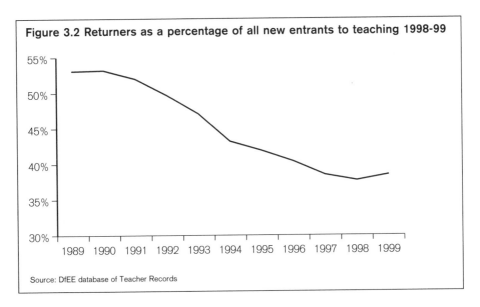

Figure 3.2 Returners as a percentage of all new entrants to teaching 1998-99

Source: DfEE database of Teacher Records

What does stand out, is the potential offered by returning teachers to solve supply problems. Teacher vacancies currently stand at 2,600 (DfES 2001). If we can restore the percentage of teachers re-entering the profession to 1989 levels, that will mean another 4,200 full-time teachers going into classrooms each year.[2]

Achieving these kind of levels would provide a long-term solution to teacher shortages. However, without more detailed information about where teacher returners come from, and what motivates and disillusions them, it is going to be very difficult to formulate successful strategies to woo back former teachers. More information about returners' length of time out of teaching, their previous job and salary, and their experiences of the non-teaching job market are needed.

A study of London's teacher supply situation (Ross 1999) found that most returners were in the their mid-30s and had come either from other employment or from a position of caring for dependents. Two-thirds of returners began their career break within eight years of qualification, and the vast majority were returning after a very short absence from the profession: over two-thirds returned to teaching within two years of departure.

Over a third of all respondents claimed that better pay would have encouraged them to return to the profession sooner. Almost 25 per cent argued that more flexible employment – making use of job share and part-time work – would have encouraged them back, while the same proportion stated that more local employment opportunities would act as an incentive to return.

UNL's study provides a useful profile of the type of people who return to teaching. There does remain significant scope, though, for further work in the area.

Current policy initiatives

The NHS provides a clear and accessible bank of information targeted at former healthcare professionals, explaining precisely how to go about re-entering the health service and what support, financial and otherwise, is available. It identifies different groups of target returners – such as parents with children, people who have been out of the profession for some time and those who have been working in the private sector – and provides returner packages tailored to their needs. They also provide detailed information about the precise requirements for re-entry to the different areas of the health service.

Although the Government actively encourages former teachers to return to the classroom, they are targeted by a much less sophisticated programme. More needs to be known about the type of people who return to teaching in order to frame specific policies catering for their needs. Current inducements are:

- *Welcome back bonus*

  As an inducement for more former teachers to return to the profession, the Government offered a one-off payment in 2001 of up to £4,000 for people returning to the classroom regardless of the route via which a teacher returns. Over 2,500 teachers registered their details (Hansard 2001).

- *Training bursaries*

  From April 2001, every participant on a refresher course is entitled to a government funded training bursary of up to £150 per week (to a maximum of £1,500 for the duration of the course) and childcare support of up to £150 per week for children aged 5 or under, and £70 per week for children aged 5-14 (up to a maximum of £1800 per child and £840 per child respectively). Introducing training bursaries to pay for childcare is a positive step towards overcoming the obstacles to returning to work faced by many parents.

- *LEA and school campaigns*

  Many LEAs and schools have active policies that aim to keep in touch with former teachers and provide them with opportunities to return to the classroom. Universities and LEAs run 'taster days', where former teachers can attend courses and get a feel for modern teaching practices. These courses make a particular effort to reach out to minority groups, and have had some success in this respect. Goldsmiths University, for example, reports high levels of participation on its taster courses from black and Asian women.

- *Keeping in touch programme*

  The Keeping in Touch Programme was launched by the TTA in autumn 1999. It compiles a database of teachers who have left the profession but wish to be kept up to date with developments. A newsletter is issued termly, providing details of training programmes and curriculum developments as well as a list of useful contacts.

Our research

In order to carry out research on the background of people who return to teaching it is necessary to be able to identify them. There are two main routes back into teaching for a person with Qualified Teacher Status. Approximately 80 per cent of teacher returners simply approach their LEA or apply directly for jobs with local schools. The alternative is more formal. The TTA sponsors 80 refresher courses around the country. Practitioners who successfully complete the course and gain a position in a school are eligible for the welcome back bonus. The TTA estimates that around 1800 people took up refresher courses by the end of 2001.

Our research concentrates on returners using the second route back to the classroom. The Social Market Foundation made an initial approach to 45 refresher course providers, explaining that we were undertaking research into the background of teacher returners and asking course supervisors for their support and participation. Twenty-six initially agreed to take part. Of these, five were running courses which started too late for the purposes of our work, leaving a total of 21 participating centres. This represents a 47 per cent response rate. In addition, Goldsmiths College, University of London, agreed to allow us access to their records on teacher returners, which stretch back to 1997. We sent out 310 questionnaires during July and August 2001, and 97 replies were received, representing a response rate of 31 per cent. In addition, two centres provided us with collated spreadsheet information about course participants.

This sample is too small to represent accurately all teachers returning to the classroom. It is intended to provide a snapshot of the situation, providing some information on the background of teacher returners, and helping to frame questions that require future research. There is a possibility that the type of people who use refresher courses as a route back into teaching are not representative of returners as a whole. It may be that the courses attract those who have been out of the profession for a long time and who feel the need to brush up on their skills before re-entering the classroom.

Findings

Age

Our data mirror the Government's official figures. The age at which women are coming back to teaching strongly suggests that they have taken a career break for family reasons. A quick look at when returners opted to leave the profession confirms this: 51 per cent of women stopped teaching between the ages of 25-34. This is the most common gap in which to have children. Around 10-15 years later, when the family is older, many women decide to resume their careers; 42 per cent of all teachers returning to the profession are women between the ages of 35-49. This has implications for the way schools employ staff, with part-time work and job share opportunities needing to be more available.

Returning men, by contrast, tend to leave teaching at a very different stage of their careers. Over a fifth (21 per cent) depart aged 50 or over. The comparable figure for women is three per cent.

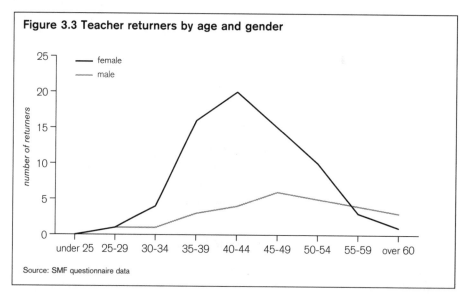

Figure 3.3 Teacher returners by age and gender

Source: SMF questionnaire data

Years out of teaching

The majority of returning teachers attending local refresher courses have been out of the profession for between six and ten years. A significant number have been out for less time. This suggests that many are reasonably up-to-date with educational developments. Returners using the Goldsmiths distance learning course, however, tend to have spent a longer period of time out of teaching. The majority of former teachers on their course have spent between 11-20 years in a different profession, with

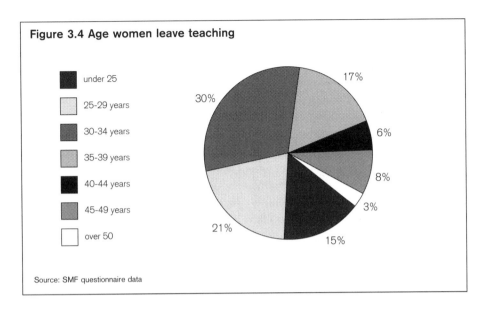

Figure 3.4 Age women leave teaching

under 25

25-29 years

30-34 years

35-39 years

40-44 years

45-49 years

over 50

17%

30%

6%

8%

3%

21%

15%

Source: SMF questionnaire data

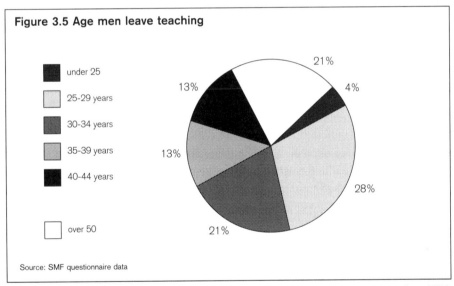

Figure 3.5 Age men leave teaching

under 25

25-29 years

30-34 years

35-39 years

40-44 years

over 50

21%

13%

4%

13%

28%

21%

Source: SMF questionnaire data

an average time away from the classroom of 16 years. Returners on other TTA sponsored courses averaged 12 years out.

The age differential between returners on the two different forms of course suggests that flexibility about the route back to the classroom is important. Some people have the time to attend a local refresher course, others prefer to minimise contact time and learn using modern communication methods. The vast majority prefer to work directly with local schools and LEAs. Promoting diversity of this

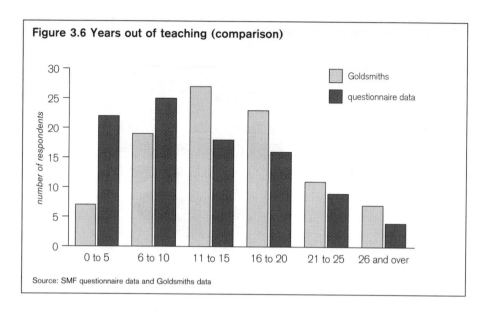

Figure 3.6 Years out of teaching (comparison)

Source: SMF questionnaire data and Goldsmiths data

kind is important if more people are to be attracted from the PIT into teaching.

Gender

The gender mix of people returning to teaching has changed over time. The ratio of female to male returners taking up places on refresher courses is 3:1, which is much lower than the Government's most recent figure for returning teachers that indicated an 8:1 male imbalance (DfEE 1998). Data for the last four years from Goldsmith College produces an even more pronounced result: over the last four years, the ratio of women to men on the Goldsmiths course has been just over 2:1.

These statistics do seem to suggest that men are coming back to the classroom in higher numbers. More men in the PIT may be amenable to the idea of returning to teaching, given the right policy incentives. This is an area on which policy makers need to concentrate.

Men overwhelmingly return to secondary and post-compulsory education. The gender ratio of re-entrants within the primary sector stands at 13:1. However, there is some evidence to suggest that flexible routes back into teaching can increase the number of men returning to primary teaching. The men who opted to take the distance learning courses run by Goldsmiths were disproportionately from the primary sector. This holds, even taking into account the higher absolute numbers of men on the course. The ratio of women to men re-entering the primary sector from Goldsmiths stands at 7:1, in contrast to the much higher figure of 13:1 for the returner courses generally. This seems to suggest that flexible ways of re-entering teaching (for

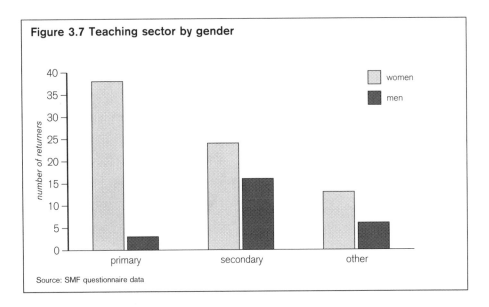

Figure 3.7 Teaching sector by gender

Source: SMF questionnaire data

example, via distance learning) not only attract more men, but attract more men from hard-to-reach groups.[3]

Career paths

When people take a break from teaching, what do they go on to do? Understanding this gives some sense of where teaching fits into a modern career path, and also which professions teaching competes with for staff.

Predictably, the answer depends on the age and gender of the person in question. It also changes over time: career paths develop new directions according to family commitments and the general economic climate.

It is important to note that the career patterns described below are particular to returning teachers. Teachers who leave the profession permanently are likely to have different job aspirations and motivations from those who are at least open to the idea of returning. While we are not arguing that every teacher who goes back to the classroom intends to do so from the outset, it seems reasonable to suppose that those who do return have different characteristics from those who leave for good. The career patterns we describe cannot be generalised.

Women

The women surveyed who take a break from teaching often become full-time parents (35 per cent) or take jobs in education or childcare (21 per cent). This last category

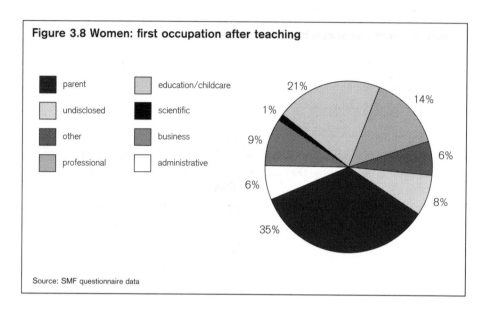

Figure 3.8 Women: first occupation after teaching

parent   education/childcare

undisclosed   scientific

other   business

professional   administrative

21%   14%

1%

9%   6%

6%   8%

35%

Source: SMF questionnaire data

includes childminding, part-time supply teaching and private tutoring but excludes any contractual position in a school.

It may seem strange for qualified teachers to leave the profession in favour of less well-paid positions in education and childcare. In fact, many do so because they intend to start a family in the near future and want a flexible, less demanding job in the meantime. If we look at how professional occupations among women change over time, this argument is supported.

A significant minority (23 per cent) of women leave teaching and go straight into business and professional careers. These include jobs like retail management and human resources, and are often pressurised, time-consuming positions. However, the percentage of women remaining in such professions diminishes over time. When we look at the occupations held by returning teachers immediately prior to their classroom re-entrance, the number of full-time parents remains almost unchanged at 34 per cent, but the proportion with business or professional careers falls from 23 per cent to 14 per cent. By contrast, the number of women working in the education or childcare sectors rises over this period from 21 per cent to 39 per cent. This increase comes almost entirely at the expense of the business, professional and administrative sectors.

The increase in the number of women working in the education and childcare sector immediately prior to returning to teaching is due to more women wanting jobs that fit around the demands of raising a family. Originally, many women left teaching in order to change career; they did not leave with the intention of having children. However, as time passed, a number of them decided to start families, and so switched

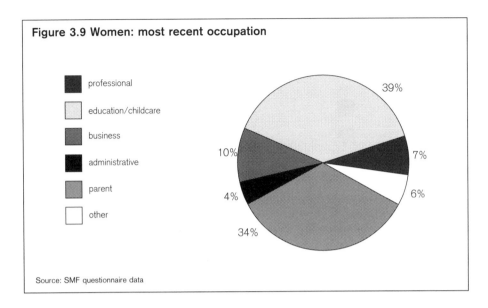

Figure 3.9 Women: most recent occupation

- professional
- education/childcare
- business
- administrative
- parent
- other

39%

10%

7%

4%

6%

34%

Source: SMF questionnaire data

from their new high-pressured jobs to ones in the education and childcare sectors that offered flexible working hours and family-friendly policies. Subsequently, when children have grown older and the pressures of raising a family have eased, many wish to swap from their education/childcare positions back to the more demanding teaching positions, while still retaining the flexibility that comes with the job.

A good example of this is one woman in her late 40s, who is currently a classroom assistant. She trained to be a teacher, but could not find a position upon qualification and so entered the civil service. After having children, she took a job as a classroom assistant to get some experience, and is now on a refresher course with the intention to teach. Another respondent left teaching to become a journalist, but gave this up when she had children. As they have now entered full-time schooling, she wants a job that provides a challenge but still fits in with her family commitments and so is returning to teaching.

Men

The biggest group of men who take a break from teaching enter jobs in the business or scientific sectors. The career path of one respondent is quite typical: he left teaching at the age of 30 because he was unhappy with his prospects for promotion. From an ICT background, he took up a job as a software engineer and then graduated to the position of programmer. Now, aged 46, he wants to return to the classroom because he loves teaching, and thinks the job now offers better promotion prospects.

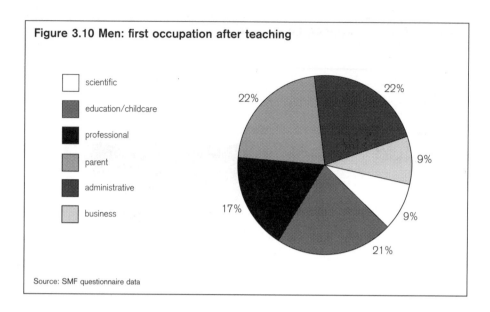

Figure 3.10 Men: first occupation after teaching

scientific
education/childcare
professional
parent
administrative
business

22%   22%   9%   9%   21%   17%

Source: SMF questionnaire data

Men's career paths change over time but in a different way from their female counterparts: 21 per cent of men leave teaching for family reasons, but few remain full-time carers. By the time they are ready to go back to the classroom, the percentage with responsibility for caring for family members has fallen to four per cent. More noticeable among men is the shift from business/scientific jobs into professional/administrative careers over time (see Figure 3.11).

Only 26 per cent of men went straight from teaching into professional or administrative jobs. Immediately prior to re-entering teaching, this percentage had grown to 57 per cent. Upon leaving the classroom, men were compelled to seek jobs that made use of their existing talents and skills. So for example, the relatively high number of people entering scientific professions can be accounted for with reference to the prevalence of science teachers who acquire a range of skills during their time in the classroom.

Similarly, positions in business make use of the transferable skills such as presentational ability, management style and effective time keeping necessary to be a good teacher. As former teachers gain more workplace experience and build up their CVs, they no longer rely so heavily upon the skills learnt in the classroom, and so are able to take up a broader range of employment opportunities.

Pay

The pay patterns of former teachers support the idea that they take jobs that are linked to their classroom specialism. A clear pay premium attaches to maths and science subjects. In our research, over 80 per cent of former teachers earning £20-30,000 a

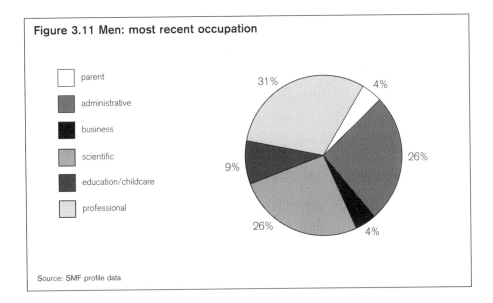

Figure 3.11 Men: most recent occupation

parent

administrative

business

scientific

education/childcare

professional

31%   4%

26%

9%

26%   4%

Source: SMF profile data

year had specialised in maths or science. By contrast, almost half of those earning under £10,000 were English and History specialists. Linguists fell somewhere in between the two, earning more than English/History teachers but less than their Maths/Science counterparts.

These earnings premiums do give credence to the idea that former teachers initially take up jobs that use their skills and specialisms as teachers. Those with a maths and scientific background are able to find jobs in the business and IT sectors, which are more highly paid than many of the careers open to teachers without transferable skills of this kind.

However, people who take a career break from teaching rarely go into highly paid jobs. The majority earn under £10,000 per annum during their time out of the classroom – reflecting the pay constraints imposed by family commitments. Part-time working women are one of the lowest paid groups in society and make up the largest single group of returning teachers. This deflates the average salary earned by teachers during their break from the classroom.

Pay differentials between teachers do open up once they enter the labour market. Primary school teachers consistently earn less in their jobs outside the classroom than their secondary counterparts. Primary teachers are the single group most likely to earn less than £10,000 a year. This is partly explained by the high concentration of women among primary teachers, but seems to be more deep rooted than that. No primary teacher in our research earned over £30,000 per annum in their subsequent career. This does suggest that primary teachers may not be perceived as having the necessary transferable skills to reach highly paid positions in the labour market.

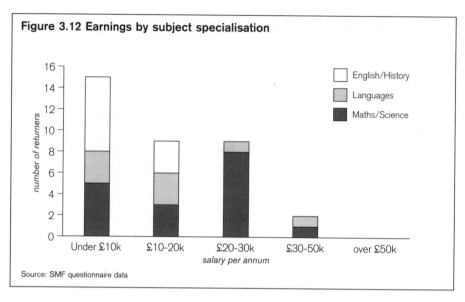

Figure 3.12 Earnings by subject specialisation

Source: SMF questionnaire data

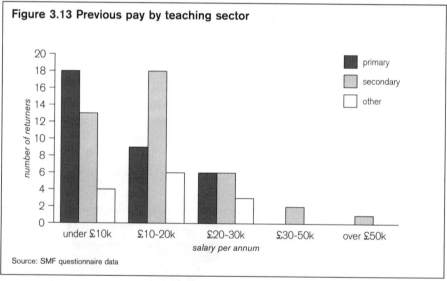

Figure 3.13 Previous pay by teaching sector

Source: SMF questionnaire data

The relatively low salaries do suggest that teachers do not leave the classroom specifically because of the pay.

Working conditions

The most common response given by people asked to compare their jobs concerned working hours. The types of jobs taken up by teachers during their time out of the classroom often involved a substantial time commitment, particularly for those people working in the business or IT sectors. However, almost without exception, respondents compared teaching unfavourably with these jobs. They complained not of the long hours, but of the way in teaching infringed upon their personal and family lives.

Other comments reflect teachers' frustration with the pay and conditions of the job. Many pointed out that although in some respects their careers outside the classroom were more pressured than teaching had been, they enjoyed excellent working conditions. This is a key point to note. The respondents were used to doing stressful jobs, and did not object to working long hours, but the working environment assumed a highly important role. If teaching is to attract back professionals, it needs to offer them working conditions that are comparable to those of other careers.

Motivations

Reasons for leaving teaching

It was found that 39 per cent of former teachers took time out of teaching for reasons to do with their family. In most cases this was either because they had recently had children, or because they were intending to start a family. In a handful of instances it was because of responsibilities towards elderly relatives.

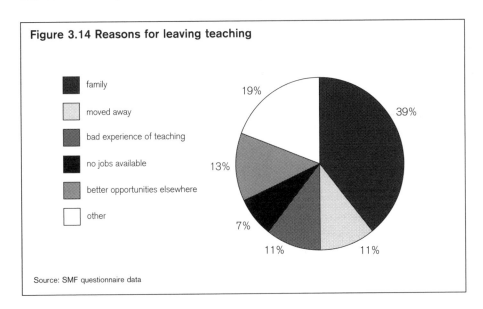

Figure 3.14 Reasons for leaving teaching

family
moved away
bad experience of teaching
no jobs available
better opportunities elsewhere
other

19%
39%
13%
7%
11%
11%

Source: SMF questionnaire data

Some people leave teaching because they simply want a change of career. The task for teaching is to attract these people back once they start looking around in their current jobs for a new challenge.

A significant minority (11 per cent) left the profession because of a bad experience in the classroom. It is easy to assume that these people are unlikely to make good teachers second time around. However, teaching as a profession has changed significantly in recent years. Whether they find the profession, as currently constructed, more or less attractive than previously is open to question.

Typical of this kind of person is an English teacher, who left the profession in 1996 after a bad experience in the classroom. Five years on, she reports, 'I feel ready to try again, and now have the time to concentrate on the job.' Clearly, with the confidence coming from a spell out of teaching and a newfound enthusiasm for the job, she believes that she can make a good teacher. Similar is a young science teacher who left teaching in her early twenties. She explains, 'I felt too young to be a teacher. I needed some "real life" experiences.' After working for ten years as a recruitment consultant, she wants a challenge and feels confident enough to go back to teaching.

The challenge for policy-makers is to capitalise on the confidence and skills gained out of the classroom. Former teachers need to be persuaded that firstly, the profession has changed for the better in their absence, and secondly, that they have valuable skills to offer. Simply because someone left disillusioned does not mean that they can never re-enter teaching and be successful.

The final reason given for leaving teaching is that there were practical problems in the way of remaining in the classroom. Some people moved away and could not find another teaching post, others left the country, and a few were simply unable to find a teaching position when they qualified, and so ended up in a different career. These people would naturally like to return to teaching, and have used the expansion of returner courses as an opportunity to do so. Part of the task facing policy makers is to remove any remaining practical hurdles that prevent willing former teachers from returning to the profession.

Why do former teachers return to the classroom?

A love for the profession

The majority of teachers return to the classroom because they enjoy teaching. Almost a third of respondents cited their love for the job as the main reason to return.

This paints a very positive picture of the teaching profession. The message coming most frequently out of questionnaire was passionate. Dozens of respondents, when asked why they were returning to teaching, simply replied 'I enjoy it'. Other typical responses include:

'I love children'
'I want an interesting and challenging job'
'I've always wanted to return'
'I miss the classroom and working with students'

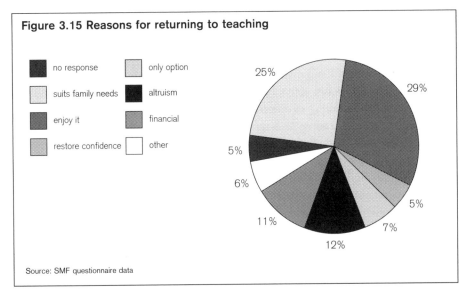

Figure 3.15 Reasons for returning to teaching

no response   only option

suits family needs   altruism

enjoy it   financial

restore confidence   other

25%   29%

5%

6%

5%

11%

7%

12%

Source: SMF questionnaire data

Altruism

Returners who cited specifically altruistic reasons that focussed on the contribution a teacher can make to society have revealing characteristics. Their salary and professional background is unrepresentative of teacher returners as a whole. 'Altruistic' returners are more wealthy and from a narrower professional background than on average. Typically, they will have left teaching during the early 1980s, and spent the next twenty years working in business or marketing. Over 70 per cent earn between £20-50,000 per annum.

One woman in her late thirties left primary teaching at the age of 22 because she felt she wasn't ready for the job. Seventeen years on, she earns between £20-30,000 as a casino manager and wants to return because 'I now feel I can be a good teacher. I want to make a difference.'

Another self-employed marketing manager is leaving her business out of a belief that 'children should be given the best start possible. I want to contribute.' A very successful foreign teacher has returned to the British classroom 'to do something meaningful.'

The characteristics of altruistic returners fit a pattern. At a certain point in life, having earned a comfortable living and achieved success in the business world, people start wanting to 'give something back' – and so return to the classroom.

Negative returners

A small percentage of former teachers return to the profession for what can be termed 'negative' reasons. The chart shows that 7 per cent take up teaching as a last resort –

it is the only career option available to them at this point in time. Other 'negative' reasons for returning do not show up in the statistics, but can be summarised as a lack of alternative job opportunities.

A good example of a negative returner comes from a woman in her mid-50s. She left teaching in 1969 because of class management problems, and entered the commercial sector, working in computer distribution. After being made redundant, she decided to take up a place on a refresher course when 'redundancy and failure to get office work coincided with the return to teaching thrust.'

It is particularly worrying if people who struggled with the job first time around are now deciding to return out of economic necessity although we should not assume that such people are not good teachers. The Government needs to encourage skilled and qualified people from the world of business to re-enter teaching. Promoting teaching as a secure and stable profession is simply playing to its strengths – and this may encourage committed people from industry to return to the classroom. It is not the same as saying that teaching is an easy job, or one which is a last resort.

Public service ethos

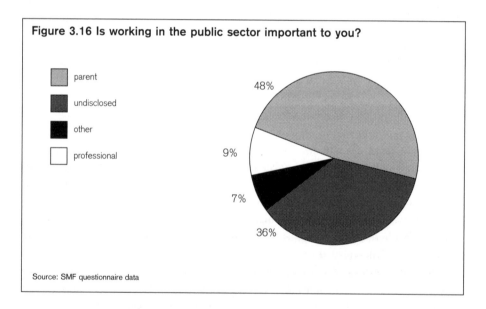

Figure 3.16 Is working in the public sector important to you?

parent

undisclosed

other

professional

48%

9%

7%

36%

Source: SMF questionnaire data

Under half of the people returning to the profession share the view that working in the public sector is important. Many of them appreciate that teaching is a valuable profession, but that it should not excuse poor working conditions. Their attachment to the public sector is not unconditional. One returning teacher remarked 'Working in the public sector is important to a certain extent, but not if this means working in overwhelming, stressful situations without support.' Another, when asked if working in the public sector was important to her replied 'In principle, yes. But if it proves too difficult I would consider alternatives'.

Interestingly, there is a gender bias in the data. Significantly more women (64 per cent to 40 per cent of men) are likely to rate working in the public sector as important. In the long-run, if the Government succeeds in its aim of encouraging more men back into primary teaching, it will have to address the issue of working conditions.

The Government has to realise that it cannot rely on the goodwill of staff indefinitely. Teachers who have spent time working in other professions have an acute understanding of how working conditions affect quality of life. They quite reasonably want teaching to meet a high standard in this respect.

Recommendations

In order to attract more former teachers back to the classroom, the profession needs to become flexible, adapting to the patterns of a modern working life. Taking a career break from teaching should be seen as a natural option for many people, enabling them to gain skills and experiences that they can bring back to the classroom when they return.

Recommendation

- Facilitate job sharing and other part time working

The Government has encouraged schools adopt job share schemes. However, no figures exist on the number of job shares in operation at present. Anecdotal evidence suggests that head teachers are not keen on the system, as it is more costly than employing a single member of staff to cover a vacancy. The Work-Life Balance Team at the Department of Trade and Industry is currently trying to calculate the extra costs associated with a job share. This information will prove important. In spite of this, the funding allocated to schools to cover teaching posts is the same, regardless of whether the post is advertised as a job share. The DfES should increase the amount of funding allocated to schools to cover teaching vacancies that become job shares.

LEAs can play a crucial role encouraging positive attitudes towards job sharing. Essex LEA makes a particular effort to encourage schools to consider appointing candidates who are willing to work on a job-share basis. LEAs also act as first point of contact for many potential returning teachers, and so will be responsible for bringing the availability of job shares to the attention of more potential returnees. The Keeping in Touch scheme could also distribute information on the possibility of working in this way.

Recommendation

●   Maintain relationships with former teachers.

Existing policies do try to capitalise on the interest teachers have in maintaining contact with the education world. There is, however, room for improvement. Schools should take the lead, and make an effort to remain in contact with former staff who left on good terms and live locally. These former teachers could then be invited along to join in some suitable training: keeping them up to date with developments in education, and ensuring that they retain good links with the school. Many teachers, however, leave the profession because they move away from their original residence. In this instance, LEAs could act as co-ordinators by matching former teachers who are new to an area with schools locally that are willing to share their INSET provision. The General Teaching Council remains in contact with a number of former teachers, as well as all existing practitioners, and could play a valuable role reinforcing the message that if you leave the profession but retain an interest in education, it makes sense to contact the local LEA.

Recommendation

●   Identify potential returners.

The education and childcare sectors are extremely popular with women wanting a gentle re-introduction to the world of work. LEAs should consider ways of targeting employees in these sectors, providing them with information about the opportunities to return to teaching.

Obviously, this needs to be handled sensitively. It would be counterproductive for schools to be seen to poach staff from the early years and childcare sectors, but it could be possible to establish a partnership between schools and pre-schools, providing a complementary service to each. LEAs may need to share information and match staff.

Recommendation

●   Use fast track to target returners.

The Fast-Track teaching scheme could explicitly target mature returners, making best use of their expertise and allowing them a rapid progression up the promotion ladder upon their return to the classroom.

At present, fast-track teaching is open to teachers of any age, but they cannot exceed point 8 on the pay spine (£23,358). This prevents some returners from applying for a place on the programme, as during their teaching career they may have exceeded this spine point. The fast-track scheme should relax this regulation, and explicitly target mature returners.

There is no published data available on the background of successful applicants to the fast-track programme. A DfES official reported to SMF that 'the majority' of people in the first cohort of fast-track students were new graduates. It would be a positive step if the second cohort included some mature returners.

Recommendation

●   Promote the profession.

The Teacher Training Agency and DfES are well aware of the importance of promoting a positive image of teaching. There have been a number of high profile advertising campaigns in recent years, and these should continue. However, as the TTA recognises, the variety of motivations requires a variety of messages, and some should be aimed explicitly at potential returners.

There should also be greater opportunities for former teachers to engage in 'taster' days. These are run at present by LEAs and University Departments, and some schools. More schools should provide courses of this type. While it may be a time-consuming commitment, schools could be encouraged to view it as a valuable opportunity to forge links with the local community. OFSTED should reward schools that set up and run taster day courses by recognising their existence in their inspection reports.

Recommendation

●   Change attitudes towards mature returners.

Many of the returning teachers in our survey mentioned that they were worried about gaining employment in schools. Because of their experience, they are entitled to a higher salary than a newly qualified teacher with whom they often compete for positions. Schools are entitled to make this choice. However, some may not be aware of the benefits of employing older staff. The General Teaching Council can play an important role in promoting the merits of mature returners. At a time when the Government is keen to attract more new recruits from outside teaching, it is imperative that no prejudice attaches to older staff.

Recommendation

● Build confidence among potential returners.

Returning to the classroom after an average 12 year break is no easy matter. Returning teachers should be offered a first year training and development package similar to an NQT's Induction Year. Schools should appoint mentors to returning teachers. An experienced member of staff would take responsibility for running the induction course and familiarising the returner with the school. This should be funded by the Government.

Recommendation

● Retain middle-aged men.

Too many men in their 40s and 50s leave teaching. Perhaps they are suffering from burn-out or staleness. Schools need to adopt explicit strategies to encourage men in this age group to remain within the profession. This must include offering a change of role and new experiences, perhaps outside the profession on a part-time or secondment basis. For example, education business partnerships place suitable candidates in positions at local firms. After a period in a different environment, staff return refreshed and with a new set of skills that can be deployed in the classroom. The Government should encourage more schools to consider secondments of this kind. It could be tied into the Davies Review which is considering ways to promote enterprise in schools. If more staff have an experience of the business world, the teaching of 'innovative' skills in the classroom is likely to be of a higher standard.

Recommendation

● Increased distance-learning courses.

There is evidence that men prefer using distance learning refresher courses. There is also evidence that distance-learning courses attract a different profile of returning teachers, namely, ones who have been out of teaching for longer.

Making routes back to teaching as accessible as possible will increase the numbers of returners each year. Since distance-learning courses demonstrably encourage a different profile of people to return, the TTA should fund more of them. Distance-learning courses are in many respects cheaper to operate than their location-based counterparts: fewer attendees will require the childcare bursaries, as learning takes place in the home.

The Teacher Training Agency should encourage more universities and LEAs to offer courses that incorporate flexible patterns of learning, making greater use of ICT and communications technology.

Conclusion

Returning teachers have the potential to dramatically ease recruitment shortages. If the number of teachers returning to the classroom after a career break can be restored to 1989 levels, another 4,200 full-time teachers will be going into classrooms each year.

The Government cannot afford to ignore the potential held by these qualified professionals. It has to realise, however, that they need special treatment. It is not enough simply to assume that standard incentives and advertising strategies will lure them back to the classroom. They have needs and requirements that first-time teachers do not yet demand. They need more flexible working practices and accessible routes back into teaching. They may need the desire to teach reawakened, or to be given the confidence to believe that they can still do the job. Or they may simply need to be convinced that schools will hire them and that promotion is a real possibility.

Increasing the number of returning teachers may also change the shape of the profession. Teaching does not have to be viewed as a job for life. It can be viewed as a career that equips practitioners with skills and experience that enable them to work in a number of exciting and dynamic fields throughout their working life. It can be taken up and left more than once. Teaching will benefit from practitioners with a whole range of different experiences and expertise – and the profession as a whole should send out this message. Experienced former teachers are welcome re-entrants.

The departure of teachers from the classroom should not be viewed as a threat, but as a positive challenge. Returners in our survey repeated time and time again that they loved teaching – and this is the message that teachers leaving the profession need to take away with them. If they do, then there is a good chance that they can be encouraged back, bringing experience and enthusiasm with them.

Endnotes

1   The data on former teachers re-entering part-time teaching is non-comparable. Part-time teacher returners will be considered in more depth further in this work.

2   This calculation assumes that the total number of entrants to teaching per year is 30,000, a figure below current recruitment levels. In 1989, 15,900 of the entrants to teaching were returners. By 1999, this number had fallen to 11,700.

3   It also suggests that more men are returning to teaching generally. Since men favour flexible, less time-demanding ways of returning to teaching, they are likely to choose to re-enter directly via a school or LEA and not take on a refresher course.

References

DfEE (1998) *Database of Teacher Records*

DfEE (2000) *Statistics of Education: Teachers* London: HMSO

DfES (2001) *Professionalism and Trust* London: Social Market Foundation

Hansard 22 October 2001 Column 40W

Ross A et al (1999) Teacher Supply and Retention in London: Phase One Report University of North London. Available at www.unl.ac.uk/ipse

TTA Press notice 11/01 9 July 2001 *Bursaries offered for return* at www.canteach.gov.uk/return/kit/index.htm

4. Supply teachers: symptom of the problem or part of the solution?

Dara Barlin and Joe Hallgarten

*Substitute teachers have remained largely absent from educational agendas...
[because of] a paucity of interest that is frequently couched in negative
pedagogic or professional terms, but, until recently, was not seen as
particularly threatening to the core work force of permanent teaching staff.*
(Morrison 1999a)

The teaching profession may be undergoing a quiet revolution. In the face of what the Chief Inspector of Schools called 'the worst teacher shortages in three decades', attention has focused on the decline in the number of people who want to become or remain teachers. Meanwhile, there has been a simultaneous, inconspicuous rise in the use of supply teachers.

This rise has provided an important tool to help schools cope with the growing demand for short term cover and long term vacancy-filling. Rather than sending children home, splitting single classes across several others, or taking away non-contact time, supply teachers have stepped into empty classrooms and continued, at least on the surface, the teaching and learning process.

Despite their now-crucial role, there is a dearth of data and research on the subject of supply teachers. Discussions about supply teaching remain marginal to policy debates. This is surprising for a number of reasons.

- First, although used throughout the system, supply teachers are most commonly employed in the schools which this Government is rightly most worried about; namely, urban secondary schools.

- Second, in recent debates over the role of the private sector in state education, a myth is often perpetuated that the private sector is only dealing with the peripheries of schools, and has yet to penetrate the core function of teaching and learning. The provision of supply teachers by private agencies refutes this. Investigating supply agencies could add clarity to the current, confused debates about the role of the private sector in the provision of public services.

- Third, freed from certain constraints, practices around supply teaching may provide new solutions to dilemmas over teacher shortages and the long term future of the profession. In particular, it challenges schools to offer more flexibility to permanent staff.

Figures on supply teachers are often inconsistent and vary greatly in definition and scope. There has, however, been an irrefutable rise in both the number of available supply teachers and the demand for their services, brought about by:

- teacher shortages

- a rise in the number of staff absences due to training and sickness

The problem of data collection

What is a supply teacher?

Terms such as occasional, temporary, floating, emergency cover, short-term supply, long-term supply, overseas, agency and non-agency, are often used interchangeably to describe supply teachers. Data gathering is therefore problematic. For instance, the DfES uses the term 'occasional' teachers, full-time teachers on contracts of less than a month. Supply agencies, however, include those on contract for more than a month, and sometimes more than a term.

An additional difficulty in assessing the situation lies in the interpretation of how teachers should be classified. Short-term agency staff are often grouped together with non-agency supply teachers; long-term agency supply teachers lumped together with permanent full-time teachers and part-time teachers confused with regular supply teachers.

The shift from LEA supply pools to supply agencies, discussed below, has made data collection more difficult. Our research has revealed little consistency in the ways different agencies compile data. This data is unlikely to be shared anyway, due to the competitive nature of the market.

It seems imperative that all parties with a vested interest have some means of centralising enough information to assess the current level of supply teacher participation. It is also essential that different institutions set standardised definitions of teachers so that terminology does not undermine the research process.

Recommendation

- There should be a strategic partnership between all interested parties to develop a common language and measurable definitions. Further, there should be encouragement to develop means by which these institutions can share information.

A review of the current figures

Table 4.1 shows a rapid rise in the number of occasional teachers since the mid-1990s, according to DfES data.

Table 4.1 Occasional teachers (000s) in England							
	1995	1996	1997	1998	1999	2000	2001
Occasional teachers	12.2	12.6	13.6	13.1	14.1	16.7	19.0
Source: DfEE (2001a)							

This represents a little less than 4.5 per cent of the overall Full-time Equivalent (FTE) workforce, but the percentage is increasing. Occasional teachers account for 2,300 of 8,000 increase in the number of teachers between 2000 and 2001 (DfEE 2001a).

Agencies estimate the participation figures of agency teachers at approximately 10 per cent of the teaching population. The discrepancy between agency figures and government statistics may be due in part to the inclusion of long-term supply teachers by the agencies. Estimates for the total number of teachers provided by agencies per annum range from 70,000 to 120,000. We are unsure how many of these teachers are being 'double counted', as many supply teachers register with multiple agencies.

A long-term supply teacher may be defined as any teacher with a contract of more than one month, but who is not directly employed by the school. The use of supply teachers in long-term contracts to fill permanent vacancies has driven recent success in the private sector. Some agencies have predicted that if the recent teacher shortages continue at the expected rates and the current practice of filling these vacancies with long-term supply staff continues, and if all other variables remain constant, by the year 2014 we could see a teacher workforce of which over 50 per cent is supply staff. Though not a realistic scenario, this illustrates the trend.

It could be argued that though many of the long-term supply teachers are recruited via an agency, in effect they are acting as full-time permanent teachers, and it is therefore justifiable to characterise the two as the same. The only difference lying between the two would be in the way the teachers are recruited and who is responsible for the contract. The danger with this type of justification is that the motivations of long-term supply teachers may differ greatly from a teacher committed to spending a significant number of years in a particular school.

Unfortunately, because the data on long-term supply staff is scarce, there is very little trend analysis which may be helpful in predicting the behaviour of long-term supply staff. In addition, whether or not the recruitment of any type of supply staff will remain at very high rates or whether other variables in the equation will remain constant is also very difficult to predict. Accurate data and further research are urgently needed on this growing constituency in the teaching workforce.

Spending on supply

Spending figures on supply teachers vary according to sources. One recruitment analyst estimates schools are now spending more than £600m annually on supply teachers (Dean 2001), approximately two thirds of which is from the private sector. If this estimate is accurate, it would amount to 3.4 per cent of the entire expenditure of LEA maintained schools in England, 5.3 per cent of the entire expenditure on teachers and twice the amount spent by schools on ICT for teaching and learning in 2000 (DfES 2001a, 2001b). One supply agency puts the figure at £650m. Both estimates includes long term supply teachers, which make up approximately half of supply teachers provided by agencies.

Another estimate was reported by the Value for Money Unit of the DfES. In the last financial year, they estimate that schools spent an average of £43.00 per pupil from their budget on short-term supply teachers, £50.78 for primary schools and £32.80 for secondary schools (VfM 2001). This equals about 2.5 per cent of pre-primary/primary expenditure, and 1.25 per cent of the secondary expenditure on maintained schools in England.

Increased demand in a competitive market is having a significant impact on supply spending. In fact, prices have been driven up so quickly over the past year that Phil Willis, Liberal Democrat Shadow Education Secretary, has formally requested the Office of Fair Trading to investigate the possibility of uncompetitive practices operating within supply teacher markets, in order 'to determine whether excess profits are being made in this privatised sector' (Willis 2001). Many agencies have responded by asserting that the prices are merely a function of the natural market.

Why choose supply teaching?

Supply teachers are most likely to be young overseas travellers, Newly Qualified Teachers or other inexperienced staff and mothers of young children. There is also evidence that 'very experienced teaching staff who simply want the flexibility of temporary work and the better pay' (Smithers 2000) are moving sectors and quickly becoming a key source of supply teachers. These diverse groups share some common motivations.

Anecdotal evidence from supply teachers, LEA recruitment managers and chief executives of supply agencies indicates that the primary reason is increased flexibility in hours and expectations. In this regard, mothers are one of the primary beneficiaries of supply work. In a 1991 School Teachers' Review Body (STRB) survey 40 per cent of former women teachers stated that flexible hours are the most important single measure which would encourage them to return to work (STRB 1992). There is no reason to assume things have changed since then. Although some schools offer part time work to returning mothers, they can rarely offer the flexibility of supply work.

Supply teaching has become a more positive choice for teachers, a career option instead of a job to take 'in between'. Many view themselves as freelance teachers. Although part time working and job sharing have become more common in schools, the rigid pay and conditions structure for teachers combined with less than innovative management styles, have left most schools unable to meet demands for flexibility. Given the current state of the labour market for teachers, the insecurity typically associated with flexible, short term contracts is significantly reduced.

An increasingly common practice is for teachers to undertake a period of supply teaching in order to find a school that they feel they can commit themselves to on a more permanent basis. This is largely positive; in fact, schools use supply teachers in a similar way, as part of a recruitment process. Thus some of the mismatches between schools and teachers can be avoided.

At a recent NQT supply teaching recruitment event, one recruitment consultant overheard several teachers agree that 'we want to teach, but we don't want to become teachers.' This typifies a growing desire to be on the fringes, rather than at the centre of the teaching profession. Chapter 2 of this book cites many reasons for the poor current status of the teaching profession, including: public criticism, poor management, worsening pupil behaviour, increased workloads and bureaucracy, low pay and the depletion of intrinsic satisfiers such as creativity and autonomy. Supply teachers are immune from none of these problems, yet may be more able to filter out their worst effects.

Relative to full-time permanent teachers, many supply teachers spend less of their time on the bureaucratic burdens associated with teaching and working hours are reduced. This provides many individuals the opportunity to teach, without shouldering the heavy burdens associated with being a permanent teacher.

Although agency teachers earn less than those on LEA contracts, the demand for supply teachers has driven up the price, particularly for the youngest and the least experienced. Some headteachers suggest they are annually paying £5000 more for an agency teacher than for a young permanent member of staff (Mansell 2001).

A global market

Over the past year, about ten thousand teachers have been brought to Britain from overseas (Elliot and Robbins 2001). One agency has recruited two thousand Australian supply teachers this year alone (Ballinger 2001). This is an international phenomenon that seems to be growing at a rapid rate. New York recruits in Austria and Chicago in Egypt. Holland recruits in Germany. England recruits in Australia, New Zealand and South Africa (Sikkes 2001). More recently, some agencies in England have now started to recruit in India, the Philippines and the US. With the current shortages, there is an increasing trend for these teachers to be hired to fill long-term vacancies.

The reason for such an increase in the international trend is two-fold. First, there is a wonderful appeal for young people who want to travel but need money to live. Second, the demand for overseas supply teachers has risen partly out of necessity, but also because of the fresh perspective and increased enthusiasm overseas teachers often bring to the classroom. Many schools have actually preferred overseas supply teachers because 'even in the toughest schools ...their attitude is "right, let's get on with it", not walking out within ten minutes saying "I'm not teaching them."' (Morrison 1999a: 179)

Unfortunately, migration of this magnitude has only exacerbated shortages in many other countries. The South African education minister, Kader Asmal, has officially requested that English schools stop luring their top qualified teachers, stating 'Such raids on the teaching profession at a critical time in our history are not helpful for the development of education in South Africa' (Elliott and Robbins 2001). The recent legislation easing the employment criteria for overseas teachers will also most likely worsen problems in other countries (Ballinger 2001).

The need to be aware and responsive to overseas recruitment in countries with teacher shortages, however, must also be balanced by the desire of individuals who want to travel and gain the enhancing experience of teaching in various parts of the world. Where the line should be drawn will need to be reviewed carefully by policymakers.

Demographic, economic and political trends' impact on supply teaching

Of course the demand for supply teachers partly mirrors the demand for permanent teachers. The more vacancies there are to fill, the more supply teachers will be needed to help fill them, on a short and long term basis.

A strong driver of current teacher shortages is the booming economy. There is much evidence to suggest that an economic downturn would lead to an increase in the number of candidates for teaching positions. The anticipated impact on supply teachers is that fewer would be used for long-term assignments (to fill vacancies). More would shift back to providing emergency cover and the overall demand for supply teachers should decrease. However, it is important not to overstate this impact. For instance, if an economic downturn coincides with the heaviest period of retirement between 2005 and 2014, the impact will be marginal. The demand for supply teachers might continue to prove a persistent element in staffing, regardless of the economy.

Poor retention rates, especially for those in the early years of their teaching career, are a major cause for concern. Causes have been documented elsewhere. In reviewing retention issues we should question to what extent full-time retention is affected by the rise of the supply teacher. While there is no quantifiable data on this yet, teacher unions, MPs, agencies and headteachers are suggesting the trend for permanent teachers to move across to the supply sector is getting stronger. In particular, when attempting to improve attrition rates in the first five years of teaching, policymakers need to know how many of these teachers are crossing into the supply sector.

The turnover of supply staff is even more excessive than that of full-time permanent teachers. The average length of service for a teacher in most agencies is six months to a year. We are unsure if supply teachers are leaving the agency or leaving the profession. Some agencies are just starting to do exit interviews, but it will be some time before results can be measured on a large scale aggregate level.

Recommendation

- The General Teaching Councils should ensure that their database and exit surveys capture information on supply teachers.

One agency, however, has estimated that close to half of its supply teachers are leaving for permanent jobs. Whether these permanent jobs are as full-time teachers in schools or in another field is still unclear. If teachers are moving from permanent positions to supply teaching and then eventually out of teaching altogether, then this process has grave implications for the future of the teaching profession. If teachers are leaving permanent posts to become supply teachers as a life career or to use supply teaching as a way of trying out different environments before settling back into a particular school, then this is a more positive trend although it must be balanced against the need for pupils to have a degree of learning continuity.

Absence due to illness continues to be a major factor in the demand for supply teachers. The DfEE report on Teacher Sickness Absence in 2000 estimates that 56 per cent of the workforce has taken some sick leave on an annual basis, at an average rate of five days per teacher in post per annum (ten days per teacher taking sick leave per annum). Trend analysis is difficult on teacher absences because statistics have only been collected since 1999. However, even in this limited time-frame, there has been a significant jump in sick leave. The DfEE reported that 10,000 more teachers took sick leave this year than last year and the total overall estimated number of sick days used has now reached well over two and a half million days (DfEE 2001b).

Some teacher unions express the increase in sick leave as a consequence of the increased workloads and stress levels for teachers resulting from recent policy reform. The DfES has requested that these figures be treated with caution, however, as some methodological problems may have skewed the estimates.[1]

Absence due to training has also grown significantly. On average, 50 teaching days per year per school require cover due to teacher training. The recent national strategies have increased the number of days missed due to training. For example, in autumn 2000 every primary maths co-ordinator was required to attend a five day training course. While the training itself may have had a positive impact on learning, schools have struggled to cope with the short-term implications of these absences.

The Government wishes a larger proportion of CPD to be undertaken outside the school day, and contractual arrangements are certain to be introduced. However, observation of good classroom practice will remain a key element of CPD, with consequent staffing demands.

Overall it can be predicted that the demand for supply teachers is highly unlikely to decline and will probably continue to increase, as will the use of temporary staff across all public services. The major potential barrier to this growth, discussed later in this paper, is the change in school practices. Schools, through necessity (insufficient number of supply teachers), creative thinking or both, can begin to explore alternatives to supply teachers, especially for emergency cover.

The rise of the supply agency

There has been a slow realisation that supply agencies have become among the largest private sector players in state education. In 1998-99, after transportation and Special Educational Needs (SEN) provisions, supply teaching made up the greatest proportion

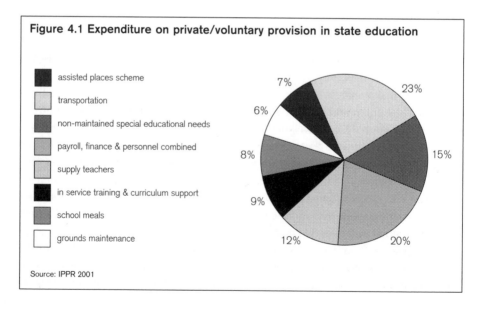

Figure 4.1 Expenditure on private/voluntary provision in state education

assisted places scheme
transportation
non-maintained special educational needs
payroll, finance & personnel combined
supply teachers
in service training & curriculum support
school meals
grounds maintenance

7%   23%
6%
8%   15%
9%
12%   20%

Source: IPPR 2001

of single private sector involvement[2] in publicly funded education with an estimated budgeted value of £210 million (IPPR 2001). Figure 4.1 describes the breakdown in greater detail. It is important to recognise that in all of the recent rhetoric about private sector involvement in education, little or nothing has been said about private sector supply agencies. The ten year experience of the rise of supply agencies must inform current, confused debates over the role of the private sector in the provision of education services.

A recent analysis estimated that in 1998-99 70 per cent of all supply teachers were provided from the private sector[3] (IPPR 2001). Further estimates have suggested that a minimum of four thousand agency teachers are employed in London on an average day, making them seven percent of all teachers in London[4] (Hutchings 2000). These numbers vary, of course, according to area and region. The experience of most agencies, however, is that while London accounts for the highest portion of client work, the effects typically spread to other cities and regions in subsequent waves.

The hegemony of supply agencies is an English phenomenon. In the US a recent poll found that agencies provide only six percent of substitute teachers. Schools rely on either District Offices to hire substitutes or on site-based resources. The director of the Substitute Training Institute at Utah State University has suggested that this is because the management of schools continues to remain at the district, rather than the school level. Schools do not have a choice as to how they will employ supply teachers, so this has enabled districts to keep control of teacher allocation and ensures that competition does not weave its way into the system. This is similar across the rest of Europe, although agencies are emerging rapidly in Australasia.

Concerns about the role of agencies have always existed and may be increasing as their presence becomes more pervasive. Some of the arguments against using agencies are detailed below.

It has been argued that agencies' ability to provide supply teachers has masked the real extent of the teacher shortage. As a union representative explains, 'If it hadn't been for Timeplan, education would have been in crisis. Had it started to collapse it would have put pressure on people to do something about it' (Hutchings 2000).

Teachers support a standard national pay system, and resent what they see as unjustifiable variations in pay rates. There is also a question of how long schools can maintain paying for agency rate teachers. In a recent survey in one agency's report, it was found that no matter how satisfied teachers are with a particular agency, they will still work for the one that pays them the highest rate. Competition between agencies for scarce labour with the increasing use of recruitment incentives may continue to drive up rates for schools.

Failing to do interviews, essential background checking (including police records) and incentive schemes which might inspire those who are not truly qualified to teach, have been practised by some agencies and create major problems for schools. 'From the perspective of delivery, the consequences of ill-equipped agents sending poorly prepared teachers were considered far more dramatic than sending a 'temporary secretary who was "a bit sloppy"'. (Morrison 1999a: 176) The same concerns have also been asserted about LEA services, however. Because of the difficulty in finding supply staff, many agencies are spending their time on finding anyone to cover a classroom and less time on weeding out those who are unfit. At the time of writing, it remains to be seen whether the Timeplan scandal of January 2002 will lead to changes in climate or regulation.

Policy is currently being finalised to introduce Quality Marks for agencies. Although this is a welcome move and should improve quality, there is already concern that the criteria are too easy to achieve.

The supply teaching sector has moved rapidly from cottage industry to big business. Whilst there are clear benefits for schools and pupils, there is concern that as agencies are taken over by large quoted companies, this will lead to increased pressure from shareholders to maximise the rate of return on their investments. It is too early to judge how this will impact on their business practices.

Can supply teachers be returned to the public sector?

The general secretary of NASUWT, discussing supply agencies, has argued that 'It is a terrible waste of public money supplying teachers in this way. It is something local authorities could do for almost nothing' (Kelly 2001). The Local Government Association has mooted the possibility of setting up its own not-for-profit agency.

The reputations of many LEAs in this field are poor, but many LEAs are trying to re-establish or improve their services. Lincolnshire, Enfield, Surrey and Sheffield are just some examples of LEAs who are re-establishing their supply pool lists, often in response to requests for such a service from their schools. Some LEAs have invested in computerised databases, to provide schools with up-to-date supply lists free of charge. Some have initiated voluntary school 'buy-in' of their service. Others have plans for strategic recruitment drives incorporating union, teacher, parent and community support. All LEAs interviewed for this research suggested it is too early to see the results, but all are confident that these improved structures will lead to an increase in supply teacher interest, and a decrease in agency use. The TTA-funded recruitment strategy managers may also play their part in restarting or improving supply pools.

The transfer of the convictions check to the Criminal Records Bureau, as from April 2002, and the requirement on the agencies to use the new procedure should end one competititive advantage to agencies. On the other hand, they remain free from adherence to national pay scales. In addition, retired teachers who are contracted through LEAs as supply teachers are not entitled to receive a combined salary and pension above their former income, a limitation which does not affect agency staff.

Many recruitment agencies already offer on-line or face to face support services, professional development seminars, accommodation services, social gatherings, and resource centres. LEAs have the infrastructure to offer such support to supply teachers but are understandably concentrating efforts on the permanent teachers in their schools. In one agency survey, 82 per cent of teachers rated the friendliness, professionalism, support and knowledge of consultants to be good or excellent. Few LEAs would get a similar satisfaction rating, even from permanent employees.

LEAs will supplant agencies only if they can convince schools that they offer better value for money. The squeeze on funding of LEA activity requires any supply teacher service to be financed almost entirely out of school budgets. Recent price increases by the agencies may have altered the economic balance. LEAs could gain further advantage by forming consortia and benefiting from economies of scale, as in the south-west region. This could be especially beneficial in London.

Although there are clear hindrances to their involvement, LEAs who wish to operate supply pools and channel 'profits' into other support services to schools deserve acknowledgement and support. Success is most likely in LEAs with good relationships with schools.

The future of supply agencies and LEAs: working together?

Recognising the difficulty LEAs will have in competing with the private sector in the future, all of the private agencies interviewed for this research suggested that it would be more productive to establish public private partnerships. Such partnerships are clearly attractive to agencies as a means of reaching out to many schools simultaneously. Perhaps the most effective partnership would be with a consortium of authorities.

One of the models for this type of partnership, and being tried in Brighton, is a contract in which one agency is responsible for the recruitment and organisation of supply allocation and the LEA is responsible for monitoring effectiveness and controlling costs. In this model, an LEA can set standards and specify guidelines which the agency must adhere to, or they will lose the contract. This might, in effect, be a plausible option for LEAs who are sympathetic to union concerns. An LEA could restrict the agency to pay-to-scale salaries and subvert the current practice of a two-tiered system of teachers' salaries. Some agencies have even expressed a preference for pay-to-scale salaries. Some LEA-agency partnerships have actually been created with the collaboration of local teacher associations.

Whether or not LEAs will be able to bring supply recruitment back to the public sector and whether or not LEAs will follow the route of developing PPPs with supply agencies will be seen in the next several years. The Government seems clear on its intention not to place universal restrictions on private agencies. Thus, unless LEAs can out-compete the private sector, the only way to control escalating costs and quality assurance is to work in co-operation with them.

Recommendation

- Exploration of LEA-managed services, or PPPs between LEAs and high-quality supply agencies should be encouraged, possibly through DfES Standards Fund money.

Ultimately, schools will determine whether any new form of provision will succeed. Even if its LEA is providing a service or is part of a PPP, a school will still be free to seek alternative provision.

Recommendation

- To ensure quality and a level playing field there should be a common regulatory framework for organisations providing supply teachers.

Are supply teachers necessary? Exploring alternatives

Compared to the rest of Europe, England appears to use more and spend more on supply teachers. This section reviews some of the main strategies in practice in England and around the world to identify alternative solutions.[5] This inevitably leads to wider questions about new directions in children's learning. All these alternatives relate only to short term and emergency cover.

As school budgets increase with consequent staffing flexibility, the floating teacher may regain popularity. The float has no fixed timetable, but is deployed according to need, covering absence being one. Cover by a member of the school community has many advantages over the use of external supply staff, but avoids the pitfalls of general internal cover. It is also worth pointing out that many headteachers used to perform this role. In their reconfiguration as managers, many have become deskilled in their classroom practice.

Recommendation

- Heads and Deputies should teach on a regular basis.

Cover being provided by other teachers and headteachers in the school is perhaps the most common type of cover in the world, for example in the Czech Republic, Spain, Slovakia, Germany, Lithuania and all UK countries. In some cases teachers are granted compensatory time off or salary augmentation for covering extra classes. Some internal cover also includes the combining of classes into one another so that teachers are expected to teach up to double the number of children.

This method has been cost-effective, but imposes an additional workload which is no longer acceptable either to teachers or to the Government. Any continuing reliance on internal cover by teachers must be on the basis of voluntary paid additional duties.

The appropriate means of covering absence is a key consideration for the Government's 'Remodelling the Profession' initiative. The combination of teacher shortage and workload concerns leads to a tendency to use staff other than teachers. There can be little doubt that staff without QTS are being used as emergency cover in lieu of qualified supply teachers. This includes lecturers, teaching assistants, student teachers, parents and occasionally friends of school staff. Private agencies have begun mass recruitment of teaching assistants. Many schools in the US now frantic to find substitutes are 'turning classes over to PTA moms, waitresses, college students and even high school students' (Elizabeth 2001). In all but one state, substitutes need no teaching certification whatsoever to take over a classroom. Other countries such as Norway, Iceland and Sweden are also utilising unqualified staff as part of their strategies to combat supply teacher shortages. In Poland, recent legislation mandates that unqualified staff are required to gain qualifications while working and in Finland unqualified personnel are required to pass a matriculation examination to be authorised cover status.

There are several benefits to employing teaching assistants. They cost less: the current rate for a teaching assistant is approximately half that of a qualified supply teacher. They often live near the school they are employed in. This tends to provide them with a stronger connection with the children and a perspective which is sensitive to the children's needs. Supply of potential teaching assistants is plentiful. One agency received well over two hundred phone calls from suitable individuals after a single newspaper advertisement.

In moving from such an ad hoc provision which, at the very least, teeters on the edge of the regulations, to a new structure, there are some other considerations. An obvious assumption is that a class in the charge of a person who is not a teacher is being supervised, not taught. What might be entailed in supervision needs further consideration.

We need more evidence as to the effectiveness of those support staff currently working with pupils. It may be that those working with individuals or small groups are more likely to be effective than those dealing with larger numbers of pupils. Midday supervisors, particularly in secondary schools, have major difficulties with control. It is arguable that large-group management is the most difficult skill of all those required of teachers. Even if teacher assistants are to be regarded as supervisors rather than teachers, they would need considerable training, which should be related to a new national qualification and national pay and conditions.

We may imagine this qualification as one element of a coherent path running from level two to QTS and beyond, available largely within the school as a workplace.

Recommendation

- A national qualification for pupil supervisors should be developed.

The status of the supply teacher

> To survive in the jungle of supply teaching you need to possess the resilience of a rubber doorstopper, the versatility of a chameleon and the hide of a pachyderm. And that's on a good day. (Jennings 2001)

The rise of the supply teacher has not been associated with a rise in the status of supply teaching. Lack of support in schools, poor behaviour of children in the classroom, and persistent references to supply teachers as 'expensive babysitters' continues to dominate discussions. The DfES has acknowledged that 'even with the best supply teachers, classes merely "tread water" in lessons covered by supply' (VfM 2001).

Whatever the future arrangements for dealing with short-term absence, supply teachers will continue to be necessary for longer-term cover. To ensure the quality of their contribution, a recognition of the poor current status is necessary and willingness to improve it imperative.

Supply teachers often do not have access to local knowledge of the school (such as what time the bell rings or where the staff room is located); information on the class; resources for the lessons; social networks in the school; the absent teacher's pedagogy; the ethos of the school; the context of the work set; information on the subject being taught, authority figures in the school or feedback on their performance. (Morrison 1999b; Dougherty 1998; Elizabeth 2001; Shilling 1990).

The Value for Money Unit has recently made recommendations for schools to provide induction material to supply teachers in the hope of engendering an atmosphere of support and encouragement.

Continuing Professional Development is possibly the most important driver of change. There has been some DfES development of distance learning packages that could prove useful to supply teachers' professional development. The framework of responsibilities for the CPD of supply teachers (DfEE 2000b) is also welcomed, although schools may need more than just 'encouragement' to include supply teachers in their training plans. Beyond this, the recent document on CPD (DfEE 2001c) made insufficient reference to the ways in which the development of supply teachers could also be improved.

Recommendation

- Supply teachers must have the same entitlement as others to contractual and paid training time.

Conclusion

It is possible to imagine a far smaller, highly skilled, trained and valued cadre of supply teachers operating in (but not necessarily run by) every local education authority, with a good knowledge of schools and the communities they serve. They would be key conduits in the sharing of best practice, and be recognised for their advisory role. The role would be so attractive that all those teaching emigrés who are now working as education consultants, inspectors, civil servants and union officials would be supply teaching part-time. As these people are mainly London-based, it would increase the pool of supply teachers in the area of highest demand.

Supply teachers with less experience would also be valued. Those from overseas would be welcomed for the unique insight they provide. Others, combining teaching with other jobs, childcare responsibilities or passions (including those many unemployed artists and actors who supply teach), would bring fresh perspectives into the classroom and staffroom, preventing insularity. And many supply teaching assistants would be on a pathway to qualified teacher status.

One reason for the decrease in the number of supply teachers would be that many of the negative factors associated with becoming a permanent teacher would have been alleviated. In particular, teachers would have greater flexibility over hours, and spend far less time on administrative and accountability-related tasks. In other words, the permanent teaching force would be more like the current supply teaching force, without the inherent insecurities.

Schools, through the use of floating teachers, some internal cover (mainly carried out by senior management and fast trackers) and new technologies, would spend a far lower proportion of their budget on supply teachers, but would ensure that those who were used contributed fully to children's learning and the life of the school. In particular, supply teachers would be valued as experts in behaviour management. A few supply teachers would be present at virtually any CPD training or INSET day. Parents and pupils, assured by quality marks for both teachers and agencies, would welcome the variety in teaching styles that supply teachers can offer. Supply teachers would be given their own mugs for tea, teachers would never be ill, and the photocopier would always work!

We are a long way from this vision, yet this chapter has aimed to outline a number of practices and policies that could contribute to it. The most important policies and practices will always be those that affect schools and teachers as a whole. However, there is still an urgent need for debates about supply teachers to relocate from the periphery to the centre of policymaking.

Endnotes

1   DfES estimates for sickness rates include 23 local education authorities that have provided either no data or incomplete figures.

2   Payroll, Finance and Personnel combined totalled £350 million, but separately each factor is assumed to be less that supply teaching total.

3   These figures are debatable. Because of the lack of information on supply teachers there is much conflicting data. One report states that 70 per cent of supply teachers in inner London and 43 per cent of teachers in outer London were supplied by agencies. (Morrison 1999a). Another report estimated in 1999, agency teachers accounted for 68 per cent of London's occasional cover, but for only 10 per cent in other parts of England and Wales. (Hutchings 2000; DfEE 2000a)

4   This figure was developed in Hutchings estimates using figures supplied by agencies; agency estimates of the proportion of their business in London; figures for agency turnover from the Capital Strategies Report (2000); and daily rates charged to schools.

5   Thanks to the Eurydice Unit in Scotland for providing much of the information about supply teachers across Europe.

References

Ballinger (2001) 'Every Australian teacher has a nightmare story to tell from England' in *The Observer* 21 January

Carvel J (1999) 'Blow to training agency as Blunkett takes control of key programmes to boost teaching' in *The Guardian* 4 February

Cousins L (1999) 'Changing regulatory frameworks and non-standard employment: A comparison of Germany, Sweden, Spain and the UK' in Felstead and Jewson *Global Trends in Flexible Labour* London: Macmillan Press

Dean C (2001) 'Hire staff and win a toaster' *Times Educational Supplement* 8 June

Dean C and Mansell W (2001) 'Supply agencies unable to fill gaps' *Times Educational Supplement* 2 March

DfEE (2000a) *Statistics of Education: Teachers England and Wales* London: DfEE

DfEE (2000b) *Supply Teachers: Meeting the Challenge* London: DfEE

DfEE (2001a) *Statistical First Release: Teachers in service and teacher vacancies* London: DfEE

DfEE (2001b) *Teacher Sickness Absence in 2000* London: DfEE

DfEE (2001c) *Learning and Teaching: A Strategy for Professional Development* London: DfEE

DfES (2001a) 'Statistics of Education. Education and training expenditure since 1991-92' *National Statistics Bulletin* 07/01 London: DfES

DfES (2001b) 'Statistics of Education: Survey of Information and Communications Technology in Schools 2001' *National Statistics Bulletin* 09/01 London: DfES

Dougherty M (1998) *The Art of Surviving in Supply Teaching* Trowbridge: Cromwell Press

Elizabeth (2001) *A Substitute for Education: When the teacher's away* post-gazette.com PG News 7 January

Elliott and Robbins (2001) '"Stealing" of teachers stirs anger abroad' *The Sunday Times* 25 February

Hallgarten (2000) *Parents exist, OK?!* London: IPPR

Hutchings M (2000) *The role of agencies in teacher supply in London* Institute for Policy Studies in Education

Commission on Public Private Partnerships (2001) *Building Better Partnerships* London: IPPR

Jennings (2001) 'Supply is demanding' *Times Educational Supplement* 16 February

Kelly (2001) 'Unions back state teacher supply agency' *Financial Times* 20 April

Mansell (2001) 'Fair trading inquiry into agency price rise claims' *Times Educational Supplement* 17 August

Morrison M (1999a) 'Temps in teaching: the role of private employment agencies in a changing labour market for teachers' *Journal of Education Policy* 14.2

NASUWT (2001a) 'Vacancies and Absences. Protection from Additional Workload' *Cover to Contract* www.nasuwt.org.uk

NASUWT (2001b) NASUWT Report 01 January 2001

NUT (2001) *Teachers' Organisations Joint Commentary & Guidelines for Schools* Available via internet??

OECD (1995) *The OECD Jobs Study: Implementing the Strategy* Paris: OECD

Revell (2000) 'Under Cover' *The Guardian* 23 May

Robbins (2000) 'Schools will recruit teachers from India' *Sunday Times* 5 November

School Teachers' Review Body (1992) *School Teachers' Review Body First Report* London: HMSO

Sikkes (2001) 'The teacher shortage' Education International www.ei-ie.org

Shilling C (1990) 'The organization of supply workers in state schools and the National Health Service: a comparison' *Journal of Education Policy* 5.2

Smithers (2000) 'Ready and Waiting' *The Guardian* 5 September

Smithers and Robinson (2000) *Talking Heads* National Union of Teachers and the Centre for Education and Employment

Thorton (2001) 'Is breaking the law good practice for schools?' *Times Educational Supplement* 21 September

TTA (2001) *£1m Boost for Local Teacher Recruitment* TTA Website Press Release 27 April

VfM Unit (2001) *Supply Teacher Study* at www.dfes.gov.uk

Willis (2001) Letter from the Liberal Democrats' Shadow Education Secretary to the Office of Fair Trading Courtesy of the Liberal Democrats

5. Learning from the US
Elle Rustique-Forrester and David Haselkorn

The attempt to learn public policy lessons from other countries is as necessary as it is difficult. Necessary, because policy problems which are unique to one country simply do not exist. Difficult, because differences in underlying cultures and processes sometimes render policy borrowing virtually impossible. The temptation is always to cherry pick exciting-looking initiatives, rather than explore the deeper reasons for another country's apparent successes or failures.

In terms of the teaching profession, learning from international experiences is becoming increasingly important, as the teaching labour market becomes globally mobile. The competition for teachers is likely to become worldwide over the next decade. The situation in the US carries particular resonance. It appears that teacher shortages are more acute in the US and in England than anywhere else. Both are simultaneously sneezing and catching colds.

An overview of US teacher supply

In recent years, a number of US policy commissions, think tanks, and educational research organisations have warned politicians about the pressing need to recruit greater numbers of qualified teachers. Reports published over the past decade on the status of the teaching profession (NCTAF 1996, 1997; Haselkorn & Harris 2001) have pointed out that demand for teachers will continue to increase over the next decade. The following long-term trends, identified by Darling-Hammond (2000) explain further why and where shortages will occur:

- More than one-quarter of teachers are at least 50 years old, and nearly half will retire over the next decade. (Hirsch, Koppich, and Knapp 2001)

- Public school enrolment in primary and middle schools rose from 29.9 million in fall 1990 to an estimated 33.5 million in fall 2000.

- Enrolment in secondary schools rose from 11.3 million in 1990 to 13.5 million in 2000. The growing numbers of young pupils that have been filling the elementary schools will cause significant increases at the secondary school level during the next decade, which is expected to rise by 4 per cent. Total school enrolment is projected to increase in the South (4 per cent) and West (11 per cent), but decrease in the Northeast (1 per cent) and Midwest (3 per cent) between 1998 and 2008 (NCES 2000). For example, by the year 2007, enrolments are projected to increase by more than 20 per cent in California and Nevada and by more than 10 per cent in many states in the West and South.

- Small applicant pools of teachers occur in some communities due to inequalities in salaries and working conditions across states and districts. Some states and districts create their own shortages through their own hiring policies and processes, for example, in lacking reciprocity of licensing requirements.

- Finally, between 30-50 per cent of new teachers leave the profession within five years of entry, and attrition rates are even higher in impoverished school districts.

According to the latest educational projections, the most well-reasoned estimates place the total demand for new entrants into teaching at around 2 to 2.5 million between 1998 and 2008, averaging over 200,000 annually (Darling-Hammond 2000). About half of these are likely to be newly prepared teachers and about half will be migrants or returnees from the reserve pool of teachers (*ibid*, see also Ingersoll 1999). The demand for two million new teachers presents a serious problem deserving national attention. However, some policy analysts, such as C Emily Feistritzer, president of the Washington-based National Center for Education Information suggest that the US has already been hiring teachers at a rate of about two million every decade. Feistritzer argues that of the 200,000 teachers who are hired each year, only about 50,000 are entering teaching for the first time. The rest are changing jobs within education, returning from years off or something similar. Darling-Hammond (2000) contends that although the teacher recruitment challenge in the US is sizeable, it is not at all impossible for America's leaders and policymakers to overcome.

First, the number of new teachers prepared in America's universities and colleges is more than enough to satisfy this demand, a dynamic similar to the UK. According to one estimate, the number of college students graduating with teaching degrees has risen in recent years – up almost 50 per cent from 1983 to 1998 – and the number of programmes offering teaching degrees has also risen. In educational areas such as general elementary teaching, there is such a surplus that a single opening, particularly in attractive suburban districts, can draw hundreds of applicants. Despite drastic shortages of teachers across some regions and in certain academic subjects, the United States annually produces many more teachers than its schools actually hire. For example:

- Only 60 per cent of newly prepared teachers enter teaching jobs after they graduate, and many report that they cannot find jobs.

- In some regions of the US, such as the Northwest, Rocky Mountains, Northeast and Middle Atlantic states, there have long been surpluses of teachers. A recent study for the Wisconsin Department of Public Instruction (2000) found a clear surplus of potential job candidates. Job prospects in elementary education, for example, were rated as 'very poor.'

Primary education has been a field of national surplus for a number of years, along with fields such as English, art, business (vocational) education, health and physical education and social studies (geography, history). On the other hand, difficulties are most common in:

- urban districts – such as Milwaukee, Wisconsin. Big cities such as New York and Los Angeles face severe shortages

- some rural areas

- many branches of special education

- math and science in many districts

- bilingual education

- areas of the US where the school population is booming and where the number of schools is comparatively small.

In some states and nationwide, there are too many people seeking jobs in 'good' schools with 'nice' kids; and too few seeking jobs where the circumstances, particularly the students themselves, are more challenging. Finding a way to attract teacher candidates to places and subjects that aren't appealing is where the real challenge of dealing with teacher shortages really lies.

With growing pressures to fill classrooms, America's inner cities often resort to hiring large numbers of inadequately prepared teachers each year. More crucially, a disproportionate number of these individuals become assigned to teach the most vulnerable students in the most highly deprived areas. In the US, these teachers are often granted, out of sheer desperation, 'emergency' licences by the state or district. But they are not fully trained or prepared to teach, especially in highly deprived areas, where children have the greatest educational needs. The bottom line? Low-income and minority students are typically the most affected by teacher shortages. The consequence of not paying attention to the preparation side of recruitment is evident in places like California, where, according to one report, one million of the state's 5.7 million students are in schools 'with so many under-qualified teachers as to make those schools dysfunctional.'

Five years ago, 25 per cent of new entrants to teaching were reported to have no licence or a substandard licence in the field they were hired to teaching (NCTAF 1996). Although many districts and states have begun reassessing such hiring policies, inner cities such as Chicago and Los Angeles still report that up to 15 per cent of teachers are unlicensed, either because teachers are awaiting test results, have out-of-state-licences, or failed the state's battery of teacher tests (Stricherz 2001).

Profile of US public climate and policy context

In their historical view, Sedlak and Schlossman (1986:39) suggest that whilst teacher shortages are not new, problems can be influenced by the present policy context. For decades, teachers and teaching in the US lacked the much-needed focus of state and national level educational policy. Many policymakers, educators and researchers debated whether the teaching profession was even worthy of substantial public resources, unsure of which school-related variables influenced student achievement. There is now substantial and compelling evidence to suggest that school-based inputs, particularly those related to teachers, such as their level of qualifications, amount and quality of preparation, class size and opportunities for professional development have an important bearing on how students learn (*Education Week* 2000). For example, Darling-Hammond's review (1999) of state policy evidence, using data from a fifty-state policy survey conducted by the National Commission on Teaching & America's Future, case studies of selected states conducted by the Center for the Study of Teaching and Policy, and national data from the National Center for Education Statistics from the Schools and Staffing Surveys (SASS) and the National Assessment of Educational Progress (NAEP), shows how state policies not only influence the quality and supply of teachers, but also influence teacher learning.

Fortunately for America's leaders and policymakers, the public's attitudes toward education indicate high levels of support for improving teaching and the teaching profession. A national study conducted by Recruiting New Teachers (RNT) (Haselkorn and Harris 2001) found overwhelming public support for increasing public investments in education. Americans not only view the teaching profession positively, but also see teachers as providing the greatest benefit to society, with public education as the pathway to the American dream. A major conclusion reached by Haselkorn and Harris (2001) is that Americans believe that policymakers should direct greater attention and investments towards improving teaching.

Recruiting and retaining teachers: a national and local responsibility

In the US there is no national policy to address issues of teacher shortages. Policies that helped to ameliorate teacher shortage in the 1960s and 1970s were rescinded by subsequent administrations. The US Department of Education maintains relatively little power over key areas of teacher policy; salary levels, professional qualifications, requirements for initial teacher preparation and ongoing professional development are left to states and districts to establish and enforce.

Far more influential in shaping teacher policy and encouraging changes in state's educational policy are the teacher unions, professional associations, and other national educational reform groups such as NBPTS (the National Board for Professional Teaching Standards), NCATE (the National Council for the Accreditation of Teacher Education), and INTASC (the Interstate New Teacher Assessment and Support Consortium). These organisations, in developing standards for teacher preparation, induction, and professional development have helped guide a number of states in developing more meaningful teacher policy strategies. Evidence suggests that states and districts like Cincinnati, Ohio; New Haven, Connecticut and New York City's District 2, which have invested heavily in improving beginning teacher induction and professional development as part of their long-term recruitment strategy have a far greater capacity to maintain an adequate supply of teachers while simultaneously ensuring that they are well prepared to teach (Rustique-Forrester 1995; Elmore 1997; and Snyder 1999).

What the US is doing to improve teacher supply and quality

Although in the US, school districts through local collective bargaining agreements and partnerships with teacher training institutions have been largely responsibly for the majority of teacher policy areas, such as recruitment and compensation (Hirsch, Koppich and Knapp 2001), more states see a greater role for enhancing the supply and quality of teachers in America's schools. This is happening through the development of a range of policies aimed at improving the capacity of schools, districts, and institutions to recruit, prepare, and retain more teachers. Combined strategies, such as those being aggressively pursued in California include a comprehensive package of teacher incentives, scholarship and internship programmes, salary raises, professional rewards and improved standards.

Federal strategies for enhancing teacher supply are aimed at helping states and districts with their own recruitment efforts. Most states and districts are choosing to pursue a 'grow your own' teacher recruitment strategy. This enables a diverse range of potential teacher recruits to meet the specific needs of the state, local areas, and communities. A number of these programmes involve the partnering of school districts with local university or community teacher preparation programmes in order to target specific groups of potential teachers – minority teachers, mid-career professionals, and highly qualified, high school and university graduates, often referred to as 'the best and brightest.' Programmes aim at recruitment, induction, compensation and professional development.

Strategy 1: Recruit teachers aggressively, using a range of incentives

The most effective recruitment strategies are those that pay attention not only to the initial set of incentives that will attract potential teachers, but that ensure that such candidates receive high-quality training and preparation in their first years of teaching and throughout their career. Within this, there are four types of strategies.

Early cultivation

In a study conducted over a decade ago, many teachers revealed that they decided to become teachers when in high school or middle school. For this reason, many school districts, colleges and national organisations are working together to help younger students learn more about teaching. Currently, twelve states have programmes that encourage high school and college students to think, early on, about a potential career in education and teaching, present positive teaching role models, provide practical teaching experiences and create opportunities to attend college.

There are over thirty academy or magnet programmes operating in the US. These programmes offer students two-to-four year programmes of study that include courses about teaching, learning, and child development, as well as practice-teaching. Many academies or magnets have partnerships with local colleges of education, allowing students to take college-credit-bearing courses while in high school. A number of high schools also offer classes developed by teachers who want to help students understand and practice the craft of teaching. Schools (and universities) can sponsor training for middle and high school teachers in these courses and offer them as social studies electives. Many high schools have also begun teaming up with colleges of education to offer dual-enrolment credits for the course. The South Carolina Center For Teacher Recruitment is one example of one such collaboration that provides information about the kinds of course offerings available in the state.

Los Angeles Unified School District offers internships to high school students who are prepared, and upon graduation, to begin teaching by first working as a para-educator (classroom assistants), whilst studying at a California State University. Participants then enrol as university students in a combined degree programme while continuing to work as para-educators in the schools. Throughout the programme, support services, such as stipends, scholarships and mentors are provided to improve the retention rate. At the completion of the programme, students not only have a bachelor's degree, but also a preliminary teaching certificate. Similar programmes are also being implemented in Los Angeles, Oakland, San Jose, and Salinas Valley.

Two successful examples of statewide programmes are in South Carolina and North Carolina. South Carolina's Teacher Cadet Program involves 148 secondary schools and centres around a yearlong course on teaching and education for which high school students can earn advanced college credit. The course has a number of noteworthy features. Participants are given structured opportunities to observe classroom teaching; to develop and try out lesson plans, and to tutor and mentor younger students. By the end of the 1997-98 school year, 21,000 students were graduates of South Carolina's Teacher Cadet programme, and about 32 per cent of the graduates were enrolled in university-level teacher preparation programmes, or already teaching.

North Carolina Teaching Fellows Program is a nationally recognised, state-based programme that has been running since 1986. The programme provides four-year college scholarships of $6,500 per year to four hundred high school graduates with an outstanding high school record of achievement and service. A unique aspect of the programme is its breadth and flexibility – scholarships are awarded to fourteen state university campuses that provide specific learning opportunities for scholarship recipients. Teaching Fellows, for example, take a trip to look firsthand at the complexity of classroom teaching, looking at the variety of districts in North Carolina to understand the diversity of school settings. The programme boasts that Fellows have been placed in 96 of the state's 100 counties. Upon acceptance of the scholarship, the student agrees to teach for four years in one of the state's schools. If the student does not fulfil the agreement, the loan is repaid to the state with ten per cent interest.

College scholarship and loan forgiveness programmes

These help to make teaching a more financially viable career option in the US, where university tuition fees and loan debt can discourage graduates from pursuing careers as teachers. They offer particular appeal to a diverse range of teacher candidates, from low-earning ethnic minorities to graduates from high-cost, private universities.

The federal government currently offers a range of loan cancellation and deferment options for teachers with student loans. With the Perkins loan, for example, teachers teaching in a disadvantaged community or subject-matter shortage area can cancel a portion of their debt, dependent on the years of service. Further, 27 states offer college scholarships or forgivable loan programmes. According to the most recent annual review of state policies, conducted by Education Week, $81 million was budgeted nationwide for scholarship and loan programmes (*Education Week* 2000).

Target recruitment at under-represented groups

To improve the quality and diversity of the teaching force, many states and districts have targeted financial incentives and packages – scholarships, loans, and grants – at specific groups. These include minorities, mid-career professionals and high-calibre university graduates.

At the national level, the teacher union, the National Education Association (NEA) has taken large steps to recruit minorities into teaching. The NEA's High School Teacher/Mentor Program has identified over 6,000 minority students who are interested in preparing to be teachers. Mentors encourage students to make plans for attending college and provide information about college entrance requirements. Students are brought to area universities to attend workshops and presentations specifically for their needs. Ten states, and school districts such as Chicago, Illinois have developed scholarships or forgivable loans specifically for minority candidates.

Another group of potential teachers is mid-career professionals. Currently, 41 states have some type of alternate route to teacher licence, which attracts this group and responds to criticism of traditional teacher education. The National Center for Education Information estimates that 75,000 people have been licensed through these programmes, with 25 states reporting an increase in the number of alternative licences granted over the last five years. One example of a state programme that targets military veterans is Kentucky, which created an alternative teaching certificate for veterans with at least five years of active duty, an honorable discharge, a bachelor's degree in the subject area for which a licence is sought and a passing score of the state's teaching exam.

High-calibre university graduates

Evidence from the US suggests that few graduates from top universities enter teacher training programmes or consider careers in teaching. Teach for America (TFA) is a national programme that seeks to attract the best and brightest university graduates to teach in deprived communities. The programme recruits teachers from prestigious universities by appealing to their idealism. Whilst the goals of the programme may be socially admirable, it has been criticised because of its inadequate training and low retention rate. One report found TFA participants lacking in pre-service classroom experience, with poor preparation, skills and pedagogical knowledge. More crucially, few participants actually stayed in teaching after a few years. Advocates of the programme, however, have suggested that the TFA experience draws its graduates into careers in education – teaching, administration, policy, research – options that perhaps would have been rejected without the experience of teaching. The potential of TFA's model is that recruitment programmes cannot always attract the best people into teaching through financial incentives alone and that combining financial incentives with a social appeal to idealism may be a better mix.

Strategy 2: Improve teachers' salaries, career benefits, and rewards

Sustaining an adequate teacher supply can only happen if future recruits and current teachers feel compelled to remain teaching. Toward this end, numerous states and districts have recognised the need to improve teachers' professional motivation and career incentives.

Although compensation has long been viewed as a primary deterrent to attracting new teachers into the profession, Hirsch, Koppich, and Knapp (2001), point to a weaker than expected link between teachers' job satisfaction and their salary and benefits. According to recent national surveys of teachers' job satisfaction (NCES 1997), work satisfaction is heavily influenced by working conditions and feelings of control. Still, in terms of attracting new candidates, low salaries can still be a major turnoff for potential teachers, and many states have begun re-examining their salary schedule and comparing them to other states.

A new trend for states is targeting the growing retired teacher workforce, and luring these veteran teachers back into teaching. Hirsch, Koppich, and Knapp's (2001) review found that a growing number of states are beginning to allow teachers to continue to draw full pension benefits and collect full salaries while working full- or part-time. In 1999, California, South Carolina, Maryland, North Carolina, Texas, and Missouri all passed legislation that created new policies or altered existing programmes that had capped retirees' salaries.

New career incentives to fill critical shortage areas and hard-to-staff regions such as inner cities include one-time signing bonuses, and offers of housing and financial assistance to relocate to cities, which are generally more costly than suburban and urban areas.

Mississippi recently passed legislation that targets teachers who are seeking to earn a master's degree, encouraging them to earn it in a shortage area. In exchange for three years of service, recipients receive a tuition scholarship towards their degree, professional development opportunities, a computer, placement in a mentoring programme, home loans, and up to $1,000 in moving expenses.

New York's 'Teachers of Tomorrow' programme offers an annual stipend of $3,400 for any certified teacher who signs a one-year contract to teach in a critical shortage area for up to three years. An annual stipend of $10,000 is granted to a 'master' teacher who does the same.

Strategy 3: Improved professional development

A major problem that compounds America's teacher shortages is the revolving door of teaching. Whilst the majority of teachers who leave the profession do so because of retirement or family reasons (pregnancy or child-rearing), a significant number leave because they are discouraged professionally, citing a lack of administrative and collegial support and disillusionment with the current conditions in schools. With national estimates of 30-50 per cent of beginning teachers leaving the profession within the first five years of teaching, states and districts have begun investing in policies that will provide teachers with a better form of induction and sustain their career development through structured opportunities for professional learning.

In the US, there can be a wide disparity in the quality and criteria of beginning teacher induction programmes as well as in the opportunities available for teachers' professional development. In Rhode Island and Massachusetts, less than 15 per cent of beginning teachers receive any kind of systematic mentoring (NCTAF 1997: 34). Yet Cincinnati, Ohio's PAEP (Peer Assistance and Evaluation programme) provides all beginning teachers with a mentor who provides assistance and also evaluates the teacher.

Recent research suggests a payoff in establishing a comprehensive teacher induction programme. For example, California's Beginning Teacher Support and Assessment Programme (BTSA) has proved to be successful in increasing the rate of teacher retention. The programme's attrition rate is nine per cent compared with 37 per cent for teachers without BTSA or a similar induction programme (Bullard 1998). The result has been support by state legislatures for programmes that provide formal induction for beginning teachers. There is also a trend towards reversing a reluctance to support policies that directly fund teachers' professional development.

A third category of state actions aimed at supporting and enhancing the profession is recognising accomplished teachers for their knowledge and skill. Over the past several decades, states and districts throughout the US have tried various forms of 'merit pay' in an attempt to link teacher salaries to performance. Many of these failed, in large part, because of the failure to develop accompanying standards that were clear and meaningful to educators. Put bluntly, there was a lack of clarity about what constituted 'merit'. Whilst the need to link pay to performance remains a popular trend amongst policymakers, there are now far better standards upon which to base such teacher rewards. A key development in this area has been the standards developed by the National Board for Professional Teaching Standards, as well as standards for beginning teachers.

Many states have begun to recognise the importance of highly skilled teachers and have begun linking salary incentives to the achievement of National Board Certification. California pays a $20,000 bonus for a National Board certified teacher who agrees to teach in a school designated as low performing. Kentucky pays an annual salary supplement of $2,000 per year for the ten-year life of a National Board certificate. Many new teacher performance pay plans can be found locally.

Strategy 4: Improve teachers' working conditions in schools

Studies show that teachers who find themselves in schools with a negative workplace environment are far more likely to become discouraged, to transfer elsewhere, or to leave teaching altogether (NFIE 1996; Stevenson 1998). Among the working conditions important to teachers are close working relationships with colleagues, time to reflect and plan, supportive administrative leadership, access to resources and advice when needed, and a manageable teaching schedule.

The national government can influence school-level reform through a federal act, called 'Title 1', which sets out a range of funding provisions which facilitates states' and districts' implementation of school-based programmes. However, the majority of strategies aimed at challenging and improving schools occur at the district level, although there are three specific areas in which state policy has tried to affect change at the school level.

Ask teachers what they need to do a better job and invariably the first response is 'more time.' time is what teachers need to meet the goals and expectations of policymakers. Despite the recognition that teachers have long been 'prisoners of time' (National Education Commission on Time and Learning 1994), few states have endeavored to address one of the perennial problems in schools: the limited time for teachers to participate in professional development. Arkansas appears to have been the only state to address the need to help schools provide more time within the school day and in 1997 began to require school districts to provide a minimum of 200 minutes of scheduled time each week for teacher conferences and instructional planning and preparation. The success of such policies, however, depends crucially on the policy environment: if schools and teachers continue to face increasing demands from new reforms, such time will not be used for professional development, but for alleviating administrative burdens.

A final set of state actions to improve schools has sought to allow school leaders and teachers to have greater freedom in redesigning the workplace environment, conducting professional development, and developing curriculum. Attempts to allow teachers and schools freedom from state requirements have occurred in some states, such as New York, where districts can request an exemption of state rules and regulations. Many of these programmes, however, are dealt with on a rule-by-rule basis, and some policy think tanks have criticised the process as being cumbersome and complicated, resulting in few districts applying for such waivers (CPRE 1998).

Future considerations

Many of the policies and practices described in this paper are succeeding not simply because they are helping to attract a greater number of potential teacher candidates, but more because such strategies are simultaneously enhancing the quality and diversity of the teaching force. Although much public attention and support focuses on making teaching a more attractive career option, the high attrition and low retention rate of new recruits are central issues for policymakers. Equally important to creating incentives for future teacher candidates are developing structures and opportunities that will support, retain and sustain the present teaching force.

There are two specific challenges for improving teacher supply and quality. One is about ensuring that well-qualified and fully prepared teachers are placed and supported in the subjects and locations in which they are needed, such as hard-to-staff schools and critical shortage areas. A second is about ensuring the allocation of equal resources so that the least advantaged schools and communities can attract high-quality candidates. Here, the flexibility and diversity of local school district and state policies can powerfully determine whether the teachers who are prepared by the range of training institutions and programmes get to where they are actually needed.

Policymakers must consider not simply how to hire enough teachers to fill vacancies each year, but for the long-term how they are prepared, where they are placed, how they are supported after arriving in the classroom, and how they are rewarded and sustained throughout their career.

Policy implications

A key lesson from the US is that whilst the pressure for change can be exerted at a national level, the ultimate impetus must come from the ground up. In the US, the assumption underlying most current teacher policy reforms is that national resources and direction are needed. However, there is clear recognition that solutions must be developed locally, professionally supported, teacher-driven and most importantly, sustained by key institutions, such as teacher unions, school districts and teacher preparation programmes.

Even with the major differences between the US and the UK in policy context and educational governance structures, many of the policy strategies described in this paper hold some promise and potential for the UK. The barriers for implementing such policies should not be seen solely in terms of resources, but rest more on the ability of policymakers to diagnose the problem fully and to construct thoughtful policies. This, in turn, depends on whether politicians are willing to recognise and acknowledge the complex dimensions of teacher supply and the needs of the teachers. A number of policy implications for addressing teacher supply are thus raised here.

- Diagnosing the problem is crucial.

- The type of policy tools used to implement change matters. Policymakers need not rely on threats and sanctioning schools to instigate change; practitioners and schools can be galvanised through the use of incentives and the development of opportunities. Investing in the knowledge, skills and potential of teachers, through such schemes as induction programmes, scholarships and professional development, can go a long, long way in sustaining and building the capacity of the profession.

- Maintaining an adequate teacher supply requires attention to standards.

- Ensure that every child is taught by a well-prepared and qualified teacher, by making sure that teachers and schools in highly-deprived areas receive greater levels of support in order to meet the standards expected for students in more affluent areas.

In Britain, solving the dilemmas of teacher supply and demand will require far more investment in and attention to how teachers are trained, hired, inducted and supported within the profession. Whether improvements in these areas can make a difference in the future will depend on two things. Firstly, the willingness of policymakers to identify weaknesses and address flaws within the system; and secondly, the capacity of those institutions which have a stake in the supply of teachers – schools, universities, unions and professional associations – to work together in formulating thoughtful policies and long-term solutions.

I conclude with a final point that is often assumed, but all too often underestimated and undervalued by policymakers. Solving the dilemmas of teacher supply will require policymakers, educators and researchers to think about and solve problems together. Linda Darling-Hammond, in describing the difficulties of educational policymaking, remarked that 'When various parts of the system are working at cross purposes, the enterprise lurches around like a carriage pulled by horses running off in different directions' (1998). For any future investment in the teaching profession to be worthwhile, the individual and institutional capacity of those affected must also be addressed. A national campaign to improve teacher supply requires concerted action and collaboration on the ground and ownership among schools, LEAS, universities and local practitioners. Even then, success will depend ultimately not on the will and effectiveness of policymakers and policy, but on the ability of Britain's teaching profession to meet the future needs of young people and schools.

Commentary by David Haselkorn

At one level the differences between the US and England with respect to the current teacher shortage crisis are really more differences of degree than of substance. All of the issues that we are facing in the US are found in England. The problem of low esteem; inadequate numbers of well qualified individuals going into the profession; the mismatch between teacher salaries and housing prices; the persistence of high teacher turnover in hard to staff schools (among others) are of as great moment in the policy discussions in the UK as they are in the US.

Recruiting New Teachers is an organisation that probably does not have an equivalent in England. We were established as an NGO back in 1986 by business and education leaders, to use public service advertising and the American media to try to raise esteem for teaching in the US.

This is something that had not been done before but there had been several conspicuously successful examples of social marketing campaigns in the US prior to ours. Seat belt use had been raised; cigarette smoking reduced, particularly among youth; highway litter had been curtailed, in part, through broad-based media campaigns that used the techniques of Madison Avenue to change public attitudes and behaviour.

The first ads (and those that followed) touched a real nerve. Over a million individuals have called 1-800-45-TEACH for information on how to pursue teaching careers, in response to them (the strongest response on record in the history of the US Advertising Council). It was a response that ultimately garnered a 39 per cent response rate from individuals of colour; this at a time when the leading policy researchers in the US were bemoaning the disappearance of the minority teacher. However, despite our success, we also quickly recognised that if we were simply recruiting greater numbers of individuals into discredited schools of education and dysfunctional urban school districts, we were not doing much of a public service at all.

So we evolved a much more active sort of research agenda to look at the ways in which we could tap into non-traditional pools of prospective teachers and prepare them in innovative ways to enter the classroom. And the kind of pools that we are talking about might include, for example, retired military personnel, mid-career transitioners from other fields, teacher aides (para-professionals already employed in poverty-impacted schools). We proposed to prepare them to become fully licensed teachers. Going down the pipeline a little further, we looked into programmes targeting middle and high school age youth. Survey data had shown that 52 per cent of American teachers had made their decision to teach before graduating from high school. Yet, while there were school-based career days where almost every kind of occupation was represented, teaching was really relegated to a rather un-robust set of future educator clubs, many were relics from the last teacher hiring boom of the late 1950s and 1960s.

By studying these and other pathways (including urban induction and mentoring programmes), RNT has been at the forefront of a movement to expand participation in teaching and improve the ways in which future teachers are recruited and prepared. For example, there are now over fifty high school teaching magnets around the country in the US. These are academically focussed college prep secondary schools that have a curricular focus on teaching and learning and really try and get students early on thinking about both college careers and careers as teachers. There are scores of new aide-to-teacher programmes, and hundreds of mid-career preparation pathways. Beyond policy research RNT began to convene stakeholders to advance the teacher recruitment, development, and diversity agenda in the States. We also began consulting with school districts, states and the federal government on developing improved human resources policies and practices in education.

More recently, RNT has established a national website under funding from the federal government, 'www.recruitingteachers.org', which is a one-stop shop for individuals looking for teaching jobs in the country or exploring teaching at an earlier stage of career awareness and development. It provides a wealth of information to individuals about how to pursue teaching careers. It links individuals to over 1500 websites, online resources, school districts, and teacher job clearing houses around our country.

Functionally, we focus most on recruitment. However, we are very much interested in issues of induction and mentoring of novice teachers in the US, in particular, because of induction's importance as a nexus between preparation and lifelong teacher development, as well as its impact on retention. The comparable figures in terms of attrition rates in the States are that we tend to lose 30 per cent to 50 per cent of our teachers within the first three to five years of urban teaching. It is a revolving door recruitment syndrome that creates a large part of the recruitment challenge in the United States.

The problem is most severe in our inner cities and in our isolated rural areas where the challenges teachers face are greatest, in terms of the paucity of resources, the poor condition of ageing schools and the problems of poverty and disadvantage that follow children into the classroom. How do we face this challenge in the US? We ensure that our most challenging classrooms and schools are staffed with our least qualified and experienced teachers.

More than two thirds of the nation's urban schools routinely hire unqualified individuals via emergency permits or under the fig leaf of quick-fix emergency certification. Too many of these paths are short cuts to the classroom that give short shrift to adequate professional standards.

So, overlaying these rather daunting recruitment challenges is a fierce ideological debate that is going on in our country as to how we prepare teachers and what constitutes a qualified teacher. Almost everyone in the political or policy community has internalised the mantra that we need qualified teachers. The real argument is over how we define quality in teaching. The National Commission on Teaching and America's Future has defined a teacher as an individual who holds an undergraduate major or minor in the subject matter they are going to teach plus a masters' degree in education or pedagogy. So they are looking at pedagogy and discipline-based knowledge as being comparable in terms of the repertoire of knowledge and skills that teachers must have.

If you look at our suburban schools, you will find some of the best-prepared, best-educated teachers in the world. If you look at our urban schools you will find, in effect, a string of short-term substitutes: new recruits who have not been well prepared, who are under-supported and who are here today and gone tomorrow. That is a huge problem.

Meanwhile the focus on policy reform in the US has been predominantly on better standards for schools and better testing regimes for students. There has been a fundamental mismatch between the predominant views on reform and the real challenges of creating the kind of autonomous profession that has been talked about. A survey that I worked on several years found that the majority of American teachers viewed themselves as targets of reform rather than agents of reform. And turning that around is a really significant problem: not just in the teaching community but also in the community at large.

Another solution that has been put on the table is recruiting overseas, particularly in hard pressed urban districts. There is a degree of madness at work here. People are looking at these solutions in a piecemeal fashion that is not addressing the need to develop teaching through a comprehensive approach that encompasses the entire lifecycle of the teacher from recruitment through preparation, selection, hiring, induction and on-going professional development throughout their career.

New York City employs around 80,000 teachers, 55,000 of whom will be eligible for retirement within the next five years. The story that exists in New York can be repeated in city after city after city. Now there are things that are being done about it. The state of California, led by a proactive governor and legislature, has taken rather dramatic action designed to provide, in a formal way, mentoring and induction of every new teacher in California over the first one to two years of teaching. It cuts down on attrition. Equally important, it can accelerate the development of accomplished teaching repertoires and skills. Unfortunately, because of the California hiring challenge and the fact that more and more unqualified teachers are being hired, (in fact, around 12 per cent of California's teachers are teaching on an emergency or substandard licence), this by and large successful induction programme is being used for triage: keeping teachers' heads above water who come into the profession unprepared, as opposed to providing a really unparalleled opportunity to continue the education of the teacher in a clinical setting which we routinely do in the fields of medicine and law. That's another problem.

The public gets it. The public in the US believes that teachers are being inadequately paid and inadequately supported and would pay more in taxes to ensure that qualified teachers are supported. The public rejects categorically allowing individuals who are unqualified to enter into the profession. Second, the public is willing to raise teacher salaries. They recognise that children of affluence and non-minority children are getting a far better shake in the country with respect to the resources they receive, and with respect to the quality of teachers that they have, and there is a growing and festering outrage about this. Teaching is still by far the profession that Americans view as being of greatest benefit to society, beating out all other professions by nearly 3:1, including that of medicine. This is a political moment that has not been adequately grasped by US politicians, and an untapped political force.

The intrinsic call to teaching still attracts individuals, but the US public at least understands, (even if their politicians don't) that teaching can no longer be pursued as a philanthropic act. So, to briefly sum up with what I feel is needed to meet the current crisis in the States. Short term: more efforts to expand the pool, improve the pipeline, increase incentives, reduce unnecessary barriers. Longer term, my version of the reform agenda is that we, at least in the US, need to address the three Cs. We need to address Conditions in the profession because teachers leave not because of the salary issues, they leave because of conditions in the classroom – not only poor discipline amongst students but also lack of administrative support and support from parents. Another is Compensation; the laws of a market-based economy do not stop at the schoolhouse door. We need to close the salary gap between teaching and other careers requiring comparable years of higher education. The average teacher in the US earns about $15,000 less than a beginning computer scientist who has had a similar length of education. The statistical gap between the salary of a teacher and a computer scientist, both of whom have masters' degrees and have been in their respective professions for fifteen years, rises to $36,000. Therefore, we need to close that gap. Finally there is the Culture of the profession itself, a culture of professionalism that supports self-directed learning, and the development of expertise that is not only honoured in the classroom, but honoured in the community, and honoured in society overall.

References

Bullard C (1998) *Qualified Teachers for All California Students: Current Issues in Recruitment, Retention, Preparation, and Professional Development* Sacramento, California Research Bureau, CRB-98-012

Consortium for Policy Research in Education (CPRE) (1998) 'States and Districts and Comprehensive School Reform' *Research Bulletin* 24

Darling-Hammond L and Loewenberg Ball (1998) *Teaching for High Standards: What Policymakers Need to Know and Be Able to Do* (published by the Consortium for Policy Research in Education and the National Commission on Teaching and America's Future, CPRE Joint Report Series, JRE-04)

Darling-Hammond L (1999) *Teacher Quality and Student Achievement: A Review of State Policy Evidence* (published by the Center for the Study of Teaching & Policy, Document R-99-1)

Darling-Hammond L (2000) *Solving the Dilemmas of Teacher Supply, Demand, and Standards: How We Can Ensure a Competent, Caring, and Qualified Teacher for Every Child* (published by The National Commission on Teaching and America's Future)

Elmore R (1997) *Investing in Teacher Learning: Staff Development and Instructional Improvement in Community School District* New York City (published by The National Commission on Teaching and America's Future)

Education Week (2000) *Quality Counts 2000: Who Should Teach?* (published by Editorial Projects in Education, Education Week)

Haselkorn and Harris (2001) *The Essential Profession: American Education at the Crossroads. A National Survey of Public Attitudes Toward Teaching, Educational Opportunity, and School Reform* Belmont, MA: Recruiting New Teachers

Hirsch, Koppich and Knapp (2001) *Revisiting What States are Doing to Improve the Quality of Teaching: An Update of Patterns and Trends* (A working paper published by the Center for the Study of Teaching and Policy, in collaboration with the National Conference of State Legislatures, Document W-10-1)

Ingersoll,R (1999) *Teacher Turnover, Teacher Shortages, and the Organization of Schools* Seattle, Washington: Center for Teaching Policy, University of Washington

National Commission on Teaching and America's Future (1996) *What Matters Most: Teaching for America's Future* New York

National Commission on Teaching and America's Future (1997) *Doing What Matters Most: Investing in Quality Teaching* New York

National Center for Education Statistics (2000) *Indicator of the Month: Elementary and Secondary School Enrolment* Washington, DC: US Department of Education

National Center for Education Statistics (1997) *Characteristics of Stayers, Movers, and Leavers. Results for the Follow-up Survey* Washington, DC: US Department of Education

National Education Commission on Time and Learning (1994) *Prisoners of Time* Washington, DC: US Government Printing Office

Rustique-Forrester E (1995) *Raising Professional Standards in Cincinnati: A Case Study of District-wide School Reform through the Professional Development of Teachers* New York: National Commission on Teaching and America's Future

Sedlak M and Schlossman S (1986) *Who Will Teach?* Santa Monica, CA: RAND Corporation (R-3472CSTP)

Stevenson HW (1999) 'Guarding Teachers' Time' *Education Week* 18:2

Stricherz, M (2001) 'Chicago Moves to Curb Unlicensed Teachers' *Education Week* 10 October

Snyder JD (1999) *New Haven Unified School District: A teaching quality system for excellent and equity* New York: National Commission on Teaching and America's Future

6. A representative profession? Ethnic minority teachers

Alistair Ross

This chapter examines the position of ethnic minority teachers within the teaching profession. It asks: why should it matter that the teaching profession reflects the ethnic composition of society? And why do we need to have teachers from the ethnic minorities? It examines the current situation (as far as this can be determined), and the way in which future members from these groups are being recruited into training (or not).

It is shown that there are insufficient teachers from these backgrounds in the profession; that insufficient numbers entering training; and that ethnic minority teachers appear to suffer discrimination in terms of promotion in their career in teaching. Barriers to change are then analysed, and some policy outcomes are suggested.

Does it matter that we have a teaching profession that represents the ethnic diversity of British society?

Why should the teaching profession be representative of the ethnic composition of the UK? We do not expect all professions (or all other workforce groups) to represent the ethnicities in the population. We have anti-discriminatory laws and policies on recruitment, training places and appointments, which should of course be upheld and enforced. But if this is done, and the teaching profession then has a smaller proportion of teachers from the ethnic minorities: does it matter?

The arguments that it is necessary arise from the particular nature of education and the way we organise learning in schools.

Learning is a formative activity conducted through a variety of processes, some of which are explicit and very visible (for example, the prescribed curriculum), and some of which are subtle, almost invisible and barely understood, even by practitioners. Processes of learning convey a wealth of meanings to young people at an impressionable and formative period in their lives: who conducts this is an important part of the process.

Learning is a social process: it takes place in the interactions between teacher and learner, and learner and learner. The people who take on the role of teacher play a critical part in determining the social relationships under which learning occurs. They are in a prominent position of authority, trust and power. Who teaches is thus critical for the learning process. Designating a person as a teacher is not undertaken lightly in any society, and important messages – to society and parents, and above all to children – are conveyed in this.

Learning is undertaken by all children/young people. Many of our other social provisions are episodic and accidental. We do not all use the health service, for example, and the use that most of us make of it tends to be transitory and intermittent. We do not expect in our lives to experience a health service in the same way that we experience educational provision.

Learning is conducted over a long period of time. Disregarding notions of life-long learning, it is a process that we require all our young people to undergo for a period of at least eleven years.

Making sure that the teaching force is simply 'representative' could be seen as simple tokenism: making sure that there are enough black faces around. But these four characteristics of education make whom we entrust to teach very important. Having a representative teaching force is critical because of the character, ubiquity, pervasiveness, duration and importance of teaching as a social activity. There are three specific reasons why we need more teachers from the ethnic minorities.

Firstly, the profession must have the capacity to reflect the full spectrum of cultural and social traditions and systems through teachers' collective professional practice. Each individual teacher brings to her or his work a set of cultural norms and expectations. Good teachers are reflective and aware of this in a self-critical way, but none of us can recognise all the culturally and socially determined mores that we carry. We have a diverse population, with a very wide range of cultures, customs, languages, faiths and beliefs, and education needs to be delivered by teams of professionals who can match that range, in explicit practice and in behaviour and attitudes. Both the formal and the hidden curriculum need to be managed and delivered in a way that reflects the varieties of social practice in our society, and this in turn demands that the teaching profession is drawn fully and explicitly from that range of cultures and ethnicities in our society. With such a range of teachers, we can aspire towards delivering an education that has the subtlety and the nuance to make each individual learner feel that her or his cultural set is acknowledged and valued, thus empowering her or him as a learner. Without such a range of teachers, this cannot even be an aspiration.

Secondly, racism and xenophobia – individual, institutional and otherwise – continue to be major issues in contemporary society. Racism in schools needs to be very explicitly and forcefully challenged: partly because this is the moment in the development of personal value systems that it can be stopped and confronted, and partly because of its effects on both minority communities and the majority community. Minorities will be disempowered and disenfranchised as learners, with all the social and economic wastage that this implies. The majority groups will develop attitudes of intolerance and an inability to value diversity. Tackling discriminatory behaviour is important in classrooms and schools: but racism is not always explicit and obvious, or even intentional. Racism is very properly an important concern for all teachers, but some of the subtleties of racist practice and behaviour will be more obvious and more capable of recognition by teachers who have themselves some direct experience of having suffered from racist behaviour. Teachers from the majority community, however well intentioned, trained and experienced they are in anti-racist work, will still be unaware of and unable to identify and analyse much of the xenophobia, chauvinism and racism in society.

Thirdly, we need aspirational role models for our pupils, particularly our ethnic minority pupils. We know that our ethnic minorities are generally poorly represented in positions of power, authority and prestige in our society. We clearly need more police officers, social workers, accountants, politicians, senior civil servants, captains of industry (and so on), from the ethnic minorities. But teachers are a particular and special category: they are the one face of civil society that every child will meet, every working day, through the whole of their formal education. It is therefore particularly critical that this 'face' of civil power be seen, visibly and explicitly, to represent all of our society. This is where such inclusiveness is essential. The presence of teachers drawn from all the ethnic groups of our society (and equally, from all the ranges of disability, from all the sexualities, from all social classes) will mean that firstly, all pupils – white majority just as much as ethnic minority – will recognise that members of the minorities have as much power and prestige as any other citizen, and secondly, that pupils who themselves come from the ethnic minorities will recognise that they too can and should aspire to excellence, esteem and authority.

How representative is the current teaching force of ethnic minorities?

Figures show 12.9 per cent of the school population in England is of children described as coming from an ethnic minority background (DfES 2001), but it is not known how many of their teachers come from such a background: it is probably less than five per cent. There have been concerns for many years at the low numbers of people from the ethnic minorities who are entering the teaching profession. A survey of eight LEAs in 1983-4 by the Commission for Racial Equality found that two per cent of the teachers in its sample were from the ethnic minorities (Ranger 1988). The sample was of LEAs that were in areas of fairly dense settlement by minorities, and might therefore perhaps be expected to have a higher proportion of ethnic minority teachers than the national level. Statistics have not been collected nationally on the numbers and distribution of ethnic minority teachers (Mahony and Hextall 2000). Joint regional conference of the TTA and the CRE in 1998 promised that ethnic minority data would be collected (TTA/CRE 1998), but this has not been done. The TTA monitors ethnic minority teachers starting Initial Teacher Education courses (TTA 2001), but there are no figures from any official source on the current level of teachers in post.

A recent survey conducted by the Institute for Policy Studies in Education for 22 LEAs found some 879 teachers who described themselves as one of a number of Black categories, or one as a number of Asian categories, or as of mixed ethnic origin (a total of 8.9 per cent) (McCreith, Ross and Hutchings 2001). These LEAs were not a random sample: 18 were in London, two in the north west and two in the south east. Given the known distribution of ethnic minority pupils (DfES 2001), it can be estimated that these 22 LEAs would include about 30 per cent of all the ethnic minority pupils in Great Britain, and that about 48 per cent of the pupils in these LEAs would be from the ethnic minorities.

Respondents categorised themselves as members of specified ethnic categories, but for the purposes of much of this paper we have aggregated the Black responses and the Asian responses into two categories. Finer-scale categories would have led to some very small groups. Where possible, this paper has used the 2001 Census categories. There are, however, many difficulties with these, and there is often much 'missing data' from individuals who have 'hyphenated identities' (Carrington *et al* 1999).

The distribution of teachers of ethnic minority origin is uneven across the LEAs that we surveyed (Table 6.1), and uneven in terms of particular minorities. The highest concentration of all the various groups of ethnic minority teachers were found in Inner London, and the lowest in the North West, but teachers of Asian origin were more widely distributed than those who described themselves as Black, who were found predominantly in Inner London.

8.9 per cent of our respondents categorised themselves in ethnic minority groups: this represents some 349 teachers who define themselves as Black, 434 who define themselves as Asian, and 96 who describe themselves as of mixed ethnicity.

Table 6.1 Ethnicity profile for all areas: percentage composition of each region

	Inner London	Outer London	London LEAs	North West	South East	Total
White	86.2	91.6	88.7	98.3	93.6	90.0
Black	6.0	2.0	4.2	0.5	1.0	3.5
Asian	5.2	4.6	4.9	0.8	4.1	4.4
Mixed	1.6	0.7	1.2			1.0
Other	1.0	1.1	1.1	1.4	1.4	1.0
N	4378	3686	8064	1042	732	9838

Source: IPSE survey of teachers in 22 LEAs, 2000-2001

Are more members of ethnic minorities entering the teaching profession?

The Teacher Training Authority is attempting to recruit more teachers from the minority communities, but it is noticeable that there are wide variations in the proportions attracted to different institutions. In 2000, only six per cent of primary student teachers, and 7.5 per cent of secondary student teachers, were from ethnic minority backgrounds: the TTA's target is for nine per cent of recruits to be from such backgrounds by 2005-6. The 6.7 per cent of student teachers should be compared with the 15 per cent of all (home) UK undergraduates who are from ethnic minority backgrounds. In Great Britain,

8.57 per cent of the population between 15 and 24 are from ethnic minority backgrounds: figures for ethnicity in England by age are not published, but it is possible to estimate that about 9.45 per cent of the English population of 15-24 years olds are from ethnic minorities (Schuman 1999). This confirms that the conception of ethnic underachievement is mythical: some ethnic minority pupils can achieve relatively higher standards than their White counterparts.

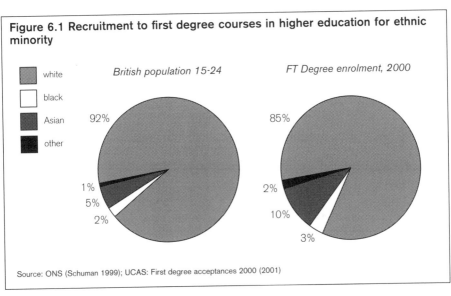

Figure 6.1 Recruitment to first degree courses in higher education for ethnic minority

Source: ONS (Schuman 1999); UCAS: First degree acceptances 2000 (2001)

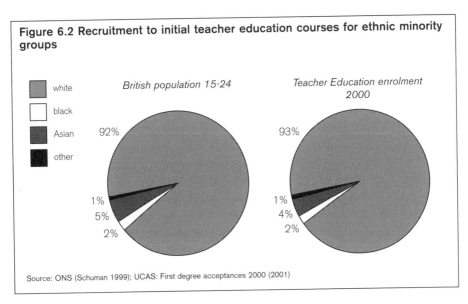

Figure 6.2 Recruitment to initial teacher education courses for ethnic minority groups

Source: ONS (Schuman 1999); UCAS: First degree acceptances 2000 (2001)

This level of participation is not matched in participation in Initial Teacher Education courses. The overall under-representation of the ethnic minority population is about 70 per cent of what might be expected (Figure 6.2).

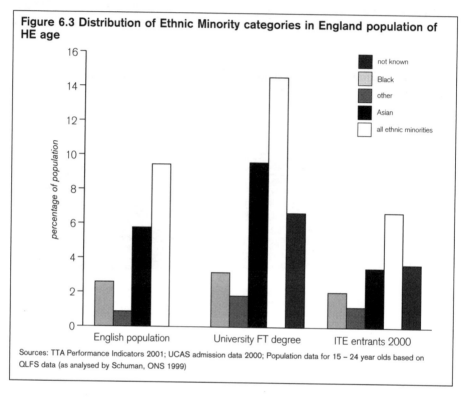

Figure 6.3 Distribution of Ethnic Minority categories in England population of HE age

Sources: TTA Performance Indicators 2001; UCAS admission data 2000; Population data for 15 – 24 year olds based on QLFS data (as analysed by Schuman, ONS 1999)

Figure 6.3 shows the percentage of ethnic minority categories, grouping them together into 'Black', 'Asian' and 'Other' (and all ethnic minorities) for a number of populations. The first set of bars (on the left) show the proportions of these categories in the approximate university-age population (15-24 year olds). The middle set show the proportion enrolling on HE courses in autumn 2000: these are all substantially larger than the figures for the whole population. The final set, on the right, show the proportions starting Initial Teacher Education course in the same year: these are all substantially lower that the figures for the whole population.

Enrolment in to teacher training is not evenly distributed between minority groups. We can calculate the number and percentages of the Great Britain population between 15 and 24 by ethnic minority, and the figures for admission to full-time first degree study by each group (taking only home students with England as their country of domicile) in 2000, and then the figures for admission to Initial Teacher Education courses in England for 2000.

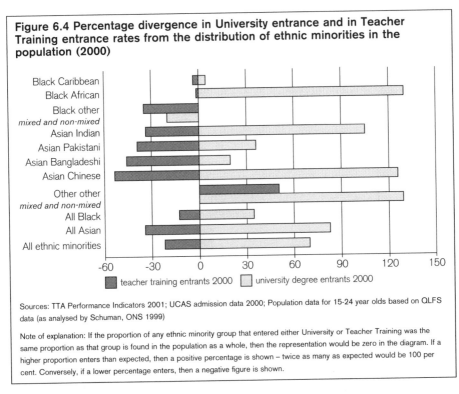

Figure 6.4 Percentage divergence in University entrance and in Teacher Training entrance rates from the distribution of ethnic minorities in the population (2000)

Sources: TTA Performance Indicators 2001; UCAS admission data 2000; Population data for 15-24 year olds based on QLFS data (as analysed by Schuman, ONS 1999)

Note of explanation: If the proportion of any ethnic minority group that entered either University or Teacher Training was the same proportion as that group is found in the population as a whole, then the representation would be zero in the diagram. If a higher proportion enters than expected, then a positive percentage is shown – twice as many as expected would be 100 per cent. Conversely, if a lower percentage enters, then a negative figure is shown.

From this data, it is possible to calculate the degree of over- or under-representation that a particular ethnic group has in Higher Education/Initial Teacher Education, based on the variance in participation rate from the representation rate in the population of HE-going age. Figure 6.4 shows this: the light bands show University enrolment, the dark band ITE enrolment. Note that for almost every ethnic minority group, a higher proportion than might be anticipated are enrolled in HE fulltime courses. Conversely, they are nearly all under-represented in Initial Teacher Education courses. This data has not been analysed for gender effects within this (the TTA goes not publish cross-tabulated data for ethnicity and gender; UCAS does, and the effect is considerable).

Distribution of ethnic minority children

The most recent analysis of the ethnic minority population by the Office for National Census (Schuman 1999) does not include predictions of population growth. But the distribution of ethnic minority pupils in the school population is very uneven across the various English regions. Figure 6.5 shows the number and distribution of pupils in maintained schools by ethnic group and Government Office region in January 2001

(DfES 2001: tables 47a and 47b). This shows the concentration of ethnic minorities generally in the London region, and, to a lesser extent, in the West Midlands. Figure 6.6 shows the same data, plotting the percentage of the school population in each group by region: this shows rather more dramatically the very uneven distribution of ethnic minorities generally, and of particular groups, by region. For example, while only 9.4 per cent of the White pupils in England are found in London schools, 61 per cent of England's Black Caribbean pupils are in London schools and 83 per cent of all Black African pupils. Inner London – with about five per cent of all pupils in England – has 46 per cent of all Bangladeshi origin pupils. Outside London there are other particular concentrations: Pakistani-origin pupils in Yorkshire and Humberside, and Pakistani and Indian pupils in the West Midlands. The North East and the South West have very low numbers of pupils from ethnic minority groups.

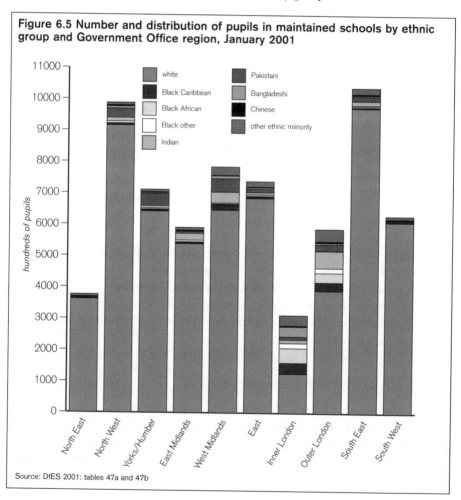

Figure 6.5 Number and distribution of pupils in maintained schools by ethnic group and Government Office region, January 2001

Source: DfES 2001: tables 47a and 47b

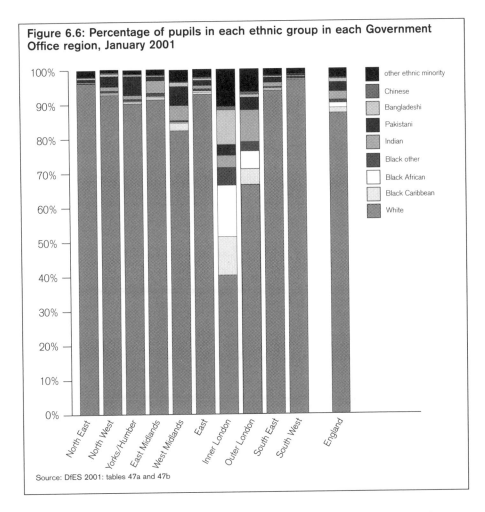

Figure 6.6: Percentage of pupils in each ethnic group in each Government Office region, January 2001

Source: DfES 2001: tables 47a and 47b

Are there demographic and professional differences between teachers from the ethnic minorities and white teachers?

Simply comparing the levels of ethnic minority teachers located in the 1983/4 CRE survey (Ranger 1988) and the IPSE survey in 2000/2001 (Ross 2001), it is clear that there has been a rise in the number and proportion of ethnic minority teachers in areas where there are large numbers of pupils (from around two per cent to around nine per cent). This change, over a period of 17 years, has resulted in a population of teachers from these ethnic minorities that differ in certain characteristics from the White teaching force. The following analysis focuses on the results of the most recent survey: it must be borne in mind that this data has a strong London orientation.

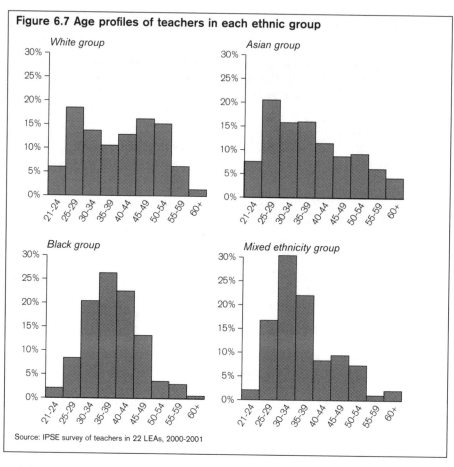

Figure 6.7 Age profiles of teachers in each ethnic group

Source: IPSE survey of teachers in 22 LEAs, 2000-2001

The age profile of the four major ethnic groups show some startling differences in the age distribution of teachers (Figure 6.7).

The White teachers (90 per cent of respondents) show the typical bi-modal distribution of the teaching force that has been demonstrated in earlier reports (Hutchings *et al* 2000). Black teachers display a single-mode distribution, in which 69 per cent of all Black teachers are aged between 30 and 45. This distribution is almost inverse to that of the population of White teachers. Black teachers comprised a mere 3.5 per cent of the total teaching population in our sample, but amongst those teachers aged between 35 and 39, 8 per cent are black. Part of this distribution is probably the result of teacher training recruitment policies in the past, where there were very few black teachers trained until about 20 years ago (such teachers now being aged 45 or more). But the low numbers of young Black teachers also suggests that there could now have been a recent fall in the recruitment of Black entrants to the teaching profession. While nearly 25 per cent of all White teachers are under 30, only just over 10 per cent of Black teachers are in this age range. But another contributory factor may be the age at which teachers qualify. Taking only those teachers who have qualified post 1989, the average age of qualification is shown in Table 6.2. The average age of qualification for Black and Asian teachers is thus between 1 and 2.3 years later than that of White teachers: this will have a marginal impact on the position of the age distributions shown in Figure 6.7 (shifting them approximately half a column to the right), but not on the shape of the distribution.

Table 6.2 Ages on qualification of post-1989 qualified teachers; average ages of all teachers

	average age on qualification (post 1989 qualified only)	average age of group (all teachers)
White	26.4	39.7
Black	28.7	38.6
Asian	27.4	38.2
Mixed ethnic origin	27.0	36.8
All	26.5	39.5

Source: IPSE survey of teachers in 22 LEAs, 2000-2001

Teachers from an Asian background show a third pattern. This appears to show a concentration of younger teachers – indeed, 28 per cent are under 30 (compared with only 24 per cent of the White teachers) – but it also shows more older teachers. 11 per cent of all Asian teachers are aged over 55, while only 7 per cent of White teachers are in this age band. While the average age of all these groups of teachers is remarkably similar (Table 6.2), this conceals significant variations in distribution.

Ethnic minority teachers tended to have qualified relatively recently. 48.4 per cent of the White teachers qualified after 1989, but 63 per cent of all Black teachers qualified in this period, 69.2 per cent of Asian teachers and 62 per cent of mixed ethnic origin teachers. There has been a particular increase in female Asian teachers over the past eleven years, and particularly into the primary phase. The patterns of when teachers qualify appears to be related more strongly to ethnic group than to gender.

Proportionally, more White females entered the profession recently, as part of the general process of feminisation that has been apparent over the past decade. Black teachers are more evenly distributed by gender than the White group, with the exception that there were proportionally many more male teachers qualifying in the early 1970s, the females having a rather similar surge in the late 1970s. But in terms of the total numbers of Black teachers currently in service in these LEAs, the intake in the 1990s dwarfs the 1970s intake. Asian teachers show a rather more uneven gender pattern in terms of date of qualification. There is very clear recent tendency (1990s) towards Asian females joining teaching: of all the Asian females now teaching, 70.5

per cent qualified since 1989 (Asian males, 68 per cent). But the number of Asian males gaining qualifications was much higher in the early 1970s (probably qualifying in the sub-continent, Ghuman 1995), with a smaller female surge in the late 1970s, in a pattern very similar to that of Black teachers.

The survey asked respondents to indicate their intentions towards maintaining a career in teaching. Did they intend to leave teaching within the next five years, to leave in the more distant future, or to stay in teaching for all of their working life? It was found in our earlier study (Hutchings *et al* 2000) that generally younger teachers were more likely to consider leaving teaching than older teachers.

More Asian teachers say that they may leave the teaching profession early in their careers, but White and (to a slightly lesser extent) Asian teachers are also more likely to say that they stay in teaching for all their professional lives (Figure 6.8).

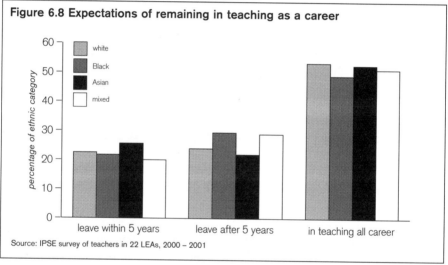

Figure 6.8 Expectations of remaining in teaching as a career

Source: IPSE survey of teachers in 22 LEAs, 2000 – 2001

The differences at this level are significant but not large, however: we can expect the Black teaching force to shrink by about 6 per cent more than the White teaching force.

It is of concern that ethnic minority teachers, who remain hard to attract into the profession, say that they are less likely to stay in teaching. Two factors may be contributing to this. Firstly, it is possible that some of those from the ethnic minorities may perceive teaching as a step on the occupational hierarchy, and intend to be upwardly mobile, advancing to careers seen as more prestigious or better rewarded than teaching. If this is an explanation, it would suggest that more Asians are intending to move on out of teaching relatively more quickly than Black teachers, but that more Black teachers intend to move onwards and upwards after five years. The second factor – which may be related to the first – is that ethnic minority teachers feel that they may not be able to achieve promotion within the hierarchies of teaching, and therefore intend to leave the profession for occupations in which they might feel less discriminated against.

But in terms of the particular LEAs that were included in this survey, there is another demographic characteristic that acts against this propensity for ethnic minority teachers to consider leaving the profession. There is a tendency for those from ethnic minority backgrounds not to move out of their local communities, where they often feel a higher level of community support, have a greater sense of security and safety, and may have more supportive family networks that they might have in a different area, with a lower proportion of ethnic minority inhabitants. This has been characterised by theories of 'choice' and restraint' (Lakey 1997; Ratcliffe 1999).

One of the reasons that teachers may leave the profession is lack of opportunities for promotion and progression, or a feeling that promotion would not be possible (see examples of this in Osler 1997, Ghuman 1995, and – at a much earlier time – Ranger 1988).

We analysed our data to see how ethnic minority teachers were represented in the various stages of career development that are open to teachers. The first point to examine was what proportion of each ethnic group filled the various levels in the teaching hierarchy: Headteacher posts, deputy Headteacher posts, the various 'posts of responsibility' (posts that have additional points attached to them, for specific responsibilities within the school), and mainscale posts. Figure 6.9 shows this distribution, and Figure 6.10 shows the position for Headteachers and deputy Headteachers more clearly. These graphs show the percentage of each ethnic group that is found at each level in the hierarchy: for example, of all the Black teachers, 48 per cent are on mainscale posts, 45 per cent in posts of responsibility, four per cent are Deputy

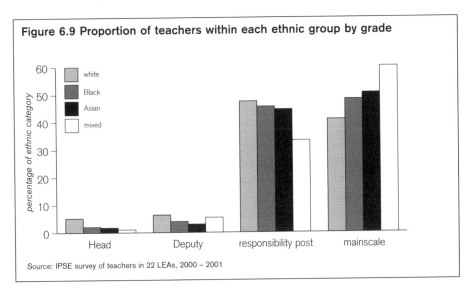

Figure 6.9 Proportion of teachers within each ethnic group by grade

Source: IPSE survey of teachers in 22 LEAs, 2000 – 2001

Heads, and two per cent are Heads. The corresponding figures for the White teacher population are 41 per cent mainscale, 48 per cent posts of responsibility, 6.4 per cent Deputy Heads and 5.2 per cent Heads.

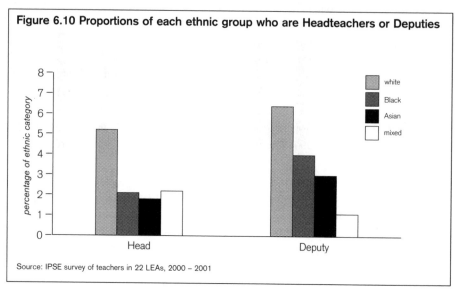

Figure 6.10 Proportions of each ethnic group who are Headteachers or Deputies

Source: IPSE survey of teachers in 22 LEAs, 2000 – 2001

It is clear that there are a preponderance of teachers from the ethnic minorities on the mainscale grades. Disparity is also found at the higher levels of responsibility. It should be noted that these percentages are of the *particular ethnic group*: because there are generally so few ethnic minority teachers, the actual disparity is much greater; our survey found 442 White Headteachers, 7 Black Headteachers and 7 Asian Headteachers.

These disparities are not evenly distributed. Examining the figures on the basis of gender, it appears that the lower proportion of ethnic minority teachers in promoted posts is particularly evident amongst male teachers. Figure 6.11 shows that 53.5 per cent of White males hold posts of responsibility, while only 47.9 per cent of Black and 47.6 per cent of Asian teachers do so. Conversely, while only 31.1 per cent of White male teachers are on the basic main grade, 46.3 per cent of Asian male, and 43.8 per cent of Black males are in this lowest category. Amongst female teachers, the distinctions are much less evident. It appears that, in respect of these two levels, male ethnic minority teachers are disadvantaged to the same degree as White female teachers are disadvantaged in comparison to White male teachers. At Headship and deputy level, while the numbers are small, White males and females dominate, with a much higher proportion of teachers in these positions.

Many ethnic minority teachers are relatively recently qualified. It could be argued that this is why there is the promotion disparity, and that when these teachers had

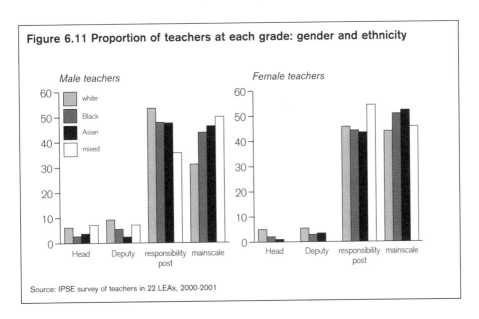

Figure 6.11 Proportion of teachers at each grade: gender and ethnicity

Source: IPSE survey of teachers in 22 LEAs, 2000-2001

acquired more experience, they too will be promoted to more responsible posts. To test this hypothesis, the following analyses select only those teachers who have had substantial experience since qualification, excluding the more recently qualified teachers.

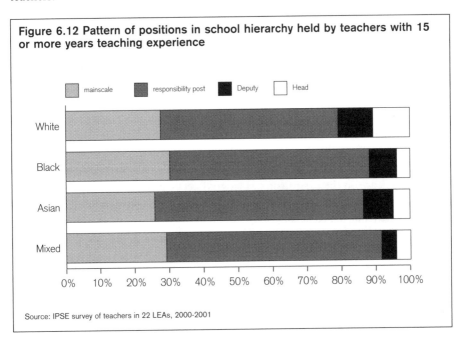

Figure 6.12 Pattern of positions in school hierarchy held by teachers with 15 or more years teaching experience

Source: IPSE survey of teachers in 22 LEAs, 2000-2001

Figure 6.13 shows teachers who qualified before 1986. Amongst even the youngest of these, we would expect to see teachers moving into Deputy Headship and even some Headship positions. Indeed, we find that of the White teaching population, some 10.7 per cent are Headteachers, and 10.1 per cent are Deputy Headteachers. But only 4.9 per cent of Asian and 3.9 per cent of Black teachers are Heads. There are a further 7.9 per cent of Black teachers who are Deputy Heads, and 8.6 per cent of Asian teachers are deputies.

It is still possible the groups being compared differ in terms of experience. Some of the white Headteachers may have had considerably more experience – given the age profiles shown in Figure 6.7, a higher proportion than is so for the ethnic minority teachers. Figure 6.13 therefore compares the positions in the hierarchy of only those teachers who have had between 15 and 25 years experience, that is, teachers who qualified between 1976 and 1986.

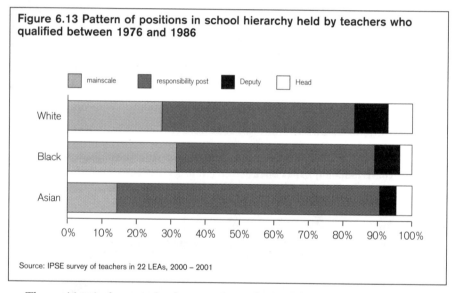

Figure 6.13 Pattern of positions in school hierarchy held by teachers who qualified between 1976 and 1986

Source: IPSE survey of teachers in 22 LEAs, 2000 – 2001

The position is the same for those teachers who qualified between these two years. 7.1 per cent of all White teachers are Headteachers compared with only 3.7 per cent of Black and 4.8 per cent of Asian teachers. This parallels the situation described by Ranger in the early 1980s (1988).

We do not know how many teachers from each ethnic group apply for posts of responsibility. It is possible – though unlikely – that Black and Asian teachers only apply half as often for posts of Head and Deputy that do their White peers (the evidence from Ranger in 1988 was that they applied for promoted posts more often that their White peers). If they do apply for promotion less often, it is a serious cause for concern that they do not feel that they can take on management roles in our schools. It is more probable that that are applying, and not being appointed. Appointments were largely made by the 932 school governing bodies represented in our survey, and even if it were possible to collect any ethnic monitoring data on applicants, there would be insufficient cases of appointment to the positions of Head or Deputy in any one school to show that discrimination had taken place.

It is most unlikely that there is such a substantial difference in the rate of applications between White and ethnic minority candidates for these posts to an extent that would explain the differences noted above. The conclusion has to be drawn that, taken as a whole, the appointment process in a proportion of these schools works in such a way that Black and Asian teachers are significantly less likely to assume positions of authority than White teachers. This outcome arises despite the fact that all the LEAs concerned have Equal Opportunity policies that require their schools to manage appointments in a non-discriminatory manner. Although there may be no conscious policy on the part of governing bodies to operate in a discriminatory way, the outcome that can be observed by aggregating all their individual acts of appointment must suggest that we are observing institutional racism in the career development process. It must be emphasised that institutional racism does not mean that conscious or deliberate acts of racism are necessarily taking place, but that the systems operate in such a way that the outcomes are discriminatory.

The experiences of ethnic minority teachers

This quantitative analysis can be supplemented and confirmed from the growing literature based on qualitative evidence from ethnic minority teachers. One of the first such accounts was the biographical narrative of Beryl Gilroy (1976), who described her personal encounters with the English educational system as a black teacher. More recently, Osler has conducted a series of detailed case histories of ethnic minority teachers (1997), and Ghuman has presented an analysis of the careers of Asian origin teachers (1995).

The narratives that are recounted present evidence of the difficulties teachers from ethnic minorities face in schools. For example, some report that they feel that they have to be better than their White counterparts in order to be equal to them (Osler 1997). Ethnic minority teachers are often called in to 'deal' with parents or children from ethnic minority backgrounds, and find themselves being expected to legitimise school decisions, or the actions of White colleagues, which they suspect may have discriminatory origins. Many of Osler's sample found that promotion was not possible in their specialist subject: they did achieve promotion if they were willing to take up posts in multicultural education, or in English as an additional language (although some reported that they then met hostility from some White colleagues when they were in such advisory units). Both Black and Asian teachers remarked that they were expected to specialise in certain areas: Asian teachers in particular are sometimes disproportionately found in teaching science and mathematics in secondary schools. Promotion may be possible in those departments, but promotion out of them – to year Head or deputy level – is much more difficult (Ghuman 1995). Such subject stereotyping to the sciences and mathematics was also noted by Ranger in the early 1980s (1988).

Barriers to joining the profession have been examined from two broad perspectives. There has firstly been several analyses of the TTA's objectives and processes (Mahony and Hextall 2000; Carrington *et al* 2000; Hextall *et al* 2001). The TTA's objective to increase the proportion of ethnic minority recruits has always been qualified: for example, the Agency's chief executive referred in her annual lecture to the Agency's desire 'to increase the diversity of entrants to teaching and teacher training, *consistent with maintaining quality*' (Millet 1996, emphasis added). The implicit assumption appears to be that if more ethnic minority recruits are admitted, somehow the overall quality of the profession will be diluted.

Similar TTA barriers are suggested in an investigation of the way in which the Agency's 'skills tests' in mathematics and English apparently discriminate against ethnic minority recruits (Hextall *et al* 2001) : the investigators conclude by cautiously suggesting that 'the outcomes of the 1999/2000 numeracy test suggest that the effect will be particularly undermining of the Agency's aspiration ... to increase the proportion of entrants into the profession from minority ethnic groups' (p236).

The second set of perspectives on the barriers to entering teaching lies in the career motivations and ambitions of young people. Osler reports some Asian female teachers as choosing teaching because it was acceptable to their parents: it often involved training locally, was a socially acceptable occupation, and did not (like, for example, nursing) involve undue proximity to males. But there are also many accounts suggesting teaching is not seen as a prestigious profession. Carrington and Tomlin report an Asian male considering primary teaching as a career being told he was 'taking a hundred steps backwards' (2000, p146). Carrington and Tomlin also suggest that this attitude may be more prevalent towards Asian young men than to young women. This would be supported by the training figures for Asian women reported above. Ghuman reports similar attitudes as being quite widespread (1995, p129). There are fewer accounts of Black pupils seeing teaching as not having sufficient status.

Another potential reason that is offered for young people from the ethnic minorities not wishing to become teachers themselves is their own experiences of the English educational system. Osler reports that some young people feel that the racist experiences that they have had at school themselves can be a deterrent to taking up a position where they will be part of this system, and where they expect to be racially harassed by pupils. On the other hand, these sorts of experiences can also act as a spur, as reported variously by Osler, Carrington and Tomlin and Ghuman. Several of those who do select teaching as a career refer to wanting to act as ethnic role models, or for other altruistic reasons (Carrington and Tomlin 2000, p144). Another possible deterrent is the nature of the curriculum which teachers are required to deliver. Some of both Osler's and Ghuman's samples report on feeling caution about having to transmit a highly euro-centric curriculum, which they feel does not relate sufficiently to their own culture or to the culture of those ethnic minority pupils they will teach (Osler p195; Ghuman p125).

Finally, there is also some evidence that students training to be teachers encounter behaviour that they find difficulties in coping with, or in being supported in dealing with by the still largely White teacher-training establishments. Siraj-Blatchford's study found ethnic minority students encountering racism particularly during teaching practice (69 per cent) and from fellow-students (64 per cent). In her study of 70 students, only five responses did not refer to incidents of racism during training (1991, p40). Showunmi and Constantine-Simms found very similar perceptions, and suggest that there is insufficient consideration of equal opportunity issues or policy issues in this area (1996, p165).

Barriers to change and policy recommendations

There is a long series of hurdles to be overcome in the attempt to increase minority ethnic participation in teaching. To begin with questions of motivation for entering the teaching profession. It was observed at the beginning of the chapter that schools are unique in that they are the only form of major social provision in our society with which almost every young person comes into contact, and that this contact is of considerable duration. Schools themselves therefore inform pupils about the nature of the educational system and the nature of teaching. Two factors emerge directly from this:

- If pupils observe that behaviour in schools is racist – whether other pupils to other pupils, other pupils to teachers, teachers to pupils, or other forms of institutional or managerial racist behaviour – then they are likely to conclude that working as a teacher will be personally stressful, and that they may well be treated in the same way.

- If pupils observe that the curriculum that they receive, and that teachers are required to deliver, is Anglo-centric to the exclusion of minority ethnic values and voices, then pupils may conclude that it is not a process in which they wish to take part.

These aspects of schooling could be addressed.

Recommendations

- Schools should continue to counter racist behaviour. Many schools are already attempting this, and have policies in place concerning pupil and staff behaviour. Discriminatory behaviour by staff is clearly still occurring (Siraj-Blatchford 1999, details students' perceptions of this on teaching practice; Osler (1998) gives various accounts from her witnesses; as does Ghuman (1995)). If schools were more explicit in tackling pupils' racist behaviour, and in supporting ethnic minority staff currently employed, this would convey clear messages about how schools would not tolerate such behaviour. Schools could also actively encourage pupils to explore racism elsewhere in society, so that it became clearer to them that schools were not the only place where such behaviour occurred, and perhaps that schools were places where anti-racist behaviour was more explicitly encouraged than in some other workplaces.

- The curriculum could be modified. Any serious attempt at social inclusion should include more active and widespread acceptance of diverse cultures. The QCA could make this a priority for all schools, not merely for those in areas which have a higher proportion of ethnic minority pupils. Different linguistic and cultural experiences should be more clearly valued, welcomed and used in schools. This would encourage pupils in the ethnic minorities to recognise that they could be part of this process if they joined the profession, and that their background would be an important complement to education. They would not then feel that they were being recruited to promote a 'White' curriculum.

More generally, teaching needs to regain its position of esteem. If ambitious pupils see teaching as a second-class aspiration, then the profession will not attract a sizeable proportion of the ethnic minority workforce. There is evidence that members of minority groups are more ambitious and have greater aspirations to succeed than members of the White population. There has been an endemic culture, for two or even three decades, of a lack of value or esteem for the teaching profession. In the last 15 years, many teachers themselves have become disillusioned, and have felt that their ability to take professional control of their lives, to be creative and to exercise professional autonomy have been seriously eroded. The responsibility for reversing this is multiple, and needs to be addressed by the Teacher Associations, the GTC, the inspectorate (HMI, OfSTED and the LEA inspectors), the DfES, local politicians, central government politicians and the media.

Ethnic minority pupils are attaining sufficiently high qualifications to enter Higher Education at a higher rate than their White peers. However, they are not entering teacher training at the same rate. There are four factors here that can be addressed:

- The TTA needs to consider how its entry requirement policies may be discriminatory in their practice. There are several points where this may occur. The Skills Tests need to be carefully monitored to ensure that they do not operate in a racialised way. The Teacher Training curriculum needs to be revised so that ethnic minority cultures are more centrally included: this would encourage applicants from the minority communities to see that they were welcomed, valued and respected. Potential students with community languages should be particularly welcomed, and courses should not only show how their skills are valued, but actively encourage them and train them to use these skills in school settings where there are multi-lingual pupils.

- The TTA needs to consider its targets for attracting ethnic minorities to the profession. If there is an apparent propensity not to move far from the home for initial teacher education on the part of ethnic minorities, then we should expect Higher Education institutions in areas where there are large proportions of ethnic minorities to attract equally large numbers of ethnic minority students. Thus, for example, such institutions in Inner London might reasonably be expected to recruit about 50 per cent of their students from the ethnic minorities.

- The Higher Education Institutions that provide teacher education need to address their working practices to ensure that, just as schools should do, they promote anti-racist behaviour. Incidents where schools visited by students on school practice are a case in point: when such incidents occur, institutions need to adopt a more overt and public manner of dealing with these. These might include, after some proper investigation to establish a prima facie case, reporting such schools to the Local Education Authority.

- Higher Education Institutions need to address how the ethnic minorities are represented in their own teaching staff. Most institutions have a teaching force and a management structure that is dominantly White, and do not represent the proportion of ethnic minorities in their own localities. This is not a welcoming signal to potential recruits from these minorities. The current age-structure of most institutions means that there could be very significant changes made in this respect over the next ten years, as relatively large numbers of existing lecturers reach retirement age.

In the current situation of shortages, most newly-qualified teachers, whatever their ethnic origin, are able to find a first appointment. Many LEAs in areas with a high proportion of ethnic minority pupils actively seek to attract teachers from an ethnic-minority background.

When it comes to teachers' career development, there are many areas that need to be addressed.

- Ethnic minority teachers should not be given curriculum ghettos, or expected to specialise in areas of 'race'. If they feel that their only opportunities for career development are in the areas of multi-cultural education or English as an additional language, then they will either become socially constructed into such roles, or they will leave the profession. Both alternatives are bad. Asian teachers need to be encouraged to be in a range of disciplines, and not stereotyped as only mathematics or science specialists.

- Staff development should be actively promoted for ethnic minority staff. If these staff continue to feel marginalised, they will either not seek professional advancement, or feel constrained to specialise in areas that appear to be 'reserved' for minorities.

- In particular, ethnic minority staff need to be encouraged to develop middle management skills at an early stage of their career. They need to be developing demonstrable skills and qualifications to take up posts of responsibility as soon as they are able, rather than feeling that they have to demonstrate that they are better than their White counterparts, or that the need to 'serve their time' before applying for such posts.

- LEAs could actively seek to encourage and support black networking groups amongst their teaching staff, to offer self-support in career development (Osler 1998, gives evidence of the success of some of these).

- OfSTED could play an important role in challenging some of the assumptions shown by some schools. Since they visit all schools on a regular basis, it would be possible for Inspecting teams to examine school staffing practices, and to ask pertinent questions of Headteachers and Chairs of Governors about the proportion of ethnic minority staff that are employed, and their levels of responsibility. This might be a particularly effective tactic in areas where there are relatively small numbers of ethnic minorities resident in the locality.

- Training for leadership is critical. The National College for School Leadership needs to have clear targets to ensure that a representative proportion of ethnic minority students are taking part in and succeeding on courses of training for Headship and leadership. Mahony and Hextall imply (2000, p 110) that much more needs to be done in this area.

- School Governors and Heads may also need explicit training in non-discriminatory appointment techniques. Any one group of Governors will make very few appointments at Headship level, and monitoring at the level of the individual school is unlikely to be helpful. But LEAs should take the responsibility for ensuring the appointment panels for senior posts are properly trained, understand the need for a non-discriminatory system of appointments, and recognise how inadvertent discrimination can take place.

- Finally, we need a far better system for ethnic monitoring across all stages of the profession. The DfES and the TTA should actively seek to require ethnic monitoring to take place in applications for training places, in appointment and promotion processes, and in employment statistics. Without this, it is very hard to show how progress is taking place.

Necessary principles underlying recruitment and retention

This paper has argued that the teaching force needs to be more representative in terms of ethnic minorities. It has suggested policy initiatives that will address this. It has also argued why this is an important issue: and it is argued the case in terms of the needs of all pupils, not only for the needs of pupils from the ethnic minorities.

It is therefore just as important that schools in the north east of England have a representation of ethnic minority teachers as do schools in Inner London. Indeed, it could be argued that, for the future health of our society, the need is greater in such areas.

Given that we currently do not even have enough ethnic minority teachers to match the range of ethnic minority pupils in areas of high concentration of minorities, such as inner London, this creates a certain dilemma. How can we simultaneously address the issues in areas where there are high levels of ethnic minorities (from which we will recruit most of our future ethnic minority teachers, and in which areas most of such recruits will probably chose to work), and at the same time ensure that pupils in areas where there are very few ethnic minorities see ethnic minority teachers in their schools?

The answer will have eventually to be that we recruit more than their proportion in the population into the profession. We probably need to be attracting ethnic minorities to be filling 15 per cent to 20 per cent of the places for teacher training, over a sustained period of a decade or two, in order to effectively address this situation. This would allow both the areas where there are many ethnic minority pupils to have a teaching force that attempts to represent their local community, and areas where there are few ethnic minority pupils to have a teaching force that represents the national community.

References

Carrington B, Nayak A *et al* (1999) *Ethnic Diversity and Teaching Policy: Policy and practice in Sixteen English Initial Teacher Training Institutions: Interim Report 2* London: Teacher Training Agency

Carrington B, Bonnett A, Nayak A, Skelton C, Smith F, Tomlin R, Short G and Demaine J (2000) 'The Recruitment of New Teachers from Minority Ethnic Groups' *International Studies in Sociology of Education* 10.1

Carrington B and Tomlin R (2000) 'Towards a more inclusive profession: teacher recruitment and ethnicity' *European Journal of Teacher Education* 23.2

DfES (2001) *Education Statistics: Schools, 2001* DfES

Ghuman PAS (1995) *Asian Teachers in British Schools* Clevedon: Multilingual Matters

Gilroy B (1976) *Black Teacher* London: Casell

Hextall I, Mahony P and Menter I (2001) Just Testing? 'An analysis of the implementation of 'skills tests' for entry into the teaching profession in England' *Journal of Education for Teaching* 27.3

Hutchings M, Ross A, Menter I and Thomson D(2000) *Teacher Supply and Retention in London: A study of Six London Boroughs, 1999-2000* London: TTA

Lakey J (1997) 'Neighbourhoods and Housing' in *Ethnic Minorities in Britain: Diversity and Disadvantage* London: Policy Studies Institute

Mahony P and Hextall I (2000) *Reconstructing Teaching: Standards, performance and accountability* Falmer Routledge

McCreith S, Ross A and Hutchings M (2001) *Teacher Supply and Retention 2001: A study of 22 Local Education Authorities* London: Teacher Training Agency

Millet A (1996) *The Chief Executive's Annual Lecture 1996* London :Teacher Training Agency.

Osler A (1997) *The Education and Careers of Black teachers: Changing identities, changing lives* Buckingham: Open University Press

Ranger C (1988) E*thnic Minority School Teachers: A survey in eight local education authorities* London: Commission for Racial Equality

Ratcliffe P (1999) 'Housing, inequality and "race": some critical reflections on the concept of "social exclusion"' *Ethnic and Racial Studies* 22.1

Ross A (2001) *Ethnic Minority Teachers in the Teaching Workforce* London: IPSE Occasional Paper

Schuman J (1999) 'The ethnic minority Populations of Great Britain – latest estimates' *Population Trends* 96 ONS

Showunmi V and Constantine-Simms D (eds) (1996) T*eachers for the Future* Stoke on Trent: Trentham Books

Siraj-Blatchford S (1991) 'A study of Black students' perceptions of Racism in Initial Teacher Education' *British Educational Research Journal* 17.1

Teacher Training Agency (2001) *Performance Indicators, 2000* London: TTA

TTA/CRE (1998) *Teaching in Multi-Ethnic Britain* London: TTA

7. A representative profession? Gender issues
Merryn Hutchings

Employment patterns in the teaching profession are strongly gendered, with long-established imbalances across phases, in promoted posts, and across subjects. In addition, there has been a gradual increase, over about the last fifteen years, in the proportion of women in teaching in all phases, positions and subjects.

Williams (1993) points out that most jobs can be identified as 'men's work' or 'women's work'. Efforts to break down gender barriers have generally focused on getting women into male fields, more highly regarded and better paid:

> Young women today are being told that to obtain decent salaries and respectability, they need to take classes in mathematics and science, and eventually enter 'men's jobs'. This advice is rarely accompanied by encouragement to young men to enter 'women's jobs'. But, clearly, eliminating segregation would require equalising the proportions of men and women in all jobs, not just the jobs that are currently male-dominated. Of course, this is all very complicated, because once men enter female dominated jobs, they tend to rise to the top, reproducing gender hierarchy within jobs (Williams,1993).

Thus the three issues of gender imbalance addressed here – shortage of male teachers, disproportionate number of male managers, and gendered subjects – are linked. They are also very resistant to change. But, as Williams argues,

> If we do not work to change the gender composition of all jobs – which means both encouraging women to be more like men and encouraging men to be more like women – we run the risk of reproducing sexist devaluation of everything female/feminine, making men the ultimate measure of success (*op cit*).

These issues are a particular concern in education because it is an institution through which gendered divisions are reproduced. Schools are the first large-scale organisations that children encounter, and the settings in which they spend a large proportion of their time. Schools offer children models of the working of gender roles and power in society; they learn that men are more often found in positions of power and authority than are women. This may impact on aspirations. Moreover, schools are implicated in the choices young people make about what to study, which then circumscribe future career choices. Thus it is crucial that we tackle the gendered composition of the teaching profession. The National Union of Teachers (NUT) sums up this argument:

> It is important educationally for all children in all schools, in all phases and throughout their school lives, to see women and men successfully filling a range of roles, teaching across the whole curriculum, and taking up senior management positions (NUT 1998).

This chapter first considers the increasing proportion of women across the profession, then focuses on each of the imbalances identified above. It concludes with a discussion of possible ways forward relating to policy at different levels.

'Feminisation' of the teaching profession

The proportion of women in teaching has been increasing over the last 15 years in every phase, at each level in the hierarchy and across subjects (Table 7.1).

Table 7.1 Percentage of male teachers, England, 1976-2000

	primary	secondary	men
1976	22.9	56.4	40.5
1985	21.9	54.2	40.5
1990	19.3	52.2	36.9
1995	17.7	49.3	33.8
1999	16.2	46.2	31.9

Sources: NUT 1980, DfES 2001a

There are about 12 per cent fewer men in both the primary and the secondary sector than there were ten years ago. This has been a steady year on year decline.

Figure 7.1 shows that the majority of the men are among the older teachers. Thus the proportion of women in the teaching profession is likely to increase simply through age retirement.

While these patterns are found across the profession, there are also regional and school factors. London and the South East generally have low proportions of male teachers (DfES 2001b). But there is also considerable variation at LEA and school level (Hutchings et al 2000).

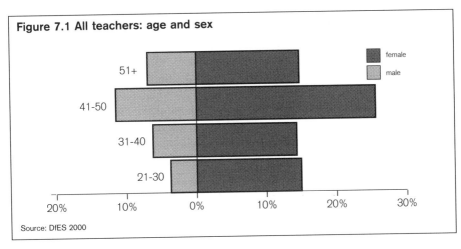

Figure 7.1 All teachers: age and sex

Source: DfES 2000

Gender and school phase

Teachers of the youngest children tend to be women and those of the oldest, men. This pattern of gender by school phase is found in the US (Allan 1993) and Australia (Lewis, Butcher and Donnan 1999) and across other European countries, as shown on Figure 7.2. Some countries recruit a higher proportion of male primary teachers, often because they have different cultural norms and expectations. For example, in Greece, primary teaching is a very acceptable career for men, and proportions of men in primary and secondary schools are similar.

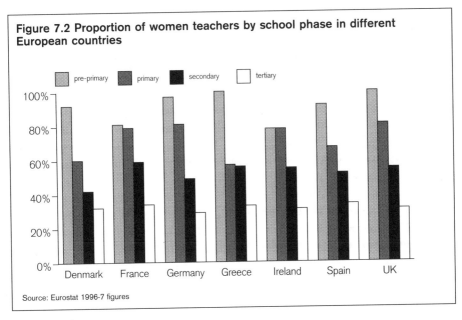

Figure 7.2 Proportion of women teachers by school phase in different European countries

Source: Eurostat 1996-7 figures

But the overall pattern is one of considerable similarity across countries. There is widespread agreement that women should work with younger children, where the role is seen as one of nurturing, and men with older pupils, who are seen as more rational. This pattern is also found within sectors: in primary schools men more often work with the older classes.

In this country, there is considerable concern about the low, and falling, proportion of men in primary schools (16.2 per cent: DfES 2001a). In 1998-9 only 13 per cent of those entering primary teacher training were male, which showed no improvement on the previous year (*TES* 1.9.00). Of those who completed teacher training in 1998 and had taken up teaching posts in maintained primary or nursery schools by March 1999, 12.6 per cent were men. Only 11.8 per cent of primary class teachers are male (there being a disproportionate number of male Headteachers and Deputy Heads) (DfES 2001b).

Why is it important to recruit men to teaching?

Numerous arguments have been put forward to support the recruitment of more men to primary and nursery teaching. One concerns representation of different groups. Anthea Millett, then Chief Executive of the Teacher Training Agency (TTA), claimed in 1996: 'A profession where one sex or other predominates to such an extent is simply not a true reflection of society today' (quoted in Mahony and Hextall 2000). The introduction to this chapter argued that schools are models of the workings of gender roles and power in society at large, and that it is therefore important that children should see men and women in all roles and at all levels.

A second argument focuses on the overall shortage of teachers. Millett continued: 'If we are to continue to attract large numbers of high quality candidates for teaching, we cannot afford to write off half the human race' (Mahoney and Hextall 2000). These two arguments are uncontroversial; however, all the other arguments are to some extent contested, and are not supported by sound research evidence. But because they are so frequently cited both by government figures and in the national press, they are examined in some detail here.

The most frequently used is the need for male role models. The notion here is quite different from that discussed above, of schools as models of the workings of society. A role model is an individual who can be admired and whose behaviour may be emulated. The argument in relation to male teachers suggests that boys will see their teachers as people they can look up to, and so will want to copy their behaviour, style of masculinity, attitude to academic work, and so on. In this argument, male teachers become the panacea to solve the problems posed by boys: loutish behaviour, truancy, delinquency, poor academic attainment, et cetera. However, there is no evidence that pupils do see teachers as role models, or that large numbers of male teachers would bring about positive changes in the attitudes, behaviour and attainment of boys.

The role model argument comes in a number of forms. Some emphasise the need for role models of hegemonic masculinity, and others, for models that challenge this. They all claim that male role models can improve behaviour and achievement.

Those favouring hegemonic masculinity argue that boys need 'real men' as role models. Anthea Millett linked this discourse explicitly to boys' underachievement:

> If boys are not exposed to some of the values that men may show, a competitive edge, for example, maybe that might result in underachievement among some boys (quoted in Pepperell and Smedley 1998: 347).

These comments also imply that boys' underachievement results from the feminised[1] culture of primary schools, which is seen as damaging to boys. Stephan Shakespeare described it as 'a cissy culture, which suited girls better than boys' (*Daily Mail*, 5.1.98, quoted in Smedley 1998: 155). Thus the message that primary schools are bad for boys is being trumpeted in the tabloid press.

This notion that boys need to associate with 'real men' is also implicit in concerns expressed about children who lack family male role models and may grow up in a totally feminised (and thus, potentially damaging) environment. The School Teachers' Pay Review Body commented in 1996:

> [We] note the views repeated to us about the educational implications of the comparatively small number of male teachers in primary schools, where a growing number of children come from single parent families with no effective male role model (quoted in Pepperell and Smedley 1998: 34).

The validity of this has been questioned; Pepperell and Smedley (1998) argue that parents are not the only male role models in most children's lives, and question whether teachers should (or can) take on the role of substitute parents.

The teacher modelling hegemonic masculinity will share boys' interests, and in particular, will be a football enthusiast. The notion that boys learn better through a curriculum permeated with football lies behind the government-sponsored scheme Playing for Success, which links schools and football clubs to develop children's literacy and numeracy skills (Skelton 2001). Skelton reports how male teachers are expected to get involved in football activities, which continue to be dominated by boys. There are some questionable assumptions here: neither all male teachers nor all boys enjoy football. Moreover, football is associated with some negative aspects of hegemonic masculinity: excessive competitiveness and hooliganism.

Male teachers are also thought to be a positive influence on boys' achievement in that they are seen as better disciplinarians. The example of a 'real' (macho) man behaving well is considered an excellent model for boys. 'Male teachers send a message to boys that education is not sissy and help issues of discipline by setting an example of appropriate behaviour' (Nick Smith, Education Minister: New Zealand Government 1999). However, research suggests that many male teachers actually adopt 'laddish' attitudes in order to construct their own masculinity and bond with their male pupils (Mills 2000; Francis 2000a; Francis and Skelton 2001).

A second version of the role model argument claims that boys need teachers who challenge hegemonic masculinity. This view emphasises the importance of children seeing men in caring and nurturing roles (for example, Weber and Mitchell 1995; Bettison 2001). They can demonstrate that reading (often seen as 'the reverse of manly', Reynolds 1996) and scholarship in general, are acceptable pursuits for men (Bleach 2001).

Another common assumption is that men are simply more effective teachers for boys. This notion informs government and TTA policy. Estelle Morris argued that recruiting more male teachers could help tackle the underachievement of boys (Furedi 2000). Ralph Tabberer, chief executive of the TTA, claimed: 'The issue of boys' underperformance is a complex problem. But we are clear that we can contribute to the solution by increasing the number of men coming into primary training' (*TES* 1.9.00).

Thus the idea that male teachers are the solution to boys' underachievement has been widely publicised and is treated as a fact. There are two problems with this. First, it implies that women teachers are to blame for boys' underachievement, which is demoralising and offensive. As Smedley puts it: 'Women teachers are thought to be nice rather than intelligent people, naturally good at working with children, yet at the same time, not actually doing a good job' (1997). Secondly, these statements rely on anecdotal rather than research, evidence. Tony Mooney wrote in *The Independent on Sunday*: 'when [my son] was taught by a man, his academic progress leapt ahead dramatically' (quoted in Pepperell and Smedley 1998). There is no doubt that particular teachers suit particular children: whether gender is automatically a factor in this would need much more investigation. There have been suggestions that boys' preferred learning styles are different from those of girls (Bleach 1998), but there is no evidence that male teachers are better at providing for these needs. In a study in Finland which sought 13-14-year-olds' views about teachers, Lahelma (2000) found that gender was seen as irrelevant. The pupils valued teachers who were friendly, relaxed and could keep order.

While the majority of those supporting the recruitment of more male teachers focus specifically on effects on pupils, there are also other arguments. For example, it has been suggested that men are 'better advocates' for the profession (Anthea Millett 1995, quoted in Smedley 1997), and that they improve staff-room dynamics, with their broad range of topics of conversation and their sense of humour (Lahelma 2000).

This section has argued that it is important to recruit more men to teaching, but that many of the arguments commonly used to support this are flawed, and are not adequately supported by research evidence. The complexity of the issues has not yet been sufficiently investigated.

Barriers to change

Far fewer boys than girls are attracted to teaching as a career, and the primary sector attracts only a small proportion of these (Lewis 2001; Johnston, McKeown and McEwen 1999a). More men than women withdraw from ITT courses (Thornton 1999a). HESA figures for 1997-8 show 8.1 per cent of women dropping out from primary PGCE courses, but 14.5 per cent of men (Lewis 2000). Reasons for withdrawal include lack of a male support network, feeling intimidated by the predominantly female peer group; and lack of support from family and friends for entry into a female-dominated profession (Thornton 1999a; Lewis 2000). Other factors include lack of commitment to teaching, perhaps compounded by insufficient experience in primary school prior to entering ITT; low levels of maturity among 18-year-old boys; and low entry qualifications accepted from male applicants. Women entering ITT tend to have a longer established commitment to teaching and greater experience in schools (Skelton 1991; Thornton 1999a). This suggests that in their efforts to recruit men, providers are perhaps lowering their standards. Emery (1997) suggests that similarly, during ITT courses; teachers assess men more generously because they consider it important that more men enter the profession.

Men are also more likely to leave the teaching profession for other employment (Lewis *et al* 1999; Hutchings *et al* 2000; McCreith *et al* 2001).

The difficulties that face attempts to increase the number of men in primary teaching are well summed up in this interchange in the House of Lords:

> *Lord Tope:* My Lords, does not the Minister agree that in addition to lousy pay and career prospects, one of the main reasons that men are not attracted to primary teaching is that primary schools are perceived to be less important and to have less status than secondary schools? Therefore it is perceived that men who wish to be primary school teachers must therefore be unambitious, effeminate or worse. What steps are the Government taking to improve that wholly wrong perception of primary school teaching?

> *Baroness Blackstone:* My Lords, I hope that any man thinking of becoming a primary school teacher would not imagine for one minute that he will be perceived as effeminate or worse.
>
> (Lords Hansard 30.11.98)

Lord Tope's assertion that the pay is 'lousy' is supported by the teaching unions, who believe that low salaries act as a deterrent to men, whereas women historically have been prepared to put up with poor pay (*TES* 2.2.01). Male ITT students put significantly more emphasis on pay levels than do women (Johnston *et al* 1999b). The NUT show that the salary for a graduate entering teaching is 14 per cent below the median graduate salary, and that the gap widens to 54 per cent after five years (Johnston *et al* 1999b) In primary schools the pay prospects are worse than in secondary because schools are smaller.

It is widely accepted that it is unnatural for men to teach young children. Other men do not take male teachers seriously because they are doing 'women's work', and female colleagues tend to push them into stereotyped masculine roles (eg mending things, sports lessons) (Kauppinen-Toropainen and Lammi 1993; Emery 1997). For many men such stereotypes, and the conflicting models of masculinity expected from male teachers, result in a continual negotiation of their masculine identities at work (Allan 1993; Smedley 1997; Skelton 1991, 2001). This can be stressful and may lead to leaving training or the teaching profession. A man may find himself the only male in a college group or primary school staff-room, and this can be uncomfortable (Emery 1997). Very similar issues are faced by male child-care workers:

> Even if the issue of which roles to model and how to do so was uncontested, a further problem arises from men workers usually being employed in a setting where they are virtually the sole representative of their sex. The man worker is faced with an impossible task. This one person may be regarded as symbolising all men, and may be expected in some way to serve as a universal all-purpose and comprehensive model (Cameron, Moss and Owen 1999: 87-88).

Male teachers may be regarded as abnormal ('effeminate or worse', in Lord Tope's words). 'A public perception is that men who teach primary grades are often either homosexuals [or] paedophiles' (King 1998: 3). They are placed in a very vulnerable position by the perception of male teachers as potential child abusers (Skelton 1994; Thornton 1999b; Furedi 2000). Johnston *et al* argue that for BEd students in their survey, media coverage of child abuse cases 'appears to cast a prohibitive shadow over having made a career choice that involves contact with young children' (1999b: 62).

Initiatives aimed at increasing numbers of men

Concern about the shortage of male primary teachers has resulted in a number of initiatives. This section identifies these, and considers whether evidence to date suggests that they are effective.

The TTA Corporate Plan 2001-4 set a target for male recruitment: by 2002-3 the proportion of male entrants to primary ITT should increase from 12.4 per cent to 15 per cent. All providers are asked to set targets for recruitment of men.

The TTA's advertising campaigns have been strongly focused towards men. *The Guardian* (14.3.98) reported that the television campaign 'No-one forgets a good teacher' was targeted at men; slots were bought in programmes that attracted a large male audience, and Tony Blair took part. Many advertisements and slogans have been based around football, and are clearly aimed at men. A postcard distributed to attract students to teaching reads: 'Every good boy deserves football'. A poster on the tube asks: 'Can you battle with the Roundheads and win? Can you manage a football team? Can you teach?'. This includes not only football, but also the male image of fighting. Another of the postcard series showed a man in a suit and a bowler hat: a rather different image of male success.

A number of TTA-funded schemes have been set up to encourage young men to consider teaching. Foster and Newman (2001) describe a scheme to counter stereotypical views of the male primary teacher; potential male recruits spent a week in school working with a male mentor. While not all the participants decided teaching was for them, they all experienced it as intrinsically enjoyable, worthwhile and interesting work. Similar TTA projects with Education Business Partnerships involve sixth form boys helping primary children to use computers. The Teacher Advocate Scheme puts serving male teacher volunteers in touch with those who are interested in entering the profession (DfEE 2000). Another initiative involves taster courses targeted at men; these have been reported to be successful (University of Wolverhampton 2000).

A number of initiatives focus on retention of male ITT students. These include men's support groups and clubs (Thornton 1999b). Single-sex groups enable men to discuss, for example, strategies around physical contact (Pepperell and Smedley 1998). However, while support groups have worked well for black teachers (Blair and Maylor 1993), those running men's groups have found them less successful. The very existence of a support group suggests male vulnerability; men are often uneasy about discussing their concerns.

While pay cannot be seen simply as an incentive for men, it is interesting to note that the government associated the introduction of training salaries with the need to recruit more men. Ralph Tabberer claimed that with the launch of training salaries, taster courses and support networks, Ministers and the TTA had made recruitment of male teachers a key priority (*TES*, 1.9.00). *The Guardian* (21.8.00) reported that 'the new £6000 training bursaries increased inquiries from male postgraduates by 50 per cent'.

However, in that the proportion of male teachers continues to fall year on year, there is little evidence that any of these initiatives has yet had any substantial impact.

Gender and promotion

While there is a widespread concern about the low recruitment of men, many writers link this to concerns about the disproportionate number of men in management, in both primary and secondary schools (for example, Acker 1989; Adler, Laney and Packer 1993; Mahony and Hextall 2000, Thornton and Bricheno 2000). As Williams (1993) argued, men entering female-dominated jobs tend to rise to the top. The majority of teachers are women, but they have not achieved a proportionate share of management and leadership roles.

Men comprise only 11.8 per cent of primary class teachers, but 41.5 per cent of primary Headteachers (see Figure 7.3) (DfES 2000). They tend to gain promotion earlier in their careers than women. Of those with over twenty years' experience, one man in every two is a Headteacher; but only one woman in five. The proportion of female Heads has been steadily increasing over the last twenty-five years, but this appears to result from the feminisation of the profession rather from any effort to reduce inequalities.

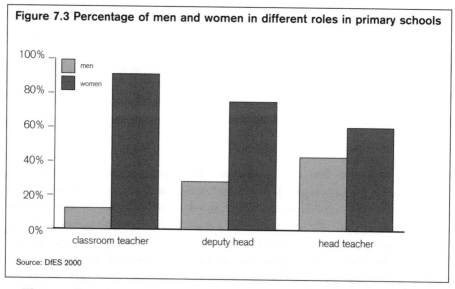

Figure 7.3 Percentage of men and women in different roles in primary schools

Source: DfES 2000

The overall gender balance in secondary schools is more even, but the proportion of women who are Headteachers remains low in comparison to men (Figure 7.4). Women are less likely to be appointed to Headships of the largest schools (Howson 2001). They are only slightly slower in gaining promotions than men, but fewer seem to take the step to Deputy Headship or Headship. Among teachers with twenty or more years experience, 15.9 per cent of men are either Heads or Deputy Heads, but only 9.2 per cent of women.

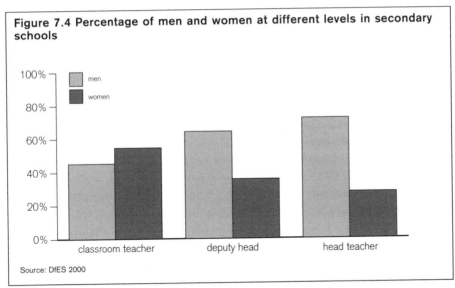

Figure 7.4 Percentage of men and women at different levels in secondary schools

Source: DfES 2000

There are also regional variations; in 1996, 40 per cent of secondary Headteachers in London were women, but only 15 per cent in the West of England and 13 per cent in the North (House of Commons Education and Employment Select Committee 1998).

Why is it important to recruit women to management posts?

These gender imbalances are a major cause for concern as a matter of social justice. Women clearly do not have equal opportunities to gain promotion in schools. Pupils are thus presented with a negative model of gender roles. They see women in subordinate positions and a disproportionate number of men in roles of power and authority. This may negatively affect girls' career aspirations, and suggest to boys that they have a natural right to positions of authority. The NUT (1998) argue that it is vital for all children to see women taking up senior management positions. Moreover, when there is an overall shortage of applications for positions of leadership, it is worrying that some women appear to be ruling themselves out of contention.

The styles of management women adopt may be beneficial to the profession; Ozga argues that they are less hierarchical and more democratic:

> Women appear more flexible and sensitive, and often more successful... Women emphasise cohesiveness. They are much less individualistic and spend time on fostering an integrative culture...women cope more readily with routine stress, and defuse conflict (Ozga 1993)

This popular discourse of women's leadership seems to converge with the 'new' management discourses that focus on good people management (Blackmore 1999).

Barriers to change

The TTA recognises the gender imbalance in leadership roles as a problem, and attributes it to the fact that 'large numbers of teachers, especially female primary teachers, are not coming forward for Headship, or even for training to become Headteachers, despite having the potential to succeed' (Millett 1998: quoted in Mahony and Hextall 2000: 116).

Men certainly appear to be more ambitious than women. Thornton and Bricheno (2000) found that men in each age group were more likely than women to say that they wanted promotion. And while Foster and Newman (2001) found that men did not rank the prospect of becoming a Headteacher as an important factor in their decision to enter primary teacher training, Button reported that many men nevertheless expected to achieve rapid promotion; 50 per cent of those entering primary teaching predicted that in ten years' time they would be Deputy Heads, and 28 per cent Headteachers (TES 29.1.99). These expectations exceed the reality of male promotion in this sector (among men with 10-14 years primary experience, 26 per cent are Deputy Heads and 18 per cent Heads, DfES 2000). The NAHT (1998) argues that fewer women become Heads because they are motivated more by quality of life than by pay.

In the NUT survey Women and Senior Management (2001) over a third of the women surveyed said that they were reluctant to apply for promoted posts because of the challenges of maintaining a work-life balance. Long hours are a particular barrier; the NUT have called for a review of the 'unlimited responsibilities and unrealistic objectives currently associated with the job' (1998). Teachers have for some years been protesting about work-load (TES 16.11.01). Those in leadership roles generally work longer hours than the average. The TES recorded that one secondary Headteacher worked 70 hours a week. This is undoubtedly a disincentive to those with dependants. Although many men now make a greater contribution in the home, the burden of household work and childcare still falls on women.

Women's careers often include breaks and/or periods of part-time work. Those who take breaks longer than the statutory maternity leave are disadvantaged in terms of future promotion. They may find themselves competing with candidates five to ten years younger than themselves, and this is likely to be regarded negatively by appointment panels. The NPHA (1998) argued that 'when they return to teaching they may well have fallen behind their male peers on the promotion ladder', and reported that women are older than men when appointed to their first Headship. Alternatively, the women themselves believe that they are past the critical age for promotion, and so do not apply (Thornton and Bricheno 2000; NUT 2001). There is evidence that women with children are less likely to become Headteachers; the NAHT (1998) reports that women Heads are less likely than men Heads to have dependent children.

Moreover, women will have noted the lack of flexibility reportedly offered to a Headteacher who wanted to work on a job-share basis on her return from maternity leave. Even after an industrial tribunal ruled that she had a right to work part-time, it proved impossible to agree terms for her return to work (*TES* 15.9.00, 8.12.00).

Some women see their work as secondary to their partner's career, which may be more highly paid. Women are often less mobile than men as a result, and can only apply for local jobs. Women may perceive promotion as a move away from their chosen career, teaching children (Thornton and Bricheno 2000). The isolation of Headship (Mercer 1997) may be a particular disincentive to women who gain much of their job satisfaction from collegiality and relationships with other members of staff.

Women may be deterred by the nature of management. A distinction has been drawn between masculine and feminine styles of management, and, while avoiding a claim of essentialist differences, many writers argue that women are deterred and disadvantaged by the styles current in education. Mahony and Hextall argue that the performance management framework privileges male 'career' orientated teachers, and that 'discourses of leadership and management tend to be masculinist in character' (2000). Also, the introduction of the market in education has 'had the effect of legitimising and encouraging assertive, instrumental and competitive behaviour' (Reay and Ball 2000). While the discourses of the National Standards for Headship are not as masculine as those current in other sectors, Mahony and Hextall argue that the management model presented is hierarchical and individualistic. Cubillo (1999) comments on the gender factors in strategies adopted to self-assess capability for leadership in the National Professional Qualification for Headship (NPQH). She found that a number of very capable women assessed themselves rather negatively, and failed to identify their collegial feminine approach as a strength. The women's lack of confidence was evident.

'Sponsorship' by Headteachers, advisors or inspectors plays an important role in encouraging teachers, and particularly women, to apply for promotion (Evetts 1989; NUT 2001). Potential sponsors are often men, and as a result women may be less well-supported than their male colleagues. The backing of peers is particularly important to women (especially in applying for an internal promotion) (Boulton and Coldron 1998). Conversely, lack of support can be a powerful deterrent. Inadequate or non-existent appraisal and mentoring systems were seen as a barrier by some women (NUT 2001).

It has also been suggested that women, more than men, like to feel that they are well-prepared for the jobs they take on. The NAHT (1998) points out that women normally progress to Headship from Deputy Headship, whereas men are more likely to leapfrog their way up the promotion ladder.

Thornton and Bricheno (2000) argue that some school governors have traditional attitudes to gendered roles and may discriminate against women, and in particular older women and married women. (It should be noted that there is also a gender imbalance in positions of leadership among governors: Keys and Fernandes 1990, reported that only 30 per cent of Chairs of school governing bodies are women.)

Initiatives aimed at increasing numbers of women in management

While there are some broad-based national initiatives to increase numbers of women in management, there are few within education. The NUT have called for more flexible career structures, support for women taking career breaks, and specific funding for LEAs to provide management training for women.

The TTA (1998) stated that in order to recruit more women to Headships it was requiring centres offering the NPQH to offer training that better matched candidates' needs and professional and personal circumstances, including supported open learning. It also stressed that women should be well represented in NPQH promotional material, and cited the recognition of female Headteachers in the honours list as an encouragement to others.

It is difficult to assess the success of these strategies. The proportion of women Heads is increasing, but this appears to result from the feminisation of the profession. The real criterion for success must be to achieve the same proportion of women in management as in the profession as a whole. By this criterion there is still a very long way to go.

Secondary subjects

The nature of the problem

Gendered subject choices and achievement patterns are long-standing. Science, mathematics and IT are seen as 'masculine', and English, languages and arts as feminine (Whitehead 1996; Francis 2000b). Mathematics and science, male and rational, are accorded a higher status, and achievement in mathematics often substitutes for overall ability or potential.

Alexander (1992) found that primary mathematics co-ordinators were frequently members of the senior management team, and were disproportionately male. In contrast subjects such as art and music were covered by staff on the Main Professional Grade who were generally female. Similarly in secondary schools, mathematics and science, taught by men, are accorded a higher status. Alexander argues:

> The linking of certain subjects to gender and status conveys, whether we like
> it or not, clear and questionable messages to children and their teachers
> about what subjects are most and least important, about where career
> advancement lies, and about which are 'male' and 'female' (1992: 35).

This appears to be a vicious circle: gender patterns in subject preference are reflected in choice of subjects at A level and in higher education. Inevitably these choices are reflected in applications for teacher training. The gender of teachers then affects pupils' perceptions and choices of subjects. The Gender and Pupil Performance Project at the University of Edinburgh, led by Linda Croxford, found that the gender of the teacher is reflected in the uptake of subjects by pupils, and may influence the gender gap in performance (McVeigh 2001).

However, there are indications of some changes in this pattern. First, recent studies have found fewer differences between girls' and boys' subject preferences than had been found in previous research (Francis 2000b; Hutchings and Francis 2001). This may offer some grounds for optimism that the pattern of gendered subjects may eventually break down.

Moreover, analysis of the teaching force suggests that gendered subject patterns will break down simply because of lack of male teachers. Ross and Thomson (1999) found that the male mathematics teachers in six London LEAs were generally older (and thus closer to retirement) than the women, and that only one tenth of those currently being appointed were men. Thus they concluded that there will be fewer male mathematics teachers in the future. It is interesting to speculate how this change will affect boys' and girls' perceptions of the subject, and their future choices.

Why is it important to achieve a gender balance?

Gendered imbalances among teachers of different subjects are a cause for concern, in that they may impact on pupils' subject choices, which ultimately circumscribe the careers available to them, and contribute to the reproduction of gendered patterns of employment and of status and power.

Within schools there are also problems implicit in the current gender divide:

> Those teaching areas constructed as feminine have been devalued to the
> extent that men who teach in these areas have to assert their masculinity in
> ways which devalue behaviour and characteristics which have become
> associated with femininity (Roulston and Mills 2000).

Thus the practice of appealing to boys, for example, through the use of their preferred styles of music, or the adoption of 'macho' images derived from competitive sport, 'are likely to legitimise homophobic and misogynist behaviour' (Roulston and Mills 2000) and to alienate those students who reject prevalent images of hegemonic masculinity.

Barriers to change

While there is a shortage of teachers in many secondary subjects, it is almost impossible to address the gender divide. The current focus must be on persuading graduates to become teachers: recruitment cannot prioritise one gender group. The scale of the problem is indicated by the observation that 'mathematics and modern foreign language targets are equivalent to around a half of the total numbers graduating specifically in those subjects' (STRB 1999).

Initiatives

Initiatives such as the Girls into Science and Technology project (GIST) (Whyte 1986), or the more recent Tapping the Talent initiative through Opportunity 2000, aimed to change girls' views about gendered subjects. Similarly some universities are recruiting more female undergraduates in 'male' subjects by offering combined degrees (*The Guardian* 3.7.01). In the long term such efforts should increase proportions of female graduates and of teachers in those subjects. However, such initiatives need to be matched by efforts to recruit boys into 'female' subjects; this does not appear to be happening at present.

Policy directions and recommendations

Education policies can certainly be used deliberately to affect the gender balance in schools. For example, in the 1930s most LEAs imposed a bar on married women teachers as a deliberate step to preserve men's jobs in a time of unemployment (Oram 1989). Other policies that have impacted on the gender balance have done so as a side-effect rather than a main intention. For example, the move to co-educational schools reduced openings for women in management as single-sex schools were replaced by mixed schools. Similarly the trend to amalgamate infant and junior schools further reduced the Headship possibilities open to women, who traditionally led infant schools. It is important always to be aware that policies will impact differentially on men and women, and to consider the potential impact of any policy in relation to gender and gendered patterns of employment. It is also important to be aware that action taken to support one gender may be construed as disadvantaging the other, and may well do so.

Attracting men to the primary and early years sector

Researchers focusing on male recruitment have made a number of suggestions for policy directions, many of which build on existing initiatives.

- Teaching should be made into a profession with high status and pay. However, it is problematic to view financial incentives solely in relation to male recruitment.

- Efforts should be made to replace the discourse that work with young children is women's work. Boys in secondary schools should have opportunities to spend time with young children and discover how enjoyable this can be. Teachers should discuss and challenge gendered work cultures with their pupils, identifying different ways of being masculine or feminine.

- Secondary schools should be encouraged to promote work experience for boys in feeder primary schools. More opportunities should be created for male teachers and ITT students to talk to school leavers.

- Positive images of men working with young children should be presented in the media (for example, in a soap), and in publicity material produced by the TTA and ITT providers. Careers advice seminars should challenge existing stereotypes of teaching (Johnston et al 1999a).

- Recruitment should focus on men of high calibre and commitment, who have had substantial contact with young children, and are likely to remain in the profession (Thornton 1999b; Foster and Newman 2001).

- In that mature male entrants often demonstrate greater commitment, recruitment should target this group (Thornton 1999b).

- Emphasis on the subject teaching aspects and the enjoyment factors in primary education might attract more (Emery 1997).

Supporting men in ITT and in schools

- Men on ITT courses should, where possible, have opportunities to work with other male teachers, and to experience teaching in Key Stage 1. This may counter men's assumptions that younger classes are not for them (Emery 1997).

- Courses should directly address assumptions and understandings of gender in teaching, and issues of sexuality. Students need to be aware of the dominant discourses that underpin classroom practice and to consider how to maximise learning for both boys and girls. Such discussions are time-consuming; the ITT curriculum needs to be adjusted to make space for this to happen. This would also involve staff development for tutors and mentors (Oyler, Jennings and Lozada 2001).

- Some issues such as guidelines about touching children, and issues of child protection, may need to be addressed in single-sex groups (Emery 1997; Thornton 1999b). Possibly these topics should be tackled as part of the curriculum, rather than in the guise of a voluntary support group, which men may not attend.

- The particular problems faced by male students should be monitored and addressed. For example, Emery (1997) found that men were less likely to attach importance to detailed planning and record keeping. The reasons for this and the requirements need to be made explicit, and male students may need extra support in this area.

- Clear nationally agreed policies should be implemented which protect both children and men working in schools. It should not be left to the individual to decide a personal policy on touching children.

- LEAs could consider running support groups for male newly qualified teachers.

- Schools should avoid perpetuating particular models of masculinity by assuming men will take a lead in sport and discipline and will carry out maintenance tasks.

Appointing women to leadership roles

- The issues of recruitment of men and promotion of women should not be seen as separate issues. Government efforts to date have focused mainly on the recruitment of male teachers. If successful, this may lead simply to a reinforcement of current gender patterns of management and power. What is needed are simultaneous efforts to recruit women into management by addressing the barriers that hold them back.

- Flexible working patterns (such as the possibility of shifting between from full- and part-time work, or of job-share) should have adequate financial support. Provision should be made for child-care, and workload reduced.

- Mentoring schemes should be developed to build women's confidence in their potential for management.

- The National College of Leadership should explicitly address gender issues including management style and differences in self-assessment.

- Governor training should address gender issues in the appointment process.

Gendered subjects

To aim to create a balance of teachers across secondary subjects is problematic at a time when there are shortages of teachers in many subjects.

- Efforts should focus as much on recruiting men to teach in 'female' subjects as on recruiting women to teach science and maths. Indeed, it is probably more important to focus on the former, because as the profession becomes more feminised simply through age retirement, men in secondary schools will become a minority.

- Attempts to redress the imbalance in secondary subject teaching need to be made at all stages in the vicious circle of subject choice at A level, in HE and for teacher training. These efforts need to focus on increasing numbers of boys in 'female' subjects just as much as increasing numbers of girls taking maths and science.

- In any curriculum changes, gender implications should be considered.

Monitoring needs

Monitoring all aspects of gender and employment in the teaching profession should be ongoing and should use transparent processes, and where necessary followed up with research. The results should be publicly available. Monitoring should include:

- ITT enquiries, acceptances, withdrawals and completions

- selection of 'fast track' teachers

- appointments of Advanced Skills Teachers and to leadership posts. This should be done at LEA level, rather than individual school level, so that patterns are more evident

- applications relating to the pay threshold and their success

- NPQH enquiries, withdrawals, and completions

- gendered changes in subject choices in the new 14-19 curriculum

- initiatives set up to bring about change in the gender balance within the teaching profession.

Research needs

- Imbalances identified through the monitoring processes outlined above should be investigated in order to identify strategies for improvement.

- Examine strategies used in countries that have changed gendered imbalances; identify effects on school culture, pupil achievement and behaviour

- Investigate schools that have succeeded in recruiting a high proportion of male teachers, and those where results show no gender gap in pupil attainment.

- Investigate the relationships between gender of pupil and gender of teacher, gendered styles of teaching and discipline used by both men and women, and how these interact with pupil achievement. Examine assumptions about the role that men can play in the light of robust evidence

- To date research has perhaps focused more on those women who are in management positions rather than those who are not (for example Evetts 1989; Hall 1996; Coleman 2000). It is also important to conduct research among those who are not applying for management posts, or who are applying and not achieving success.

- Carry out further investigation of pupil subject and career choices, including pupils in single-sex and mixed schools, and academic and vocational subjects, in relation to teacher gender.

In conclusion

This chapter has identified a range of possible ways in which policy and practice could be addressed at different levels to create a more representative profession. To bring about substantial change, traditional (and often unfounded) beliefs about men and women teachers' roles and aptitudes must be abandoned. A cultural change is needed in schools. But while there has been a great deal of concern about the shortage of men in primary schools and the feminisation of the profession, it must also be remembered that men's earnings in the teaching profession are higher than those of women, and that men hold a majority of the positions of power. It is therefore essential that a holistic view is taken and that the various gendered imbalances are considered together, so that strategies taken to ameliorate one do not unintentionally worsen another. Simply to focus on the recruitment of men is an inadequate response.

However, if these issues are tackled successfully in the teaching profession, the result could be a much wider change in the gendered inequalities in society.

Endnote

1   The word feminised is used here not simply in a statistical sense, as it is elsewhere in this paper, but rather to describe an environment that is biased towards females, and disadvantages males (Skelton 2002).

References

Acker S (ed) (1989) *Teachers, Gender and Careers* London: Falmer.

Adler S, Laney J and Packer M (1993) *Managing Women: Feminism and power in educational management* Buckingham: Open University Press.

Alexander R (1992) *Policy and Practice in Primary Education* London: Routledge.

Allan J (1993) 'Male elementary teachers: experiences and perspectives' in Williams CL (ed) *Doing 'Women's Work': Men in non-traditional occupations* Newbury Park: Ca: Sage

Bettison L (2001) Fewer men going into teaching. *The Australian* 23 May.

Blackmore J (1999) *Troubling Women: Feminism, Leadership and Educational Change* Buckingham: Open University Press

Blair M and Maylor U (1993) 'Issues of concern for black women teachers in training' in Siraj-Blatchford I (ed) *'Race', Gender and the Education of Teachers* Buckingham: Open University Press

Bleach K (1998) 'What difference does it make?' in Bleach K (ed) *Raising Boys' Achievement in Schools* Stoke-on-Trent: Trentham.

Bleach K (2001) Introductory speech at the Network Training Conference, Raising Boys' Achievement, Birmingham, 27 March.

Boulton P and Coldron J (1998) 'Why women teachers say 'stuff it' to promotion: a failure of equal opportunities?' *Gender and Education* 10.2

Cameron C, Moss P and Owen C (1999) *Men in the Nursery: Gender and caring work* London: Paul Chapman Publishing

Coleman M (2000) 'The female secondary Headteacher in England and Wales: leadership and management styles' *Educational Research* 42.1

Cubillo L (1999) Gender and leadership in the National Professional Qualification for Head Teachers: an opportunity lost? *Journal of In-service Education* 25.3

DfEE (2000) Let's make teaching one of the top three professions (interview with R Tabberer) www.dfee.gov.uk/teacher/data/modprof/data/top3_07.htm

DfES (2000) *Statistics of Education: Teachers England and Wales* London: The Stationery Office.

DfES (2001a) *Statistics of Education: Teachers England and Wales* London: The Stationery Office.

DfES (2001b) *Statistics of Education: Schools in England* London: The Stationery Office.

Emery H (1997) 'Men into primary teaching' *British Journal of Curriculum and Assessment* 7.2

Eurostat (1999) *Education across the European Union: Statistics and Indicators* Luxembourg: Office for Official Publications of the European Communities

Evetts J (1989) 'The internal labour market for primary teachers' in Acker S (ed) (1989) *Teachers, Gender and Careers* London: Falmer

Foster T and Newman E (2001) *Men mentoring and masculinity: the role of mentoring in the recruitment of young men into primary teaching* Paper presented at the Teacher Supply and Retention: Emerging Issues, University of North London, 12 June

Francis B (2000a) *Boys, Girls and Achievement: Addressing the classroom issues* London: Falmer Routledge

Francis B (2000b) 'The gendered subject: students' subject preferences and discussions of gender and subject' *Oxford Review of Education* 26.1

Francis B and Skelton C (2001) 'Men teachers and the construction of heterosexual masculinity in the classroom' *Sex Education* 1.1

Furedi F (2000) 'An unsuitable job for a man' *The Independent* 12 October.

Guardian (2000) 'The trouble with boys' (Leader) *The Guardian* 21 August.

Guardian (2001) 'What women want in the maths department' *The Guardian* 3 July.

Hall V (1996) *Dancing on the Ceiling: A study of women managers in education* London: Paul Chapman.

House of Commons Education and Employment Committee (1998) *The Role of Headteachers: (Ninth Report)* London: The Stationery Office.

Howson J (2001) *State of the labour market 2001: Report to NAHT/SHA* Education Data Services / NAHT.

Hutchings M, Menter I, Ross A, Thomson D, with Bedford D (2000) *Teacher Supply and Retention in Six London Boroughs* TTA.

Hutchings M and Francis B (2001) *The practice of teaching and learning in girls' schools* Paper presented at the Association of Maintained Girls' Schools Conference, Bournemouth, October.

Johnston J, McKeown E and McEwen A (1999a) 'Primary teaching as a career choice: the views of male and female sixth-form students' *Research Papers in Education* 14.2

Johnston J, McKeown E and McEwen A. (1999b) 'Choosing Primary Teaching as a career: the perspectives of males and females in training' *Journal of Education for Teaching* 25.1

Kauppinen-Toropainen K and Lammi J (1993) 'Men in female-dominated occupations: a cross-cultural comparison' in Williams CL (ed) *Doing 'Women's Work': Men in non-traditional occupations* Newbury Park: Ca: Sage.

Keys W and Fernandes C (1990) *A Survey of School Governing Bodies, Vol 1* NFER

King J (1998) *Uncommon Caring: Learning from men who teach young children* New York: College Teachers Press

Lahelma E (2000) 'Lack of male teachers: a problem for students or teachers?' *Pedagogy. Culture and Society* 8.2

Lewis E, Butcher J and Donnan P (1999) *Men in primary teaching: an endangered species?* Paper presented at the Australian Association for Educational Research Conference www.aare.au/99/pap/but99238.htm

Lewis P (2000) *An enquiry into male wastage from primary ITE courses at a University College and success indicators for retention* Paper presented at Regional Issues in Teacher Supply and Retention conference, University of North London, January

Lewis P (2001) *Overcoming barriers and dispelling myths about being a male teacher in an early years context* Paper presented at Teacher Supply and Retention: Emerging Issues conference, University of North London, 12 June

Lords Hansard text for 30 November 1998.

Mahony P and Hextall I (2000) *Reconstructing Teaching: Standards, performance and accountability* London: Falmer Routledge

McCreith S, Ross A and Hutchings M (2001) *Teacher Supply and Retention 2000-1: a study of 22 Local Education Authorities* Institute for Policy Studies in Education, University of North London

McVeigh T (2001) 'Boys lagging in class for years' *The Observer* 23 September.

Mercer D (1997) 'The secondary Headteacher and time-in-post: a study of job satisfaction' *Journal of Educational Administration* 35.3

Mills M (2000) 'Issues in implementing boys' programmes in schools: male teachers and empowerment' *Gender and Education* 12.2

NAHT (1998) Memorandum from the National Association of Head Teachers. Appendix 6 to the *Select Committee of Education and Employment Ninth Report, The Role of Headteachers* London: The Stationery Office

New Zealand Government (1999) *Push for more male primary teachers* Press release www.scoop.co.nz/stories/PA9907/S00603.htm

NPHA (1998) Memorandum from the National Primary Headteachers' Association, Appendix 5 to the *Select Committee of Education and Employment Ninth Report, The Role of Headteachers* London: The Stationery Office

NUT (1980) *Promotion and the Woman Teacher* National Union of Teachers/Equal Opportunities Commission.

NUT (1998) Memorandum from the National Union of Teachers, Appendix 12 to the *Select Committee of Education and Employment Ninth Report, The Role of Headteachers* London: The Stationery Office

NUT (2001) *Women and Senior Management: an NUT survey* National Union of Teachers

Oram A (1989) 'A master should not serve under a mistress: women and men teachers 1900-1970' in Acker S (ed) (1989) *Teachers, Gender and Careers* London: Falmer.

Oyler C, Jennings G and Lozada P (2001) 'Silenced gender: the construction of a male primary educator' *Teaching and Teacher Education* 17

Ozga J (1993) *Women in Educational Management* Buckingham: Open University Press.

Pepperell S and Smedley S (1998) 'Calls for more men in primary teaching: problematising the issues' *International Journal of Inclusive Education* 2.4

Reay D and Ball SJ (2000) 'Essentials of female management: women's ways of working in the education market place?' *Educational Management and Administration* 28.2

Reynolds K (1996) 'He's got to be so macho' *The Guardian* 8 October.

Ross A and Thomson D (2000) *The future of maths teaching: a feminised workforce?* Unpublished manuscript, Teacher Supply and Retention Project, University of North London

Roulston K and Mills M (2000) 'Male teachers in feminised teaching areas: marching to the beat of men's movement drums?' *Oxford Review of Education* 26.2

Skelton C (1991) A study of the career perspectives of male teachers of young children' *Gender and Education* 3.3

Skelton C (1994) 'Sex, male teachers and young children' *Gender and Education* 6.1

Skelton C (2001) *Schooling the Boys: Masculinities and primary education* Buckingham: Open University Press.

Skelton C (2002) *The 'feminisation of schooling'? Masculinism and primary education* Paper presented at Globalisation, Policy Change, Teachers and Teaching: International Sociology of Education Conference, Sheffield, January

Smedley S (1997) 'Men on the margins: male student primary teachers' *Changing English* 4.2

Smedley S (1998) 'Perspectives on male student primary teachers' *Changing English* 5.2

STRB (1999) *Eighth report* DfEE www.dfee.gov.uk/review-body

Teacher Training Agency *Corporate plan 2001-4*

Teacher Training Agency (1998) Memorandum from Teacher Training Agency, Appendix 3 to the *Select Committee of Education and Employment Ninth Report, The Role of Headteachers* London: The Stationery Office

TES (1999) 'Children draw men into teaching' *Times Educational Supplement* 29 January

TES (2000) 'More male teachers needed to help boys' *Times Educational Supplement* 1 September

TES (2000) 'Primary schools go on a manhunt' *Times Educational Supplement* 3 March

TES (2000) 'Head wins right to job-share' *Times Educational Supplement* 15 September

TES (2000) 'Job-share Head seeks six-figure sum' *Times Educational Supplement* 8 December

TES (2001) 'The male role models who listen' *Times Educational Supplement* 2 February

TES (2001) 'Workload action on the cards again' *Times Educational Supplement* 16 November

Thornton M (1999a) 'Men into primary teaching: Who goes where? Dilemmas of entry, survival and career prospects' *Education 3.13*

Thornton M (1999b) 'Reducing wastage among men student teachers in primary courses: a male club approach' *Journal of Education for Teaching* 25.1

Thornton M and Bricheno P (2000) 'Primary school teachers' careers in England and Wales: the relationship between gender, role, position and promotion aspirations' *Pedagogy, Culture and Society* 8.2

University of Wolverhampton (2000) *University urges men to consider career as a primary school teacher* Press release, 7 February

Weber S and Mitchell C (1995) *That's Funny, You Don't Look Like a Teacher* London: Falmer

Whitehead J (1996) 'Sex stereotypes, gender identity and subject choice at A level' *Educational Research 38*

Whyte J (1986) *Girls into science and technology: the story of a project* London: Routledge and Kegan Paul.

Williams CL (ed) (1993) *Doing 'Women's Work': Men in non-traditional occupations* Newbury Park: Ca: Sage

8. From ivory towers to chalkface: recruiting teachers from the élite universities

Steve Haines and Joe Hallgarten

> We will know when we have succeeded (in transforming education) when 'too clever by half' is no longer an insult, and when teaching is recognised alongside the law or business as a profession of the highest status and regard.
>
> Tony Blair in *Prospect* March 2001

> When I asked about PGCEs the careers officer said that 'Imperial students don't go into teaching'.
>
> Imperial Graduate, Class of 1999

The purpose of this chapter is to evaluate the role that the country's so-called 'elite' universities play in teacher recruitment. It examines whether graduates from the Russell Group universities (institutions which have high entry and research standards) are choosing teaching as a career. To do this it looks at:

- the background of the debate about teacher recruitment in terms of quantity and quality

- the number of first degree graduates from the Russell group universities who are enrolling on PGCE courses as their first destination after graduation

- qualitative research from individual careers centres about students' views of teaching as a profession

- what is being done and could be done to address the situation

- the policy implications of the findings

Background

Graduate recruitment: quantity

This Government came to power with an inherited problem concerning teacher recruitment. Falling levels of applications to teacher training in the preceding years, and increasing problems with retaining sufficient teachers have been described in Chapter 2.

In particular, the last two decades has seen a decline in both the numbers and percentage of graduates who enrol on post-graduate teacher training courses. The first destinations of university graduates enrolling on teacher training dropped from 7.9 per cent in 1980/81 to 4.2 per cent in 1990/91. By 1999/2000 the figure had still fallen, but not so dramatically, to 3.7 per cent (Higher Education Statistics Agency 2000; Universities' Statistical Record 1991 and 1981). The legacy left to Blair's administration was a critical situation, where the number of graduates entering the profession was insufficient to meet demand.

The reasons for this decline have also been widely explored. The 1997 report of the Education and Employment Select Committee, *Teacher recruitment: what can be done?* noted that 'many other professions have a more attractive image than teaching; pay is felt to be better in many other jobs and employers in other fields generally pay for their employee's training; and the working conditions are also seen as better in other walks of life' (House of Commons Education and Employment Committee 1997). In a buoyant economy corporate organisations are able to offer more attractive incentives that may take potential teachers into other professions. However, as the report notes, the low starting salaries of careers in the media show that the problem is not just one of incentives or salary. The problem is also one of how the profession is perceived.

A survey conducted by MORI has reflected some of the reasons why graduates are not choosing teaching as a career. In their report on the perception of the teaching profession 47 per cent said teachers are badly paid, and 42 per cent of graduates said that the public does not hold teachers in high esteem (MORI 2001). The perception of the profession is unattractive financially and offers little kudos. However, perceptions often only reflect uninformed opinions. If significant numbers of graduates who are able to choose from a wide range of careers were seen to be entering teaching it would boost the kudos of the profession.

To some extent, the Government's drive to increase the number of teachers has been successful. In November 2001 the Teacher Training Agency (TTA) announced that 'almost 29,000 people are expected to start initial teacher training courses in England this year – a rise for the second year in succession and the highest number since 1994-5' (TTA 2001b). Estelle Morris claimed that 'this rise reflects two things. Firstly, that teaching continues to be the first choice profession for graduates; and secondly, that our targeted recruitment policies are working well' (DfES 2001b). These recruitment strategies have been relatively successful, although are still not keeping up with the increased demand for teachers that has been caused by increased investment and attrition rates in the existing teaching population.

The Government is aware that 'the teaching profession is competing for graduates in a very tight market' (DfES 2001c). Corporate companies are able to offer high salaries and levels of support, whilst other professions such as law or medicine are respected as challenging and rewarding. In addition to this, the perception of the teaching profession has been consistently negative and this image continues to deter graduates. Yet, the reality of the situation is that teacher's pay has increased by 25 per cent since 1997 (DfES 2001c) and is able to compete with the average starting salaries of many graduates. This increase has improved the situation, but this is only part of the picture of how graduates can be attracted into the profession.

Graduate recruitment: quality

The first strategic aim in the TTA's corporate plan is to 'increase the number and quality of recruits to teaching' (TTA 2001c). While recent figures show an increase in entry to PGCE, this does not necessarily show that the quality of graduates is also improving.

The most obvious way to evaluate the quality of teaching recruits is to look at the degree results of PGCE students. The higher education statistics agency (HESA) records the degree grade of those entering PGCE courses. Two caveats to remember with this data are that the degree grade for a number of PGCEs was unknown and the remaining percentage for all graduates was listed as unclassified. The percentages listed apply to all known and classified degree results.

Table 8.1

	1997-98		1999-2000	
	PGCE Students	All Graduates	PGCE Students	All Graduates
First	5.0%	8.0%	5.8%	9.1%
Upper Second	47.0%	47.0%	47.7%	48.7%
Lower Second	39.0%	37.0%	39.2%	35.6%
Third/Pass	9.0%	8.0%	7.2%	6.6%

There are a number of noticeable points about these figures. The percentage difference between the two years is minor and PGCE students as a group seem to follow the overall trends. In both cases those achieving a First are under represented in the PGCE cohorts, whilst those with Thirds and below are over-represented.

Teachers and the élite universities

It is clearly hoped that recruitment initiatives intended to improve the attractiveness of teaching as a career will lead to a greater number of applications from the countries' top graduates. Estelle Morris recently spelt out the Government's view that 'action is needed now to ensure that teaching secures and retains its position as a trusted, high quality profession, backed by effective support and reward systems, a profession capable of attracting and retaining the nation's best and brightest individuals' (Morris 2001). The Fast Track Scheme that has been introduced as a specific response to the goal of recruiting high quality graduates, but the Government has not yet targeted the sources of these graduates.

Our data

The aim of our research was to explore whether the university a student attended would make a significant difference to the likelihood that a student would enrol on a PGCE course as their first destination after graduation. There is no clear definition of an 'élite' university. We chose the Russell Group, a self-appointed body that claims to represent research institutions of the highest quality in the country. Although some of its members are not often thought of as 'élite' it is often assumed that this group provides many of the country's top graduates.

Unfortunately, the Graduate Teacher Training Register (GTTR) chooses not to collect data on the location of any applicant's first degree. Instead, the data was collected through the careers' offices of the Russell Group universities, and then compared with data from the HESA 'First Destinations' data sets.

Requesting data directly from careers centres allowed collection of both quantitative and qualitative data about the first-degree graduates. The universities were asked about how many of their graduates were enrolling on PGCEs as their first destination and also asked to offer some reasons why others may not be.

The data is to be evaluated with a number of caveats in mind:

- These statistics do not take into account graduates who enrol on a PGCE course at any other time than immediately after graduating. However, there is no reason to suspect that if data including graduates who enrolled later had been compared with similar baseline data, that our results would have been significantly different.

- Of those universities who supplied figures on the comprehensiveness of their returns, most registered a return rate of between 80-90 per cent. The return rates for HESA first destinations for 1999/2000 was 77 per cent.

- A comparison over time was not always available and data from pre-1995 was not easily obtainable.

- Two of the 19 Russell Group Universities (Liverpool and Manchester) did not return their data.

Findings

Data for all graduates

- The number of applicants for PGCEs rose by 3 per cent during the previous year, from 20,993 in 1999/2000 to 22,349 in 2000/2001 (DfES 2001b).

- HESA records the total number of the first destination of undergraduates in 1999/2000, who are classified under the 'teaching professional' category of those undertaking further training or study, as 6,340 of 170,752. This represents a total of 3.7 per cent of all known first destinations.

Data for Russell Group University graduates

Figure 8.1 below shows the number of graduates in 1999/2000 who enrol on PGCE courses as their first destination as a percentage of all destinations. There is a comparison between the percentage of all universities, on the far left labelled HESA, and data collected from 17 of the 19 Russell Group universities.

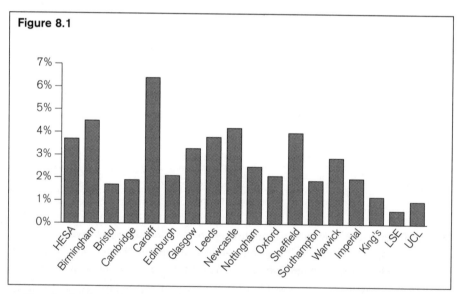

Figure 8.1

Despite the high figures of some of the universities, the average percentage of first destinations from the listed élite universities who go on to do PGCEs is 2.7 per cent. This compares to the HESA average of 3.7 per cent.

However, when viewing the data it must be remembered that results can be affected by the intake of these universities. LSE for example has a high proportion of overseas students. It is also worth considering why students choose these universities and the geographical trends associated with choice. In some cases, these universities specialise in vocational courses which are designed to train for a specific profession such as medicine or law. The incidence of students taking these courses can significantly reduce the number of potential of applicants to PGCE courses.

Figure 8.1 shows that twelve of the seventeen Russell Group universities whose figures were available are below the HESA average. Both Oxford and Cambridge fall short of the HESA average by over a half. London universities similarly produce low quantities of graduates. Yet, other universities above the HESA average prove that high numbers of graduates from elite universities are willing to enter PGCEs as a first destination.

It is worth noting how the figures change over time. Year on year data was not always available for universities, but where it was the percentages did show continuity in some cases. Cardiff consistently produced a high percentage: 6.4 per cent in 1998/1999, 6.4 per cent in 1997/1998, 7.1 per cent in 1997/1996 and Oxford a consistently below average 2.1 per cent, 2.9 per cent and 2.7 per cent respectively.

However, the data did not always follow an expected trend. This is shown by the Bristol statistics in Table 8.2.

Table 8.2 Bristol University: graduates taking PGCE

	actual number	percentage of known destinations
1996	66	2.75%
1997	45	2.1%
1998	27	1.1%
1999	40	1.6%
2000	44	1.7%

Although the percentage change between 1996 and 2000 suggests a downturn in applications, the fluctuation in the intervening years shows that the change does not follow a smooth trend line. It may be the case that this variation has more to do with the financial climate of the time than the attractiveness of PGCEs as a first destination. The numbers are so low that although they show the teaching profession is only attracting a very small number of graduates, it is difficult to chart a progression; the percentage change can be affected dramatically by a small number of graduates. Without better data, it is impossible to say whether the number or percentage of graduates entering teaching from the elite universities has declined.

In spite of the possible inaccuracies, the picture is still revealing. There can be little doubt that graduates from these universities are less likely to go on to PGCE courses and become teachers. It is also noticeable that some of the highest profile universities display consistently below average figures. As a whole this data highlights an untapped pool of potential graduates who could fill the TTA's aims of quantity and quality.

Why are these graduates not entering the teaching profession?

Graduate opinions

Many of the reasons why graduates from these universities do not enter PGCEs as their first destination are intuitive. They are highly regarded by employers, simply have more choices than the average student, and are not choosing teaching.

Anecdotal evidence from careers' offices gives a picture similar to the general perception of the profession. The media portrayal of teachers, and the coverage of current shortages were noted to have an impact. At Birmingham University, the profession 'is viewed by many who might otherwise consider it as a career as a low status/low reward occupation'. Views included: 'the universal perception is that teachers struggle under a huge bureaucratic load'; 'the inspection regime is hostile and punitive'; and 'many teachers spending most of their time on crowd control rather than facilitating learning'.

Cardiff noted that:

> Students' opinions on teaching as a career tend to go from 'I couldn't do all the discipline thing' and 'my mum's a teacher and I could never go through what she goes through' to 'I love kids and really want to make a difference in this world'.

The careers' office at Birmingham argued that 'serving teachers seem to tell their offspring to avoid like the plague following in their footsteps'. It seems that the views of serving teachers themselves are detrimental to the graduate perception of teaching as a career choice.

Sheffield found a further problem arising with students who had taken a PGCE but dropped out during the course or in their first year of teaching. Problems associated with the job were 'the sheer amount of time that the job demands with consequent exhaustion and depression and no time for any life outside work' and 'having to teach subjects far removed from one's own to cover for absent colleagues'. This disillusionment then spread back to the graduate final year cohort making their career choices.

Contributing factors

Without qualitative research, it is impossible to tell whether students from the elite universities are motivated by different factors from other institutions. In particular, it would be interesting to know whether the way in which teaching and schooling has changed in the last decade has had particular impact on these students. For instance, does the perceived loss of autonomy and creativity turn these students off more than others? As one participant said at a recent IPPR seminar 'the last thing anyone with a passion for physics would want to do is to teach Key Stage 3 physics'.

Another possible factor may be that a larger percentage of these students are privately educated. It is not known whether privately educated students are more or less likely to go into teaching. What is known, however, is that many of those who wish to teach go straight to teaching at private schools, where Qualified Teacher Status is not always deemed necessary.

It is also significant to look at where these graduates are going instead. Data regarding other first destinations of graduates from Nottingham shows that by far the largest employer was financial services. This trend was supported by Oxford who showed a significant rise in employment in this sector from 4.8 per cent in 1996 to 7.3 per cent in 2000. Similar percentage increases in the field of professional and commercial services could be seen in Warwick's data. However, graduates are not motivated by financial gain alone and many were shown to be entering low paid positions as a first destination, most notably in the media industry.

The qualitative data shows that teaching has a low appeal in the élite universities, stemming from the poor perception of the profession by the graduates themselves. This poor perception appears to come from a variety of sources, ranging from teachers themselves to social influences. In order to reach the Government's aim of quantity and quality, these universities should be leading the recruitment drive into the teaching profession, rather than lagging behind.

Does this matter?

On one level, compared to degree class, degree origin could be seen as irrelevant: the aim should be to attract high quality graduates from wherever they emerge. Never mind the *alma mater*, feel the quality. However, the statistics above should be concerning to the education world for the following reasons.

Impact on quality

The figures appear to reveal an untapped pool of potential teachers coming out of the élite universities. Unless more PGCE students are recruited from these universities, it is unlikely that the Government and the TTA will be able to meet the ambition to attract sufficient high quality graduates into the profession. This data shows that it is clearly the case that more could be done. Either the teaching profession is not attracting these graduates or élite universities are not being targeted as a potential recruitment area.

In a more significant way than degree grade, if top graduates are seen to not be choosing teaching as a career, then this may deprive the profession of those with the best education in their subject. The desirability of an education at one of the élite universities should be reflected in their ability to provide the best students with the best training. These students are the best placed to be bringing their understanding and enthusiasm for their subject into the classroom.

Impact on status

These universities are still the places that those who rise to influence often attend. The networks that are formed at these universities, and continue into working life, are excluding teachers. This will impact on the status of the profession.

Impact on school-university networks

If fewer graduates from elite universities are becoming teachers there are fewer role models to encourage school leavers to apply to these universities. The lack of role models who can encourage pupils who might not otherwise have thought of applying to élite universities may mean that these pupils are less likely to consider applying. This is especially true for those universities with a certain, and often unfair, reputation that can put off many pupils. A recent study by the NFER showed that 'teachers may be contributing to the problem by giving bright working-class students the impression that top universities are not for them' (Mansell 2001). The presence of teachers who are graduates from these universities could go some way to address this. This link is difficult to prove, but is still worthy of consideration.

There has been widespread concern about the fact that a disproportionate percentage of many students at leading universities come from private schools, and are unlikely to be from low income families. At the same time, if the number of teachers who attended the élite universities is declining then so is the number of permanent role models in these schools. After the Laura Spence affair, where a state school pupil claimed to have been discriminated against because she was educated at a state school, universities have been keen to dispel this myth. However, Estelle Morris recently renewed Chancellor Gordon Brown's attack on university admissions, announcing a 'wide ranging and fundamental review of higher education' (Hayes 2001) to address these inequalities.

Universities are doing more than ever to improve this situation, investing in various linking and outreach schemes, particularly with inner city comprehensives. Schemes such as the Oxford Access scheme are designed to encourage elite university students to create links with schools by visiting them and inviting pupils to shadow students. The introduction of schemes such as this show the importance of links and role models to schools in encouraging students to apply to the elite universities.

Impact on Universities

Ultimately, these universities should have a vested interest in encouraging their students to spend some of their career teaching. Without the enthusiasm of skilled subject specialists in our secondary schools, it is unlikely that these universities will receive a sufficient number of quality applicants for their undergraduate courses.

There are ways of addressing this that need to be considered outside of increasing the recruitment figures. The Government's White Paper *Schools: achieving success* outlines a future for the teaching profession that does not represent the job for life. The Paper also states that 'in the 21st century, it is questionable to suggest that a full-time teacher is the only option for filling a vacancy' (DfES 2001c). The White Paper proposals to improve the teaching profession rely on 'floating teachers' who take on contact time and 'trained learning support assistants leading part of a lesson' (DfES 2001c). However, schemes that take subject specialists out of the classroom may exacerbate the problem of the impact on universities.

The situation addressed in the data above should therefore concern all education stakeholders. Appropriate policy responses are outlined below.

What is being done or could be done?

Clearly, the Government is putting a lot of work into improving the attractiveness of teaching as a profession. Some of this may change attitudes, but it is the assertion of this chapter that, without careful targeting, it is highly unlikely that PGCE students will become representative of the graduate population as a whole.

At the same time, there is no guarantee that such targeting will work. The choices that students from the elite universities have on graduating are far greater than the average student, as are the pay differentials between many of these choices and teaching. It may be that the solution to attracting graduates from the elite universities is to catch them older, at a mid point in their careers, or even through early retirement.

The role of the universities

Measures can be introduced at the university level that would help attract graduates to the teaching profession. The careers centres often did not want to be seen as showing bias towards certain career choices. For example, Birmingham saw its role as 'that of the independent broker helping students to identify and achieve career paths that are suitable to them as individuals'. Edinburgh pointed out that 'as careers professionals, we offer non-directive guidance, and do not "encourage" graduates to enter any particular career'.

Both Warwick and Oxford pointed out the benefits of a close relationship with their own Schools of Education in encouraging graduates to consider a career in teaching. A possible way forward for recruitment at this level would be for all universities to forge a link with an institution that offers PGCEs. This link could help promote teaching as a career.

Cardiff also noted the use of student tutoring schemes whereby undergraduates spend an allotted time each week helping out in local schools. This allows the students to gain the experience that is requested on the GTTR forms. All universities have similar community outreach schemes, or use organisations such as Community Service Volunteers (CSV). Here exist pools of undergraduates in the élite universities that are probably more likely to consider teaching, and thus could be encouraged towards enrolling on PGCEs.

Finally, Imperial College's proposed teaching assistant scheme aims to encourage science and engineering post-doctoral students who are employed as research assistants to teach part-time in state schools. The scheme proposes that up to 50 per cent of the research assistants' three-year contract would be spent assisting teachers 'who would supervise the teaching assistants and maintain discipline'. The aim is that schools would benefit from this input and the close links with the university in the short term.

Ultimately, it is hoped that a small fraction of these assistants may also be encouraged to become teachers themselves. The scheme proposes to create the twofold effect: 'school pupils would benefit through being taught by a recently qualified subject specialist and by being made aware of the opportunities that universities offer'. It is hoped that 'the teaching assistants would stimulate an interest in science and, to an extent, act as role models'. A similar scheme at Cambridge University called STIMULUS has brought about 70 volunteers into 30 schools each year.

For such a scheme to be successful, it may need financial input from the DfES. The STIMULUS scheme has had to survive on sponsorship funding from a number of charitable sources and industry. As an incentive, Imperial College proposes the clearing of student loans for those taking part in the scheme. It is also hoped that the Government would finance the research element if normal research sponsors or HEFCE money were not available.

The Role of Government

Fast Track

This year the first cohort of Fast Track teachers are taking their PGCE courses. The programme aims to recruit 'able graduates' and 'trainee teachers with high potential' into the profession (DfES 2001a). The scheme is designed to 'inspire, attract, retain and reward the most dedicated, enthusiastic and able people' (Fast

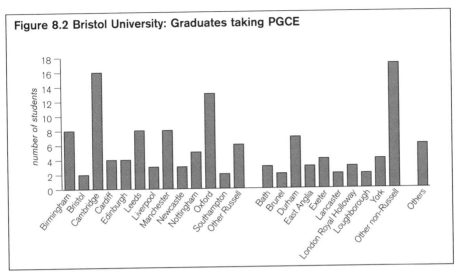

Figure 8.2 Bristol University: Graduates taking PGCE

Track 2001). In return for a larger training salary and accelerated progression, Fast Track teachers are expected to take on extra training and accept placements and jobs in specified schools. The number of applications to the first year of Fast Track was lower than anticipated. At a cost of £80,000 per graduate only 110 graduates were recruited in 2001 (Charter 2001). It seems that even with the improved prospects, the Fast Track Scheme does not yet attract the numbers of, for instance, the similar civil service fast stream.

Although the Fast Track Scheme has come under criticism, it appears to be making inroads into attracting students from the 'élite' universities. All those offered places had a 2.1 or equivalent, and at least 22 UCAS points or equivalent. Although data is not yet available on the degree origins of all 1574 applicants, 61 per cent of this year's Fast Track cohort attended Russell Group universities.

Clearly, the Fast Track Scheme will never be large enough to redress the imbalances that this paper describes, but it does appear to be attracting elite university students into the profession. Oxford and Cambridge both notably contribute the highest numbers to the Fast Track intake, whilst both showed poor figures in the previous data on PGCEs as a whole. However, one issue that has arisen regarding the Fast Track procedure is that many of those whose application is not successful choose not to go into teaching as a result.

Recommendation

- The Fast Track application procedure should be delayed until the PGCE year, with the extra money and training coming on stream during induction years.

Encouraging School-University Links

The Government's White Paper *Schools: achieving success* proposes that the communication between schools and higher education institutions is developed. Advanced beacon and training schools will 'link to Higher Education institutions and to each other and will be given a responsibility to spread their good practice widely' (DfES 2001c). In addition to this, advanced specialist colleges are to be developed that 'will work with us to develop the role and to see how they can play a greater role in training teachers' (DfES 2001c). These specialised schools will require teachers who will be able to maximise the use of these links. This involvement will give the profession a new visibility in universities that could encourage more graduates to enter teaching. But, as this chapter suggests, the reality of the modern teaching profession needs to be attractive to these graduates.

The élite universities who seem most successful at producing future PGCE students are those who develop strong links with their own PGCE course providers. For those universities who do not have this, it would be useful to develop the links mentioned above as a breeding ground, not only for potential students, but also to encourage existing students to consider teaching as a career.

The Government recently announced a scheme in its White Paper that 'allows students to gain credits towards Qualified Teacher Status while studying for the first degree' (DfES 2001c). This scheme forges a link between the education departments and the university as a whole, or brings in ITT providers who do not offer a QTS programme (TTA 2001a). However, these schemes do not necessarily mean that the élite universities will be targeted, as not all operate a modular system that the schemes can easily work within.

Funding

Although there are no firm proposals, the Government is currently considering radical options for reform of the way £5 billion of public money is allocated to universities. Education Minister Margaret Hodge has declared that 'I want to see diversity amongst universities. They could excel in research, teaching, outreach to the community, links with industry, many things' (Kelly 2001). Rather than rewarding and categorising inputs, one option could be to create funding incentives for universities to increase the number of their degree students who go on to take PGCE courses, or who choose to enter other public service professions where shortages exist. How they managed to do this would be entirely at their discretion.

Conclusion

Although the picture is not complete, the results of this research highlight some important challenges facing teacher recruitment. It is clear that graduates from the 'élite' universities hold teaching in low esteem and that these universities are not producing high numbers of PGCE entrants. These findings should concern the Government both in the short term for attracting bright graduates into the profession, and in the long term for the impact this will have on the profession and the networks of the education system as a whole.

A specific policy aspiration to attract graduates from elite universities deserves consideration. If this is a real concern, these graduates will require effective targeting.

Recommendations

- Effective targeting of universities that provide few entrants to PGCE courses.

- Encouraging greater links between the élite universities, ITE providers and schools themselves

- Developing the Fast Track model of recruitment focus on those already on PGCE courses.

- Encouraging those who may be interested in a career as a teacher, such as community service volunteers or research assistants.

- Developing new funding incentives for universities to increase the number of their degree students who go on to take PGCE courses, or who choose to enter other public service professions where shortages exist.

References

Blair T (2001) *Prospect* 3.1

Charter D (2001) 'Graduates spurn teaching fast track' *The Times* 5 November

DfES (2001a) *Schools: building on success* London: DfES

DfES (2001b) *Recruitment to teacher training hits seven year high* Morris Press Release 1 November

DfES (2001c) *Schools: achieving success* London: DfES

Fast Track (2001) www.fasttrackteaching.gov.uk

Hayes, D (2001) 'Estelle announces fundamental review of higher education' *Times Educational Supplement* 22 October

Higher Education Statistics Agency (2000) *First destinations of students leaving higher education institutions* Higher Education Statistics Agency

House of Commons Education and Employment Committee (1997) *Teacher Recruitment: What can be done? First report* HMSO

Kelly J (2001) 'Government to reform funding of universities' *Financial Times* 9 November

Mansell W (2001) 'Fear of university debt puts off thousands' *Times Educational Supplement* 30 November

MORI social research institute (2001) 'Graduates Find Teaching Career "Unappealing"' 10 August

Morris E (2001) *Professionalism and Trust – the future of teachers and teaching* A speech to the Social Market Foundation 12 November

Teacher Training Agency (2001a) 'Credits for students as new route into teaching is piloted' Press Release 18 November

Teacher Training Agency (2001b) 'Trainee teacher numbers are highest for seven years' Press Release 1 November

Universities' Statistical Record (1981) *University statistics 2: First destinations of university graduates* Universities' Statistical Record

Universities' Statistical Record (1991) *University statistics 2: First destinations of university graduates* Universities' Statistical Record

9. Visions for the profession
Jodie Reed and Joe Hallgarten

In January 2002 IPPR, in collaboration with the Future Education Network, launched an online survey, a 'call for visions' on the future of the teaching profession.

'Teachers and Teaching in 2010' aimed to provide an opportunity for everyone passionate about learning to add their voices to the national debate. IPPR and FEN developed an online tool that enabled all to contribute their perspectives on teachers and teaching as individuals or groups. As well as an instant comment box and a longer survey, a set of resources was created that could be used in the classroom, the staffroom, or any other group meeting. These resources included a discussion guide for group leaders and a sheet containing a selection of others' views on the future of the profession. Launching the survey, we stated that

> for too long, those involved in education have been told about their futures, rather than asked about them. Whether you are a pupil, parent, school governor or member of staff, we want your views on teachers and teaching and your sense of what the teacher, and the school, of tomorrow should look like.

We received more than five hundred responses to the survey. The majority of respondents were current or former teachers, but we also received responses from other school staff, parents, governors and students.

We are aware that the responses do not constitute a representative sample, and that this chapter can only offer a selected snapshot of these responses. Nonetheless, the 'call for visions' elicited some fascinating ideas and ideals. Drawing on the survey, this chapter will reflect feeling on the ground about teaching and draw out positive visions of the future of the profession.

A longer report of the survey, and the full database containing all responses is available on both the FEN and ippr websites.

The standing of the teaching profession today

While many respondents painted a picture of a profession in crisis, comments related diverse opinions on the standing of the profession.

> *Demoralised and demotivated and undervalued and defensive* Educational Researcher

Excellent: very forward thinking – Lecturer

In considering views about the standing of the teaching profession today, the substantial difficulties facing the profession must clearly be taken into account. The standing of the profession should not, however, be seen to directly mirror levels of problems it faces or might face in the future. Through bearing in mind views on what or who lies at the root of these problems and recognising differences in how the profession is perceived amongst different groups, a more honest and positive image of the standing of the profession emerges.

A profession in crisis

Current problems

Those who saw teaching as a profession afflicted by substantial difficulties, identified certain problems with notable frequency. When questioned on the three most important things which could be done now to transform the teaching profession, the issue of pay was most frequently the first thing mentioned. Many felt that current rates were undermining the value of teacher's work, damaging recruitment retention.

> *Teachers work the same hours as city bankers and doctors and are (at least!) equally worthwhile. This needs to be reflected in pay* Experienced teacher

> *Raise salaries. It is very rare for 'top' graduates to enter the teaching profession. One of the reasons for this and the perceived lack of status of the profession is undoubtedly money* Experienced teacher

> *Government should pay a decent salary, especially to long-service staff without whom no school can do without* School senior manager

> *I want a profession that is better rewarded both financially and by respect within the community* Parent/Trainee teacher

Pay was not always seen as a problem. Those who prioritised working conditions sometimes saw the pay issue as a distraction from more pressing areas in need of funding. Many respondents commented on the need to take action on poor working environments, the deluge of paperwork and insufficient non-contact time in which to deal with this paperwork work.

> *It is not about pay but conditions of service which are the problem. Limit working hours and workload, pay overtime* School senior manager

Make schools smaller and less like prisons. Schools should be nurturing environments Parent

Increase non-contact time to reduce burden of workload and improve teacher efficiency Ex-teacher

I would like to see someone who is not bogged down with a myriad of forms to complete Parent

Blaming teachers

Of those whose comments reflected a vision of a profession in crisis, some did feel that teachers themselves were largely to blame. Critics of the profession tended to accuse teachers of being anachronistic and reluctant to embrace change and more concerned with their own needs than those of children.

They have been stubborn and refused to move on from the stance that public sector organisations had in the 1960s when they could do what they liked and no-one measured their effectiveness Researcher/Teacher

In the future I would like to see a much more professional one that embraced change in a society; that valued the concessions made almost uniquely to them University teacher

The misconception on the part of the teaching profession that work-based or vocational learning is only for those who lack academic ability...serves to lower the standing of the profession within engineering and business circles Engineering Employers' Federation

A profession far too worried about status. A profession which has shown little sense of independence Experienced teacher

In the future teachers should be committed to organising schools as mindful, nurturing places around the needs of the children and their communities rather than around the convenience of teachers Parent

Hopefully teachers who aren't making the grades will be unable to languish in the safety of a permanent contract – these should be conditional on required standards being attained Parent

Some respondents reflected an opinion that teachers had failed, in part, to take sufficient steps to ensure positive relations with parents.

> *In the future teachers need to gain the ability to recognise the need to involve parents in their children's learning, and have the skills to communicate with parents* Governor/FE student

> *The biggest single improvement would be joint acceptance by teachers and parents that they each have rights and responsibilities* School senior manager

Blaming the Government

Frequently respondents did not attribute failings to teachers but lay blame primarily at the Government's door for engendering a collective crisis of confidence. This was seen as both an obstacle to their educational capacities and, to their ability to project out a positive image of themselves.

> *They should be invested with trust from above and they may gain it from below* FE Student/Teacher

> *hampered by our declining confidence in our relationships with children* Parent

> *It appears that sometimes, we are viewed as the 'enemy' rather than as facilitators of learning. This is in part our own fault. We have allowed ourselves to fall into a morass of self-doubt, as evidenced by our continuing change of standards and expectations* Experienced teacher

> *We are still not good at advocating how good we are at coping with the complex diversities of what is education in this country* School senior manager

> *We need to have our confidence restored and our horizons broadened* Teacher

Three factors were seen as crucial in identifying the reasons that teachers felt the Government was undermining them. Firstly, a tendency was noted for government and media to use teachers as a convenient scapegoat for deep-rooted social problems.

> *Teachers are no longer seen as the role models for future generations, but the scapegoats of some children failing to achieve in societal rites of passage* Trainee teacher

Both government and media assume perfect pupil motivation and rant accordingly Experienced teacher

Secondly, teaching was seen to suffer through being an outlet for inconsistent, and frequently divisive, political agendas.

Pulled in many directions from Government Policy advisor

We're seen as an easy target for politicians wanting to make their mark, so we get a period of stability to actually get on with the job Teacher

I would like to see a profession that controls itself rather than being controlled by political whims Trainee teacher

Thirdly, there were widely held views that the current political agenda in particular serves to undermine the profession. Its derision of outmoded models of teaching, emphasis on targets (exemplified in league tables) and crisis management approach was often seen as leaving teachers with an utter lack of control over the content of learning and impotent to effect change.

trying to reassert its professionalism in the aftermath of its 'de-skilling' through constant implications that teaching methods in the past were inadequate and that the current models of what makes an effective teacher are the only ones Parent/School senior manager

Dominated by assessment of surface learning. Dominated by central policies that are educationally superficial. Reflecting a siege mentality at times – and with some justification! Education lecturer

Government should get off the backs of teachers and ensure that school inspections are less frequent, more constructive and much less stressful Parent

each school needs to have more control over its priorities and should be allowed to pursue them if they can be justified Retired school senior manager

Crisis management is over burdening teachers with repetitive paperwork Teacher/Parent

I would like to see a profession in control of its own destiny. One which is consulted on and involved in curriculum change, when that change is

necessary, but is in a position to say when that change is not necessary
Teacher

I would like to see teachers becoming experts in learning again rather than being deliverers of someone else's content School senior manager/parent

Fears were even expressed that externally enforced rigidity and redistribution of teaching duties and lack of appreciation was, or would soon be, driving many more experienced older teachers out.

The constraints of the 'frameworks' suit strategists but the passion has gone as the older teachers who worked with their hearts as well as their heads are moving on Teacher

Giving the best bits of the job (the children) to Classroom Assistants will drive many more out of the profession Teacher

I hope the teaching force of 2010 are better paid, respected and given more credit for their hard work and dedication. If so I might just remain one of them Experienced teacher

Surviving the crisis

In spite of all the criticisms and obstacles highlighted above, there were strong signs that, for many, the standing of the profession itself remained high. One teacher said;

My work as a teacher today is characterised by doubt and scepticism and regulation externally, but by care, curiosity and passion internally Experienced teacher

A distinction was made between the profession's standing amongst government and its standing amongst the general public and more specifically, parents. A strong degree of support from the general public and parents was recognised fairly consistently. Where a feeling of public support was not explicitly stated, public sympathy frequently was, with the notion of success in the face of government adversity implicit in many responses.

In the views of parents, [the standing of the profession is] generally good. In the view of 'managers' – governmental LEA or in school – always 'never good enough' Trainee teacher

Most parents remain realistic and faithful but are leaning towards the unachievable hype and expectations paraded by vote thirsty government School senior manager

I find it constantly surprising that there are so many great teachers given that the pay and conditions are so bad HE student

Viewed as a selfless or martyr type role Experienced teacher

Support for teachers was underscored by those commentators who believed that that teacher's skills should not be emphasised as an area of future development should not be put on teacher's skills. They saw current skills as adequate.

I don't believe that there is a great problem with knowledge, skills attitudes and abilities. We need to leave behind the technocratisation of the profession and look at ourselves as agents of social improvement School senior manager

In the main [future teachers will require], the same knowledge, skills, attitudes and abilities which good teachers have always possessed Teacher

Looking forward

This degree of support was made all the more promising by the considerable number of respondents who felt that the standing of teaching had turned a corner and was beginning to improve.

Hopefully, just past an all time low Teacher trainer

Probably better than five years ago Educational consultant

The general public view the teaching profession more favourably than they did ten years age Teacher

Looking to the future, further affirmation of this new confidence could be seen. In reference to the skills needed by the teacher of the future, answers frequently suggested a need for a capacity to think about the bigger picture. This indicates a belief that teachers will be more empowered to contribute to future decision making.

The ability to reflect on practice and ask questions about teaching and learning that go beyond how to make the government's agenda work Former teacher/Teacher trainer

The ability to analyse and be critical in a positive environment. Head of LEA Teaching services

A capacity for critical thinking about ideas and initiatives in education; skills of handling change Teacher trainer

Envisioning a better profession in 2010

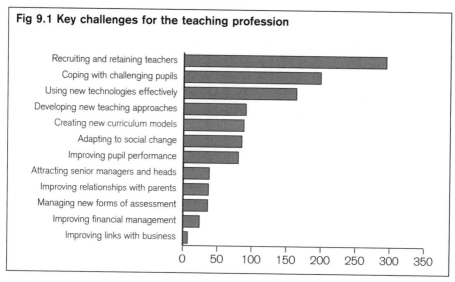

Fig 9.1 Key challenges for the teaching profession

Asked to select from a list, respondents were able to look forward in positive ways to the challenges to be faced over the next decade. The results are shown in Figure 9.1.

Respondents envisioned positive outcomes in the future resulting both from the successful overcoming of current difficulties discussed above, and also a whole array of changes resulting from new ways of thinking about teaching.

Benefits of overcoming current problems

Empowering teachers

There was a strong evidence that teacher empowerment was seen as more than an end in itself and that restoring teacher's abilities as agents of change would encourage more creativity, innovation and diversity in education in the future.

A profession that is able to make its own decisions about how it teaches. This will promote a context in which schools can again be different from each other and parents and children will have some kind of choice HE lecturer/parent

I would be keen to see increased creativity amongst teachers – perhaps restructuring the outcomes to which they must presently conform (eg results, exclusion figures, etc) to incorporate 'softer' outcomes as well Research and information officer

Free to return to inventive and exciting curriculum development Teacher

Further, it was felt that asserting teacher confidence and would allow teachers to provide a more flexible, high quality service. This would thereby increase professionalism.

Professional. One which engenders a common set of moral standards, self-confidence and the ability to articulate meaning clearly in all its learners Manager in FE

A vibrant robust autonomous group of professionals, confident in their professional knowledge, skills and understanding and in their recognition by society...and committed to their continuing professional development Teacher trainer

A more mobile professional group. Moving flexibly between more educational units Reading recovery tutor

Leaving targets behind

A rolling back of what has been described as 'crisis management' and decreased emphasis on mechanisms for testing standards was seen to have a number of benefits for future teaching. In the short term, respondents envisioned a profession that has time to be more child-orientated or even child-led.

A group whose first and, perhaps only, question will be, 'How will this aid my students?' Teacher

One that balances standards with the needs of youngsters Retired school senior manager

*Teachers in the future need to be positive about children and involve children
more in the decision making process in a school – not in a tokenistic way but
with real influence over things that are important to them* Experienced teacher

Looking more to the long term, a learning culture which revolved less around meeting
targets was connected with a notion of a profession which draws on a broad range of
recruits with diverse backgrounds, ages and skills. This was sometimes seen to require
more flexible working approaches.

It should be seen as a profession for intelligent, imaginative people of all ages
Speech therapy student on school placement

*We would like many more teachers in the future but they may not all have a
PGCE and work permanently in schools* Engineering Employers' Federation

Fewer teachers but with a greater variety of experiences and abilities
Teacher/Parent

More teachers who have worked outside education before they enter teaching
Parent governor

*A flexible profession where teachers came from a greater variety of
backgrounds* School governor

Conflicting opinions were expressed however on the issue of the level of academic
accomplishment which should be expected of teachers.

*I would like to see well qualified staff but with an emphasis on the skills of
teaching not so much the academic background* Teacher

In the top third of graduates in their subjects from top class universities
Researcher

*A good honours degree – if the profession is to become a real profession
again, then only people with first or second class honours degrees should be
accepted* School senior manager

Well qualified but degree subject should not matter as much Trainee teacher

*More varied. Less emphasis on good honours graduates – especially for less
academic kids* Parent governor

New ways of thinking about teaching

For many, envisioning a better profession in the future entailed more fundamental questioning of the contexts in which teachers see their work, leading to new ideas for changing practice.

Considering context

Taking first the question of context, many respondents felt that in order to make teaching more relevant there was a need for teachers to be less introspective and view themselves as situated within a broader modern social context. There was a hope expressed that in the future, teachers would see themselves and their students as integral parts of wider environments and communities. In one sense this meant seeing themselves as part of an extended learning community.

> *A profession that acknowledges that we are part of a huge learning community and that we can all learn in many different ways and circumstances* School senior manager

> *Teachers should be viewed as the portal to learning* Teacher

> *The other important factor is to lose the idea that learning will take place within defined age limits (5-16, 18 or 21) and realise that learning will be a life-long skill and re-training will be a fact of life for most people* Lecturer in education

> *Teachers must learn to take account of prior learning (and learning out of school which currently gets little or no recognition)* University senior manager working in education

In another sense, the communities referred to were local or physical communities. This meant recognition of the factors in the external environment as drivers of learning needs and a greater recognition that children will form the basis of tomorrow's society.

> *A teaching practice driven as much by strong community links and awareness as by evidence* Education lecturer/Parent

> *I would like to see teachers who were vibrant, fully contributing to the social order and, producing individuals who have a sense of intellectual responsibility and curiosity about the world* HE course leader

We need to develop an approach to social improvement and see ourselves as key players in that game School senior manager

They must develop a clear understanding of the concept of sustainable development in order to allow them to develop the whole child; to encourage children to take part in prudent decision making and adept their role as citizens for the future County council officer providing a service to schools

Teachers should see themselves as a higher form of community worker, interesting themselves in students' lives and being able to direct their academic development on a more individual basis HE student

Changing practice

The consideration of context places a whole new set of delivery challenges on teachers. Following from recognition of teachers and students as part of a wider community, the need to involve the community in education was highlighted. This need could be seen as partially served by the recruitment of teachers from more diverse backgrounds as described above. In other instances, it could be served by improving relations with outsiders or, more radical recommendations for bringing non-teachers into education and actually changing teaching practice.

I would like to see more involvement in the community, and with local business Teacher

Teachers in the future should have the capacity to liase with other professional disciplines – medical, religious, legal etc Teacher governor

There should be more flexibility of terms and conditions so that citizens play their part as teachers, eg two half-days a week alongside other employment, and teachers play their part as citizens, because they're not bound to 20 hours per week of contact time Teacher

A greater willingness to 'open' up the school to more people Parent

Teachers, and their schools should be more engaged with their communities which would tend towards smaller schools and sites (perhaps facilitated by technology or even the sense that some children could attend more than one school at a time, depending on their needs) School governor

Schools should build relationships with employers and companies wherever possible, including opening the doors to people who have relevant experience and knowledge to share but who may not have a PGCE Engineering Employers' Federation

Encourage citizens to see as a civic duty their involvement in the process of 'education, education, and education' Experienced teacher

Thinking about teaching in the context of the modern environment led some respondents to advocate a total re-think of the curriculum and modes of assessment. Many comments reflected a belief that the current curriculum is outdated, narrow and places too much emphasis on knowledge and not enough on thought process.

There are real problems with our system of education because it is basically unchanged over the past century. We must accept that its current rate of change is too slow for modern society Trainee teacher

We must concentrate on the needs of process learning rather than product to ensure that our children get the strategies and skills necessary to perform numerous tasks. Educators alike need to acknowledge, that the needs of future generations will be contingent upon providing strategies to adequately handle varying circumstances Experienced teacher

We must look to the future and produce a curriculum for the 21st century Teacher governor

Completely overhaul the current 5 key stage curriculum, which culminates in academic exams, in order to provide basic skills education through traditional subjects early on, as usual, but to work with businesses to provide apprentice opportunities for 14-16 year old who are ill suited to GCSEs. GNVQ teacher

By the year 2010, I would hope that we have all matured enough to dump the politics and apply the science to those factors which affect and often severely limit, achievement, I would hope there is more flexibility in the curriculum Experienced teacher

Outmoded curriculum models Education lecturer

Finally, some comments reflected an opinion that new ways of contextualising teaching would also demand a re-think of teaching and learning methodologies to incorporate less knowledge-based approaches.

> *Learning methodologies are archaic and irrelevant. Information gathering is not education; we are drowning in the stuff* Experienced teacher

> *In the future the main move will be away from a knowledge based process to a cognitive process which will also change the nature of assessment as well as learning* Lecturer in education

> *I would like a sea-change in the advancement of new methods of teaching, particularly based on brain-based research: children need to be taught how their brains work and how best to maximise their potential, instead of being left with information overload* Recently qualified teacher

Knowledge, skills, attitudes and abilities of the future teacher

A more empowered, less target orientated profession which operates within, and in collaboration with, a rapidly changing environment will have to constantly take on board new knowledge, skills, attitudes and abilities. Recognition of need for constant renewal was given by the frequent call for teachers to be given the time and space for continuing professional development.

> *Long established staff need time to update their skills* Teacher/School senior manager

> *Treat the first 3 to 4 years of new teachers' careers as a distinct stage of further professional development, with a guaranteed entitlement to reduced timetables, opportunities to work with teachers in other schools or contexts to develop their understanding of best practice; meet regularly with peers to sustain a reflective approach to practice* University-based teacher

> *Teachers are expected to keep up with the changing curriculum update skills and teach full time... Teachers should be given time to develop as teachers and to look at updating there skills every two years and be paid for this time* Teacher

Building on future visions described above, respondents showed the need for a renewed profession which puts emphasis on new types of qualities.

Taking on new contexts

Changing students

Given the enormous socio-cultural changes that continue to occur, many stressed the importance for future teachers of gaining the knowledge and skills to deal with the increasingly complex needs and problems of students. This could involve more sociological and psychological focus in training or improved mechanisms for dealing with difficult students.

> *I think that as society is changing so rapidly at the moment, teachers will need to have studied sociology at a deeper level in order to connect properly with their students* Experienced teacher

> *The teacher of the future needs to know more about what is important to his/her student. This might include new media, drug use and group dynamics, especially the problem of managing bullying* Experienced teacher

> *Greater cultural understanding as our students become more and more diverse* Teacher

> *Ways of coping with the changing nature of childhood and parenting* Parent

> *Ability to enthuse, entertain and maintain the interest of a generation with a smaller concentration span* Teacher

> *A knowledge of how to help children become emotionally literate and able to control their anger* Teacher

> *We will need more back up and procedures when dealing with the increasingly difficult students encountered* Teacher

> *Forethought as unfortunately more and more instances are arising of teachers being sued etc for errors of judgement etc* Trainee teacher

Technological society

The need to improve technological skills and adopt positive attitudes toward new learning tools was consistently emphasised. This was seen as crucial in dispelling negative, anachronistic images of teachers and also for adapting methods to meet the new, broader based, learning agenda.

A modern forward thinking technologically aware profession which has awareness and understanding *of modern society's needs* Teacher/Parent

So the future teacher must be a person who knows about the scientific developments, different methods of teaching, psychology of the learner, and should give importance to human values Teacher

Where most people are excited by new technologies, rather than afraid of them Teacher

Government must fund training for teachers and new technologies so that all schools can develop a new approach Senior school manager

I believe that in the next ten years our teachers will be fewer in number and have a greater need for ICT skills as more an more resources will be available for learning and testing on-line. I think that the government can help by providing funding and time for teachers to keep abreast of these new skills as well as ensuring that teacher training is kept to a very high standard right through our education system from nursery to HE Experienced teacher

Taking on new practices

Adaptability and flexibility

Accepting that the rate of change in the external environment is set to continue, and hence the flow of new teaching practices, teachers of the future will need the adaptability and flexibility to handle change. Support for continual professional development was supplemented by the view that teachers must start seeing themselves as learners as well as their students.

Future teachers should have strength, patience and the ability to dance on a moving carpet Teacher/Governor

Future teachers must be fast and adaptable learners School senior manager

They must have the skills of handling change Teacher trainer

Being in touch with new teaching and learning styles. It is important as a teacher not to get stuck teaching one way – trying out new techniques is a quality of a good teacher Trainee teacher

A force which is far more flexible, where there are a far greater number of educators with clearly defined separate roles but where people move between roles during their career Non-teacher working in school

In some instances, adaptability and flexibility were also seen as crucial in adopting new, cross-curricular teaching practices.

We need to have our skills base increased and our cross-curricular approaches consolidated in the curriculum Teacher

Teachers must start looking at cross-curricular links so that children see the relevance in what they are covering School senior manager

Must be able to be a team player, able to share skills and resources. Must have feet in tradition and eyes and ears for new initiatives they can adapt for use in their subjects that they feel comfortable with Teacher governor

Teachers as managers and specialists

In contrast, a different view of how the role of teachers would develop attached importance to honing more specific skills. Many respondents supported, or at least saw as inevitable, the notion of a future where teachers are fewer and many of the supervisory and more basic teaching tasks are left to teaching assistants. In these cases, the need for the profession to improve managerial skills and develop specialist expertise was highlighted.

Fewer, more professional teachers supported by more teaching assistants Parent governor

Experts who can be called upon as needed Parent

I think that teachers will become managers of large numbers of children. The real teaching will be done by class room assistants Reading recovery tutor

They will need some management skills to be able to manage a budget and support staff Teacher

I also think that there needs to be room to allow teachers to specialise more in the primary sector Teacher

The managerial role was also seen as advantageous to those who stressed the need for children to become autonomous learners.

> *If pupils are to become autonomous learners teachers need to work towards that with them in every possible way... Teachers will need to learn how to use more effectively a range of support staff – eg technicians, clerical/communications officers, data processing officers* Experienced teacher

Teachers as enablers

Underpinning all of these new roles for teachers was a sense that in the future teachers should be see themselves as enablers. As their role expands beyond its traditional remit of information dissemination, they will need to acquire and develop their capacities as facilitators of learning.

> *Above all, the ability to enable students to find information. The ability to transmit it will/should be redundant* School senior manager

> *Teachers need to learn to show kids how to find things out for themselves ...to be creative with the advantages of new technology rather than passive learners* University senior manager working in education

> *The teacher of the future will be just a senior friend of the student who has more knowledge in his subject and by virtue of being experienced. He only facilitates and guides a student for developing independent critical thought* School senior manager

10. Reinventing the teacher: the impact of pervasive technology
Chris Yapp[1]

The time is September 2010. Elene and Attila are taking the twins Peter and Oliver for their first day at St Graham's school, Ringshall in Hants, a proud moment in any parent's life. They have with them the parental contract that opens the individual learning account, (ILA) for each of the boys.

They meet the new Headteacher Julie Kirsch, who goes through the contract with them. Attila is of Hungarian descent and Elene of Norwegian extraction. The new contract, which covers the years of compulsory education, obliges the school to provide two modern foreign languages of pupil choice, among other entitlements over the boys' period at the school. All languages of the EU countries, along with languages of the local community, are available to parents on request. With Hungary's vote to join the EU in the previous summer, Hungarian is now on the list.

The Headteacher proudly announces that this means that the school will now be teaching thirty languages to its 250 pupils, a far cry from what was possible when she started teaching. She tells the parents that she will contact the LEA, the Language Education Authority, to identify the teachers and resources available for Hungarian.

Elena asks about the optional Spanish at 11, for which a parental contribution is required. The school will email the details in the next week. She is happy. Attila asks what will happen if he moves his job as he may do in the next two years. He is told that the Language contract will be transferred along with the resources, if this is necessary. The procedures have been in place for two years and work well.

They leave the boys to start their schooling.

Introduction

The story above describes a vision of a more flexible and personalised education service that will deliver world class outputs for the new society and economy. Whether you believe the story or not, or believe that it might be possible but not until 2020, bear with me for a little while. What the story illustrates is that the impact of ICT in education does not start and stop with a teacher in a classroom. It also impacts the organisation of the school itself, along with the supporting agencies of education such as local authorities and indeed the overall system at the regional and national level.

The above story is entirely feasible, though the timing may be difficult to achieve. The approach is very different from current practice, but many of today's teachers will be working in schools in 2010. Also, some of the pupils in school today will be teachers by that time. In the rest of this chapter, I aim to provide a model for describing the role of teachers in a pervasive ICT environment and a look at the impact on teaching and learning. The influence that this will have on the training and development of a professional educational workforce will also be explored. In addition, I want to suggest how we start on the road towards implementing this model.

Learning on demand

Before dealing with the roles of teachers, I wish to outline here a series of thoughts about the system of education within which the teaching profession will operate by 2010. In practice, looking at other sectors that have been transformed by technology, we should by 2010 see serious transition in place, but it will take fifteen to twenty years for the kind of examples that I wish to describe here to be commonplace. What I have attempted to do is to look at a view of the top half of schools rather than just the leading edge, in order to identify that a critical mass has been established that will transform the rest of the sector over the next few years.

As technology becomes more and more pervasive, it is essential to understand the factors that distinguish those organisations that reap benefits from investment in technology and those that do not. If two schools invest the same amount on hardware, software and teacher training, will they get the same benefits? The answer is no.

What matters most is that the organisations that get the greatest benefits are those that can answer the question: 'In the light of ICT developments what can we now do that was not possible before and what can we do differently?'

Those that simply try to emulate on computers what they do currently are those that frequently fail to realise the benefits of ICT in quality, cost or performance. It was this recognition in the late 1980s to the term 're-engineering', in that the greatest benefits from new technologies are through the close integration of the organisational strategy to the managerial processes and then to ICT. That is to say, there is no direct link between ICT and strategy.

Successful deployment of ICT systems also has a number of key characteristics. The first is a move from supply-side push to user-pull. In manufacturing, for example, moving from manufacturing-to-stock to manufacturing-on-demand, or 'just-in-time' manufacturing. Technology is making possible David Blunkett's desire to 'put the learner at the heart of the system'. Much research into ICT's impact on learning has shown an increase in learner empowerment. This is essential if creativity is to be more central to the practice of education. Before they attend school, children learn through play and after graduation they go back to playing, but call it research. New technologies can enable schooling to become increasingly research-led not teaching led, without the downsides of the lack of rigour in many earlier experiments in child-centred learning.

Second, there is frequently a move away from the individual to small teamwork: a re-organisation of work. It is my contention that teamwork in teaching will be key to a world-class education system. It is presently undervalued in assessment of the current provision of both pupil and teacher performance.

Finally, there is a move increasingly towards fuzzy boundaries instead of silos. We are familiar with this in our every day life where cashback facilities in supermarkets have blurred banking and retailing. We will see blurring of boundaries between primary, secondary and tertiary institutions along with libraries and other educational facilities, to create networked learning communities. What often holds back discussions of 'classrooms of the future' is that we still tend to lapse into a vision of schools as vertically-integrated organisations, with all available resources being 'owned' or 'employed' by the institution. This can lead to a simple definition of roles – teachers are people employed in schools, librarians in libraries and lecturers in colleges.

For these reasons, the model outlined in this paper is based on teamwork across multiple locations and organisations to deliver a system of learning on demand.

Looking at other sectors, this transition has typically taken twenty years or more to fully bed in under competitive pressure. My picture of 2010 is realistic if education can manage change on a par with other large-scale institutions. My experience of the last decade shows no reason to believe that it will be slower.

Understanding teaching roles

Looking back to the early 1990s, I can remember many voices arguing that computers in education were a bad idea. In particular, the notion that 'education was not a factory' was used on me on a number of occasions. Unfortunately for too many, the experience of education is too much like an old factory run on Fordist lines.

A child enters the production line at four or five years old and is processed for a number of years, with those needing the most help leaving the production line earliest, labelled low-quality 'rejects'. This is Fordism. That the school day consists of a lesson of Geography followed by Maths and Literacy then RE, is a perfect example of the division of labour. I recognise that I exaggerate here for effect, but I would draw to the readers' attention that this model of factory is fifty years out of date. High productivity with technology is reflected in high-quality organisation.

There are two major problems that I wish to address before going into my analysis. First, a great fallacy is that:

New teacher = Old teacher + ICT

What concerns me is that training teachers in the use of ICT in their own curriculum areas should be the start of the transformation process, not its completion. The second problem is that the view that teachers will change from being a 'sage on the stage' to a 'guide on the side' as a reflection of the role of the technology in the teaching and learning processes.

Learning is, at its heart, a social and a socialising experience. Technology will have profound impacts on teaching and learning because it has profound impacts on the organisation of teaching and learning, not simply on the 'delivery' of lessons. In my discussions and observation of schools over the last five years, I have tried to discern a series of reasonably separable roles that teachers fulfil, to see whether it is practical for a richer professional model to exist than teacher plus classroom assistant or teacher and paraprofessional.

What I propose is a series of teaching roles which I will list and then explore to flesh out what the new model might be like in action. These roles are as follows:

- Master Teachers/Narrators

- Learning Resource Managers

- Learning Coaches

- Curriculum Managers/Agents

- Staff Development Managers

- Advice and Guidance Professionals

- Educational Administrators

- Trainees

Some may look at this and ask why it requires ICT. Surely this could be done anyway. I wish to be clear that the subtlety of the link is not lost. Earlier, in describing on demand systems, it is important to note that manufacturing 'just-in-time' was created as a principle without computers. However, it is the development of technology that has made it increasingly economic and scaleable. While most people focus on applications of ICT – the short-term costs and benefits – it is the long-term impact on organisational design that is most significant.

Organisational design is simple in principle. First, divide the organisation up into tasks (Primary, Secondary, English, PE for example). Second, put in the co-ordinating mechanisms (for example, reporting, monitoring, and quality control). Most technologies impact either the doing of work or it's co-ordination. The significance of ICT is that it impacts both dimensions of organisational design.

In the long run, pervasive technology offers the potential to re-engineer significantly what is done in the classroom, in the community and at regional and national level. This is far from risk free and requires long-term commitment.

Let us look at each of these roles in turn.

Master teachers/narrators

This is the most obvious role, and is that of the 'subject' expert. Given the increased availability of digital learning resources, the role will change over a period of time. The ability to teach, inspire, and lecture will remain central, but with the content available digitally, the increased importance will be placed on context and joining knowledge together to create learning constructs. It will also be possible for the best teachers to be available remotely to a range of schools so that small rural schools, for instance, will not necessarily be disadvantaged by teaching shortage in certain subjects. Also, the ability of experts in museums, galleries, libraries and industry to make their expertise available to schools with technology will increase the expertise available to all schools and children.

Learning resource managers

With the increased availability of digital learning materials, the role of the school librarian along with Design and Technology technicians, ICT support staff and other paraprofessionals will evolve into this new role of creating learning environments for the students. For example, an education broadcast on history and its associated web site might be linked to web sites relevant to the local community to create rich navigable systems for learners. These teachers must be able to understand when physical or virtual resources best support the learner. For instance, in a chemistry experiment, when will the real lab environment be needed and how can a virtual simulation enhance or prepare a learner for the lab environment?

These staff will also be responsible for the introduction of external initiatives, evaluating and employing resources offered by public, private and voluntary sectors.

Educators would be expected to develop the idea of teachers as content creators. I see this as a role shared with master teachers. Let me illustrate this by example. In a revision of the science curriculum at secondary level a new topic is introduced to the syllabus. There is a shortage of material on this area and many teachers need to be trained in the new subject. This is of course an area where there is a specialist shortage, so taking teachers out of the classroom for training may exacerbate the problem. I would foresee a group of master teachers and learning resource managers spending a period at a Teacher Training establishment. The group would work together on the new area and create a curriculum resources web site. After the work is completed this site would go live along with chat rooms to allow for the creators to stay in touch and develop the site based on experience in the classroom. This resource would then be available to any teacher in the country. The teachers involved in the creation of this site could be eligible for additional payments. This type of approach could also be used by museums and galleries, to ensure that the sites they create are both educationally sound and relevant to the curriculum. Such research and peer development would mark the maturity of the virtual teacher centre. Moving from virtual teacher centres to virtual teacher networking, is again an important feature of the move towards a more dynamic professional model.

Learning coaches

This group is key to flexibility and made up of specialists in transferable skills. In the new environment, all children have special learning needs. This group would be responsible for the identification of individual learning styles and needs. The introduction of 'thinking skills', Gardner's multiple intelligence theory and other approaches would be facilitated by the learning coaches. A child working in a group on a Geography project who needed help with spreadsheets would seek help from a learning coach. In the early years, these professionals would be responsible for early identification of barriers to learning, and working with the learning resource managers would identify resources appropriate to the condition.

As children mature, the learning coaches would concentrate increasingly on study skills, communication skills and personal knowledge including teamwork skills.

Curriculum managers/agents

Putting the learner at the centre of the system means the evolution of the national curriculum to a national framework for personal curricula, benchmarked to international standards. It will, in my view, be increasingly hard to assess by age. For example, there are six year-olds in my village with their own web sites alongside fifteen year-olds with no access at home. How a system that tests this group at fourteen is fair on either group is a moot point.

In the way that actors or authors have agents, professionalising the learning environment for the learner will entail working between the agent and the student to agree both what is studied and the targets to be set. This 'learning prospectus' is then available to the other teaching roles, to parents and later on to employers as a record of achievement, progress file, and as an electronic CV.

Staff development managers

It is often said that if a teacher of 1900 were catapulted into a class of 2000 they would recognise it and be able to perform, unlike, for instance, a surgeon or a train driver. If there is some truth in this, we need to understand why. Over the last twenty years our knowledge of the human brain, the way it works as well as our understanding of language acquisition and other matters has grown enormously. However, it is also fair to say that there is much left to be learned. Yet, how much of this has been taught to teachers? How much of the educational research based on what works has been translated into general practice? In my model, teachers are themselves viewed as lifelong learners and the role of the staff development manager is to act as a bridge between the external knowledge base and the learning needs of the other roles.

Teachers would also be responsible for identification and training outreach and community staff who contribute to schooling including religious leaders, police and health professionals.

The approach outlined above for virtual teacher networking in the section on learning resource managers could build a closer connection between the educational research field and classroom practitioners.

Advice and guidance/counselling professionals

Careers advice is an obvious example of this teaching role. I would broaden this out to cover a wider range of advice and guidance roles, including personal and sexual health, drugs, religious, spiritual, and family guidance.

The increasing divorce rate and changing family structures have increased the pressure on teachers over the last generation to provide caring services in schools of greater diversity and complexity.

This in turn leads to the potential for greater 'joined-up working' with other children's professionals. The development of common curriculum and qualifications within these areas would allow Youth and Social workers to move into education with much lower barriers and allow teachers similar opportunities to transfer to other 'children's' professions during their careers.

Educational administrators

Excellent administration is an essential part of any world-class education system. These professionals would be responsible for the oversight of progress files and assessment of school quality reporting. They would be responsible for identifying both individual and organisational issues and improvement plans. According to the story at the start of this chapter, they would also be responsible for matters such as school transfers and the individual learning accounts.

It would be increasingly possible for Ofsted to move from the somewhat monolithic audits externally imposed on schools to targeted interventions at a school's request. For instance, if a school was having difficulty, say, in written English with a particular age group, while improving elsewhere, then an Ofsted specialist could be called in to help. The move from an externally imposed to an internally driven model of self-evaluation would do wonders for morale in the teaching profession. As long as this was done along the lines of principle 'intervention in inverse proportion to achievement'; and then this should not compromise commitment to standards. Ofsted staff would increasingly be drawn from serving teachers. I would see the Advanced Skills Teachers; for instance, earning salary top-ups when called in to support another educational establishment.

Trainees

Any system will, of course, need new blood entering it. In this model, I would see new teachers starting on a 'GP'-type course for teachers before choosing whether to go towards a specialist role, as described in the preceding paragraphs, or a GP-style teaching role.

Some readers, looking at the above, will find that there is little or nothing new. I agree! The problem that I see on my visits to schools is that individual teachers are attempting to perform all these roles. This lies at the heart of the teacher stress and motivation issues in many schools. The job today is too broad and complex to be done by a real human being. Even compared to another stressful position, that of the health GP, the role is complex and the backup to front line staff is underdeveloped compared to medicine (though medicine has its own problems!). What I am suggesting is that individual teachers and indeed individual institutions need to map their needs and plans against the roles outlined. What I am not suggesting is that teachers should be pigeonholed into one or other of these roles. They should be encouraged to develop both depth and breadth in the roles, and also to work with others as needed to create a rich learning environment.

Impact on the organisation of schooling

Some years ago, I remember Sir Christopher Ball suggesting that the ideal teacher to pupil ratio could be estimated by doubling the child's age. I think that this is not a bad starting point.

What I envisage is a fall in the teacher pupil ratio in early years with an increase later in secondary years. While all the roles are needed in all schools, there would be different patterns with age, with learning coaches needed most at the earliest stages of schooling. I would suggest that primary schooling would continue to have a tightly focussed common curriculum, but that increased resources would be used to introduce flexibility into learning approaches, creativity and early diagnosis of strengths and weaknesses. On top of basic standards for literacy and numeracy, the transition from primary to secondary education would be based around the young person having acquired a group of basic learning-to-learn, study and thinking skills.

As the secondary curriculum becomes more flexible and personalised, curriculum agents become more central to the system. Also, the advice and guidance professionals would tend to be more concentrated in secondary education.

What is clear is that this kind of system cannot be achieved on a school by school basis within a reasonable period of time, either educationally or economically. For this reason, I would suggest that the Education Action Zone model is of the right scale to balance flexibility and comprehensive provision. The typical EAZ is around twenty schools with around two to three secondary schools and fifteen or more primary schools. For the system to be comprehensive, the components should be specialised. Michael Barber has used the famous '1066 and all that' description of the Cavaliers (wrong but romantic) and Roundheads (right but repulsive) to describe much of educational policy debate. What he has described as the goal is to be right and romantic, or in educational speak, equality with diversity. Restructuring the teaching profession along the lines envisaged here would contribute to making that a realistic proposition.

Impact on teacher training and development

What is clear is that if this model is to be in any way implemented the Teacher Training institutions and the General Teaching Council need to be central to fleshing out the recruitment, training and development implications.

Earlier, I described the trainee role as starting with a general practitioner course to get a view of the overall system and a personal profile and development plan agreed with the trainee teacher. This then becomes their own professional progress file, against which new depth and breadth of competencies can be accumulated over time.

Importantly, I would envisage the greatest change in professional development rather than initial teacher training. I gave an example of roles working together in the creation of content with a teacher training establishment, or possibly a museum or gallery. In the area of vocational training, this role might be extended to working with companies to create learning resources pertinent to real-world problem solving. This would be motivational for specialists where they have little day to day contact with other experts in their own sphere of knowledge.

I find it easier to split the current ITT and INSET into ITT, Early Career Development (ECD) and Continuing Professional Development (CPD). In ITT, the teacher would cover the 'GP' model of width across the roles and understanding how the overall approach works. In ECD, there would be a plan to experience the roles that the teacher is keen and able to develop so that the distinctive competencies are developed and any weaknesses tackled. The move from ECD to CPD would occur once the individual was clear as to whether they wished to become a specialist in one or more of the roles, or develop a career across a broader portfolio of the roles.

Also, the link between INSET and educational researchers in the Teacher Training institutions could help the goal of teaching becoming a research-based profession. By working with industry, museums and galleries, the researchers would also have the opportunity to broaden their horizons with a better understanding of the kind of world children are being educated for. One of the frustrations of the current approach is that, rightly or wrongly, education in the classroom is seen as distant from real-world learning. This broader link between industry and schools of education in HE would help to break down many myths about education.

First steps

I do not see the roles outlined above as a pay scale with master teachers being paid more than learning coaches, for example. I do see the development of depth and/or breadth as part of the pay scales, but I am agnostic on relative values of the different roles.

What I would see as the first key step towards this type of approach is the development of an appraisal and development process for current teachers in order to understand what we currently have as well as where the gaps are both personally and across the profession. I also feel that giving a teacher a broader set of criteria than the current Ofsted rating of one through five is more realistic, motivational and helpful to target learning plans for individuals and school communities. Also, the use of staff in other organisations, such as libraries and museums, if more clearly co-ordinated could add value to mainstream staff in schools. The example of joined-up professionalism with youth and social work lower barriers for mobility across the professions to good effect.

The framework as outlined above could also be used in research to diffuse what works across the broader provision from early successful pilots. Obviously, the framework would itself evolve over time. Indeed if it did not, it would run the risk of becoming a new set of silos.

Some key issues have not been addressed here. For example, the link between the 'new teacher' and new models of curriculum and assessment are vital. Joining up the many initiatives in education to create an initial template for a system of learning on demand is central to building a practical pathway to delivering a world class education service. This holistic approach to policy, supported by individual short-term actions, is essential if we are to build a scaleable education service economically, rather than just a few good examples followed by exhortation to the rest.

Summary and conclusion

What I have attempted to do above is to describe what might happen to school age education as technology becomes increasingly pervasive, borrowing from experience in other sectors. As an approach, this is open to criticism on a number of fronts. For example, the role definitions themselves are open to challenge.

However, I would hope that the kind of approach outlined above would make change management in education both more effective and humane. The new teaching roles could contribute to morale within the profession and a world-class approach to teaching in a pervasive technology environment.

Endnote

1   This chapter was published in an earlier format by IPPR in ICTeachers (2000).

11. Chasing the wrong dream? The quest for teacher professionalism in the age of the citizenship school

Tony Breslin

Teachers as under-paid, under-valued and under pressure

Self perceptions and shifting realities

A cursory reading of the press or taking part in a conversation in almost any staffroom is likely to reveal that, whatever their standing among others, teachers feel themselves to be under paid and under valued for the work that they do. Certainly, as a working teacher for over a decade, my own impression is one of an occupational group constantly battling with a status crisis that serves to undermine its own practice. In this context, the regular and extensively reported pronouncements of the former Chief Inspector for Schools, Chris Woodhead, and a succession of Secretaries of State for Education about incompetent teachers, the emergence of Ofsted, the arrival of the National Curriculum and benchmark testing, the publication of school examination results, unfavourable comparisons with overseas competitors, the emergence of the targets culture, and the focus on children's and parents' rights (Wilby 1997) all contribute to a moral panic around teachers' and schools' performance and a culture of blame such that, in the terminology of one eminent commentator, teachers have become electricity substations, feeding out knowledge that has been generated elsewhere, but still getting the blame for low voltage (Kogan 1997 cited in Wilby 1997). The recent addition of performance management, while coming with a cash reward has done little to alleviate the problem.

Behind this moral panic lies, as is so often the case, the perception of a golden past. In this era teachers were, apparently, highly thought of in society, held a particular status within their local communities and were masters within the classroom. While some have questioned exactly how golden this age was, and, indeed, who it was golden for, the image is a powerful one and is comparable to that constructed by Braverman (1974) of the skilled manual worker. Critics of Braverman have suggested that any process of deskilling and proletarianisation is far more complex than his image of a linear and chronological reduction of craft artisans to production line operatives. And a similar point might be made about the evolution of the modern teacher. Thus, what teachers, government ministers and the general public, in their different ways, believe teachers once were retains an importance whatever the objectivity of the view and the spin placed upon it.

The 'golden age' thesis used both by teachers and against them serves, then, to emphasise the extent of the current crisis around their status and identity. Certainly, whatever their recollection of the distant past, the experience of teachers over the past twenty-five years has been characterised by changing contexts and increased scrutiny. If occupational stability is the hallmark of personal security, teachers have experienced neither over the past two decades. Dating from James Callaghan's speech at Ruskin College, Oxford, the education service in the United Kingdom has seen a range of changes that have impacted directly on teachers and the contexts in which they operate. These shifting sands might be summarised in terms of three processes: routinisation, marketisation and casualisation.

Within this framework, the National Curriculum and the consequent focus on the generation of schemes of work, the meeting of attainment targets, the development of planned outcomes and their standardised assessment has introduced a formal routine to, and curtailed much of the autonomy around, teachers' classroom practice (Hoyle and John 1995). The claim that 'the teacher's classroom is his professional castle' (Wilby 1997) begins to look rather empty in the face of a standardised curriculum and testing regime. Coupled with the emergence, in the late 1980s, of 'directed time', the association of the teacher with the line operative begins to look less far fetched. Indeed, once the language of 'performance management' enters the frame, the Taylorite tradition appears complete in its re-emergence.

If the National Curriculum and directed time have been among those forces routinising the work of teachers, marketisation (Whitty 1997) has drawn teachers closer to the daily insecurities of the private sector workforce. Thus, the introduction of localised school management and the development of schools as quasi-businesses, with subject departments operating as 'cost centres' within them, has fundamentally altered the economic context within which teachers work. Teacher redundancies, or the threat of them, almost unheard of in earlier times, were a common feature of the early 1990s, and the replacement of older, more expensive staff with less expensive and experienced employees has become a standard, and rather more insidious, route to a goal based on common cost, rather than pedagogy. Moreover, the publication of inspection reports and examination results and the shift towards open enrolment, per capita funding and frameworks of parental choice (Ball *et al* 1995) have ensured that this marketisation is not a purely 'internal' phenomenon. With results published in the local and national press, and notions of 'successful' and 'failing' schools quickly enshrined in both political discourse and academic literature, education is becoming less a public issue and more a 'private consumption good' (Whitty 1997). As with all such goods, it appears that the more affluent and articulate are able to consume more and better (Ball *et al* 1995) such that 'poor schools' are left to serve the 'poor', for they can attract nobody else.

The third development of the context within which teachers work is the emergence of casualisation as a major employment form. It introduces the kind of labour flexibility to the classroom that multinationals have been busily developing in their workplaces over the last three decades, a flexibility that struggling schools with falling rolls and declining budgets are most likely to need, whatever the educational outcomes. This is now underway across three domains. Firstly, the increased use of supply staff, not simply to cover for daily absence but to fill posts for up to twelve months or more, and the emergence of national private sector supply agencies is creating an additional, marginalised, and non-unionised tier of non-contract staff on the fringe of school and college life (Shilling 1991). Secondly, the emergence of a broader range of routes into the classroom, has, whatever its actual impact, served to support the idea that 'anybody can teach' and, as such, has both undermined and affronted professional claims (Barton *et al* 1994; Jenkins 1997). Thirdly, the increasing reliance on non-teaching staff to support curriculum delivery, especially in the primary classroom and in vocational areas, raises questions about the centrality of teachers' professional practice to what goes on in the classroom. The revolutionary impact of classroom assistants in many primary classrooms and the growing use of mentors in primary and secondary settings reveals the potential of involving non-teachers in the classroom. However, when teachers feel that they are under valued, under paid and under pressure and when the newcomers are perceived to be 'filling in' at a time of teacher shortage, their welcome is likely to be cool indeed.

It is the joining of these three processes – routinisation, marketisation and casualisation – with an environment characterised by the increased surveillance of what teachers do and how they do it that does most to undermine both the perceived public status and the personal self esteem of teachers. Here, the formation of Ofsted and the launch of 'league' tables in the early 1990s has been a catalyst for establishing a new, if flawed, transparency around the practice of teachers and schools. Moreover, it has masked an ideological shift to a focus on teachers and schools as the major reason for the success or otherwise of students. Where previously home background, parental income or cultural attitudes might have been offered as explanations for poor educational performance, they are seen now as no more than challenges which the teacher is expected to meet. In recent years the debate has been closed and teachers have been castigated for raising such explanations, accused of promoting them as excuses for poor performance. In fairness, the focus on parents by the current Secretary of State for Education, Estelle Morris, that appears to be emerging as this chapter goes to press may herald a change of direction, or at least of scapegoat. However, it does little strategically to challenge the culture of teacher blame that teachers, or at least those in 'challenging' schools, have felt to be dominant for the past decade.

This focus on teacher and classroom practice has had a broader impact. Some commentators (Barton *et al* 1994; Whitty 1997) have seen the shift to more school based training on PGCE courses and the introduction of objectified 'competencies' (Hustler and McIntyre 1996) as laying the foundations for an atheoretical approach to pedagogy such that:

...teachers focus on the development of craft skills rather than professional understanding

(Barton *et al* 1994)

Within this framework Barton and his co-authors cite Buchmann and Schville in their support:

First-hand experience is seen as the best teacher. It is trusted implicitly as both the means and the content of education. It is supposed to be down-to-earth, 'personal and practical'.

(Barton *et al* 1994)

Given the introduction of 'performance management', the concentration on competency in training, the focus on classroom performance during inspection and moves to 'fast track' 'bad' teachers out of the profession, it is not surprising that teachers have at times felt, in one writer's phrase, 'vilified by the state' such that there is 'no vision, only failure' (Lawn 1996). Even the creation of the General Teaching Council (GTC) seems clouded with suspicion and carries the allegation of poor practice. Thus, when the then School Standards' Minister, Stephen Byers (1997) conceded that 'teachers have for too long now had too little say in how their profession develops' he could only do so while qualifying this by asking for a GTC that involves parents, governors and representatives from industry and the churches before clarifying more boldly what this body should not be:

We are not interested in a talking shop for teachers or a body to defend the way things are.

(Byers 1997)

Whatever the function of a GTC, it has yet to prove that it can offer teachers autonomy or that it can shield them from the type of attack that is implicit in Byer's statement. This ability to resist attack is a key explanation for the increasingly desperate quest by teachers to assert their professionalism, their professionality and their desire for further professionalisation.

Professionality, professionalism and professionalisation

Debates around teacher professionalism, professionalisation and professionality are riven with difficulties around the definition of the central concepts themselves. Apple (1997), Hoyle and John (1995) and Popkewitz (1994) all reflect on the persistent ambiguities in terminology that is continually under reappraisal and reconstruction. In this context, Hoyle and John's opening comment that 'professional is an essentially contested concept' is nicely understated. Moreover, the realisation that we are dealing not simply with the notion of 'professional' but with a set of distinct but related concepts – professional, professionality, professionalism, professionalisation – provides an indication of the complexity of the terms involved.

At a literal level, the term 'professional' can simply be taken to indicate an activity that brings payment. In turn, the fact that, as a society, we tend to express value in monetary terms indicates that those goods or services for which we are prepared to pay are of a higher value than those goods or services for which we are not. Professionals are paid, usually relatively well (except perhaps in public services such as teaching), and, therefore, professional practice is seen as valued practice. Thus, the professional footballer is presumed to be better than his amateur counterpart and the paid parliamentarian might be expected to display a greater level of competence than the unpaid councillor. Here, the concept of the 'professional job', as used, for example, by a building site manager inspecting the quality of a bricklayer's work is useful. The appraisal is not so much about the bricklayer's status but about the quality of their work, their competence in the task and their ability to reach targets. In short, the focus is on professionality (Hoyle and John 1995). The level of 'professionality' that an individual displays in their work can be applied to almost any given situation that requires the completion of a task or the delivery of a service.

Generally, though, the term professional has a more exclusive application (Abercrombie *et al* 1988; Ginsburg 1997). 'Professional' as an adjective, that is professional as professionality, may be shared by plumbers, footballers and cleaners to describe their performance in a given situation but 'professional' as a noun has long been applied to, if not deliberately colonised by, an exclusive cluster of white collar occupations: law, medicine and certain aspects of commerce and public service. Here, the professional is seen as a holder of formally qualified and officially accredited expertise. Through this expertise professionals hold authority, operate autonomously, secure relatively high levels of pay, experience comparatively good conditions of service and enjoy access to privileged knowledge both in a professional capacity and as part of a social network or as Popkewitz puts it:

> The label 'profession' is used by occupational groups to signify a highly trained, competent, specialised, and dedicated group that is effectively and efficiently serving the public good. But the label 'professional' is more than a declaration of public trust: it is a social category that also imputes status and privilege to an occupational group.

> (Popkewitz 1994)

Popkewitz's closing point has significance because it begins to clearly mark off the professional from other mortals; to be a 'professional' is to occupy a specific position in the social scale. This 'marking off' of professionals is critical to the argument that will be developed in due course for it helps to explain why such a status might be actively sought and why it may be singularly inappropriate for teachers, and other public servants, as an occupational status.

If the concepts of professional and professionality can be distinguished with some clarity, the distinction between these terms and *professionalism* is more subtle. Indeed, some writers claim or imply that professionalism and professionality are synonymous (Hoyle and John 1995). I want to argue to the contrary and propose that the level of exclusivity, and the ability to maintain this exclusivity, is at the core of the distinction. Thus, whereas the notion of professionality, as demonstrated above, might be applied to the performance of any individual worker, the notion of professionalism refers more narrowly to the expected behaviour of those who hold or claim professional status. Moreover, the trade union legislation introduced by the Thatcher governments, articulated as an attack on restrictive (rather than professional) practice, in the 1980s can be seen as having disabled non-professionals from developing and asserting something akin to this professionalism within their own occupational identities. Thus, while professionality can be claimed by all, professionalism has been reined in and reasserted as the preserve of professionals themselves.

Professionalism is, then, an attitudinal outlook, a way of engaging with the world rooted in one's occupational location and operationalised through a code of ethics, implicit and explicit, that derive from, and through, this location. Critically, in going beyond task or service competence to expected and accepted behaviour, the suggestion is that such 'behaviour' relates not only to task or service delivery but to the membership of the professional group. Moreover, not all of the norms, mores and rules of the professional group relate to delivery; some are distinctly about group membership itself.

In this context, the shift to competency-based approaches in teacher training and the focus on such competencies within appraisal and inspection frameworks identified earlier (Barton *et al* 1994; Whitty 1997) take on a particular importance. At one level, they can be seen as an attempt to insert professionality over professionalism and to aid the process of teacher deprofessionalisation in so doing. At another, they can be seen as providing a guarantee of substance that serves to underpin claims on professional status and the expression of professionalism. For while professionality ('doing a good job') does not necessarily lead to professional status and the assertion of professionalism, professionalism must be based on the ability to do such a job: professionality. *Professional status and the assertion of professionalism do not necessarily flow from professionality but cannot live without it.*

This distinction between professionality and professionalism offers a template for the battleground on which disputes about teacher status over the past two decades have been fought. In these disputes, teachers, individually and collectively, have sought to assert their status as professionals through, with one eye to the golden age, *reprofessionalising* their position within the occupational and social structure. Within this framework, and so as to clarify the definition of this final term, 'professionalisation' (or 'reprofessionalisation') describes the journey that teachers have attempted to make to realise the professional dream. Here, professionalisation is the occupational status to which teachers have clung serving once again as:

> ...a manifestation of the historical and social ambition of an occupational group to achieve status and a position in society.
>
> (Englund 1996)

It is to the appropriateness of this ambition that I now turn.

Professional identity as a double-edged sword

Conceptions of the classic 'profession' are inextricably bound up with the models of professionalism practised by those in the legal and medical professions. Pronouncements from key figures at the Teacher Training Agency and the GTC seem to emphasise this point with their focus on the explicit objective to make teaching one of the 'top three professions' within a framework where the other two are clearly law and medicine. Somerville (1986), citing Millerson (1964), is clear about the strategy being used here and observes that:

> Much of the conventional literature is characterised by what has been called a 'trait approach'. This begins by defining the characteristics of an ideal-typical profession and then becomes the measure by which other occupational groups aspiring to professional status are assessed.
>
> (Somerville 1986)

However, the fact that this ideal-typical model is essentially made up of 'elements abstracted from' established and classically framed professions, such as those developed around law and medicine, poses, for Somerville, a difficulty:

> No other occupational group, developing under different circumstances, is ever likely to duplicate these characteristics and, therefore, will always fail the test.
>
> (Somerville 1986)

If the status of the established professions remained intact, the pursuit of their professionalism, and all of its trappings, might at least be understandable. Thus, teachers might aspire to benefit from their rightful place in a traditional meritocracy, one in which the classic value consensus emerges: professionals gain public consent for both their endeavours and for the rewards that these endeavours bring through the marrying of their expertise to the altruistic inclinations that they display during the course of the working week.

The truth, though, is that the status of the established professions has never been as questioned as it is today and herein lies the first drawback of an occupational strategy based around teacher professionalisation: *professionals are losing their popularity*. The Teacher Training Agency's attempt to enhance the esteem in which teachers are held, and, as a consequence, to broaden the appeal of teaching as a career is laudable (Jenkins 1997) but it may be that the attempt to reposition teaching within the occupational hierarchy is misplaced, not least because it amounts to a pursuit of the professionalism bandwagon at precisely the time when its wheels appear to be coming off. Bottery (1996), Hoyle and John (1995) and Lunt (1997) have been among those to point out that, for professionals, the past decade has not been a good one. Moreover, the attacks have come from both left and right.

From the left, the longstanding criticism that the professions amount to a set of self serving and bourgeois groups closely aligned to the business classes and implicitly associated with the bureaucratisation that accompanies modernistic employment structures has been given new energy by the emergence of the green movement, the further development of feminism and the emergence of 'new age' approaches that draw on these trends. Thus, the emergence of 'alternative' medicine and the reappraisal of the medicalisation of events such as childbirth question the authority of a largely male professionalism (Davies 1996) and explicitly reject the impersonalism of those managerial structures that it operates within. In this respect, writers such as Schon (1983) acknowledge the emergence of a new phenomenon: the 'counter professional'. Seen, perhaps, first in the squatters' movement of the 1960s, the counter professional is epitomised in the 1990s eco-warrior and anti-roads protester, 'Swampy'; articulate, educated and of middle class background but questioning constantly the decisions and 'taken for granted' assumptions of 'professional society' and offering solutions that appear at least as sensible and considered as those that emerge from professional 'officialdom'.

From the right, market-focused strategies that are critical of unions, professional associations, cartels and, to some degree, certain forms of corporatism while focusing on accountability and client or customer empowerment have brought a populist angle to the attack on professionalism, one that New Labour has done little to distance itself from. In this context, Apple and Oliver (1996) describe how a community faced with an unresponsive local schooling authority 'become Right' as they struggle with a bureaucracy apparently more dedicated to protecting professional self-interest than promoting educational standards. As such, they offer a potent warning to those who foreground professionalisation ahead of educational outcomes or, indeed, its core professionality.

At the heart of these recent criticisms, then, lie well-established and more profound concerns about the practice of professionals that are *intrinsic* to professional practice itself. Critically, the allegations are that the process of professionalisation serves to distance the professional from the client and that it does so on the basis of self-interest. Bernard Shaw was able to talk about professionalism as a 'conspiracy against the laity' while Illich (1979) argues that professional groups capture and monopolise certain areas of knowledge, and practise and develop them to the advantage of the group to the disadvantage of everyone else (Gomm 1986). Whatever the extent of this distancing, of this 'marking off' of the professional from the mass (Parry *et al* 1974), it clearly does impact on the ability of professionals to provide service. In short, the expression of professionalism, because of the social distancing that this involves, undermines the very professionality on which the claim of professional status is based. Thus, this phenomenon of 'distancing' and subsequent social positioning opens up key tensions within the notion of professionalism, indeed questioning the concept's intellectual integrity, and provokes dilemmas for those occupational groups embarked upon strategies of professionalisation for while the practice of professionals is wrapped up in notions of service to the wider society, the professionals' reward is to be socially detached from this society. To put it bluntly, on their days off one might expect to find professionals with other professionals and not with the more disadvantaged of their client base.

Against this background, the spectre of enlightened self-interest haunts any claim of altruistic intent: personal reward is an intrinsic part of the professional's contract with his or her client and, thus, there is always the danger that when the promise of reward clashes with the promise of service, the former will emerge victorious, with the professional exercising a particular form of 'insider dealing', holding onto knowledge so that the community's need for service remains. Behind every criticism of the lawyer's or the doctor's jargon and behind the emergence of alternative therapies and of self-help groups lurks the suspicion that professionals are not so much elites offering service as they are self serving elites. It is this suspicion, far more than a dissatisfaction with corporatist structures, that has fuelled the criticism of professionals, from all political angles, in recent years.

And for no occupational group is this phenomenon of 'social distancing', this charge of self interest, more profound than teachers. Central to the very process of teaching is the giving away of knowledge, both substantive and pedagogic. The issue is plain enough: the role of the subject teacher is to pass on a knowledge of his or her subject. Increasingly, though, the teacher's role goes beyond the filling of empty vessels.

Shifts towards mixed ability teaching and student centred learning in the 1970s, integrated curriculum and records of achievement in the 1980s, vocational courses and distance learning in the 1990s and the emergence of online learning through the internet have pushed teachers both to develop the range of their pedagogic skills (their 'professionality') and to share these with their students. The 'secret garden' is no more; now the focus is on study skills, independent learning, supported self study, assistance programmes for parents who wish to support their offspring's educational progress and so on. Indeed, it might be argued that in as far as teachers have adopted a professional language, they have undermined this requirement to share their professionality especially amongst working class and ethnic minority students and their families. Thus, if the 'elaborated' code sometimes drawn on by educationalists is relabelled as a professional code used by middle class teachers, and by schools as middle class institutions, a powerful argument for not adopting a specialist language for the education professional, akin to that used by the doctor and the lawyer, emerges (Bernstein 1971 cited in Burgess 1985). Such a language can serve only to reinforce barriers of demarcation and exclusivity that are themselves likely to undermine the pedagogic rationale that informs teaching itself (Goodson and Hargreaves 1996).

The growing unpopularity of professionals, the elitism and subsequent social distancing that seems to accompany the professionalisation process and the pedagogic implications of professionalisation all serve to warn teachers away from any professionalisation project. There is, though, a final sense in which the prize of professionalism might be deemed a double-edged sword: the relationship between teachers collectively and the state and teachers individually, at school and college level, and those who manage them. Within this framework, the badge of 'professional' itself becomes a device through which the professionality of the individual is viewed and managed. Here, the shift to competence in teacher training, the focus on poor teachers and poor schools, the introduction of teacher appraisal, the micro-focused ethos of many 'school improvement' strategies and the school inspection process, all cited earlier as challenges to teacher professionalism, are claimed to be measuring devices of, and therefore necessarily accompany, the professionalism initiative. Thus, various state and quasi-state bodies claim to be the agents of teacher professionalisation rather than part of some deprofessionalising conspiracy. Given this additional concern, it may be wise to ask who best this new professionalism is likely to serve. Indeed, it may be wise to ask whether professionalism is the dream to pursue.

Towards new contexts and new identities

Professional identity, then, howsoever defined, arrives with considerable baggage. It is my central contention that this baggage may be too cumbersome to carry. Any professionalisation project is sure to be bound up with concerns over the declining status of professionals in recent years, allegations of elitism and self interest and the risk of managerial abuse on both a macro and micro level. Thus, the need is to consider new and progressive models of professionalism and to assess any post-professionalist model that might move beyond the current conception of a professional identity for teachers as an occupational group.

While progressive exponents of teacher professionalisation (Avis 1991; Barnett 1997; Bottery and Wright 1996; Lunt 1997; Whitty 1997) have acknowledged that the traditional model of professionalism is flawed in just these ways, they have refused to condemn a professionalist strategy out of hand. Instead, they have argued, variously, for a model that is democratic, jargon free, interdisciplinary, collaborative and participative, one that rejects both the old professionalism and 'the 'old' politics of education' (Whitty 1997). Partly, this rejection is based on the failings of the older model and its notable tendency to exclude parents, pupils and other interest groups from discussions of educational purpose and partly it constitutes a recognition of a new framework within which the education service must grow.

Barnett (1997) identifies the key task of the new professionalism as the management of incoherence. Rather than being tied to the predictability of the 'modern' era, professionality, professionalism and professionalisation offer strategies for dealing with the constant confusion and upheaval that characterise post-modernity. Thus, the emergence of 'niche' schooling, initially with the launch of city technology colleges and grant maintained status, and now through a much broader specialist schools programme and an associated city learning academy initiative, the reality of a 'core and periphery' dual labour market in education and the emergence of the New Public Management (Bottery 1996) demand rather than marginalise or undermine professionalist approaches in teaching. These developments are aided by further changes at both curricular and institutional level such as the already cited growth in distance learning, the expansion of further education and the promotion of life long learning. Together they call forth a new professionalism, based on the teacher as a facilitator of learning and characterised by a range of qualities, notably permissiveness of practice and pluralism of context, that might not traditionally have been associated with the term (Hargreaves 1994).

My contention is, though, that to suggest such a profound reworking of what we have always meant by professionalism is, frankly, to ignore the daily usage and understanding of the term. In marketing speak, the professionalism brand is being stretched too far. To promote a professionalism that is democratic, inclusive, collaborative and jargon free is actually to promote something else, something that retains only the stated altruistic claims, albeit the original ones, of professionalism while dispensing with the rest. Thus, to hold with the terminology of, and around, professionalism is to cling to exactly the traditional model criticised by progressive writers such as Barnett (1997) and Avis (1991). The terminology itself is too closely wedded to exclusivity, elitism, social demarcation and the rest to be reinvented and, therefore, it serves only to frustrate the sort of occupational practice that these theorists would implore teachers to pursue. Rather like the suburban comprehensive school that retains the term 'grammar' in its title, the old associations remain, and the suspicion is that these are intended to serve a small clique at the expense of a wider population of potential and needy beneficiaries. My suggestion is that, in clinging to the pursuit of a 'professional' identity, teachers themselves may damage rather than enhance their claims for a new and different status. As Ginsburg puts it:

> Adopting professionalism as a model for educators' engagement with/in communities may be inappropriate because of the undemocratic tendency within many versions of the ideology, not only to distance teachers from parents, students and other members of the community but to establish a hierarchical relation between professionals and the lay public.
>
> (Ginsburg 1997)

Further, teachers and schools risk developing this distance at a time when the aloofness of those standard-bearers for professionalism, doctors and lawyers, is being called into question by a post Alder Hey population, no longer willing to accept professional myths and the client dependency that these develop.

Instead there is a need to establish a new occupational identity for teachers with a collaborative altruism as its cornerstone, seeking something akin to Ginsburg's (1997) promotion of democratic politics, and a role for teachers within it, rather than a quasi-democratic attempt at professionalisation as an occupational strategy. This approach allows teachers to construct a new identity rather than to struggle with one that is beginning, on a much broader level, to wane. In so doing, teachers are encouraged to establish their own dream rather than to follow one that barely fits those most keen to wear it and one that translates, all too easily, into a management tool of control and deskilling. New working contexts demand new occupational identities even if the final rejection of the old identity, or at least its pursuit, creates insecurity and anomie in the short term. Herein lies the route to a longer term autonomy and authority for educators and with it the sort of *post-professional* identity that teachers now require.

Post-professional identity: reflections from a practitioner

To make the academic case for a post-professional identity is insufficient by itself, especially when such a case is largely made through a critique of the current professionalist strategy. The question is one of practical operationalisation; in plain terms, 'how do we do this?'

There is a key constraint on change. In Britain, arguably to a greater degree than in other western countries, the mainstream mass education system has been derived from one constructed for an elite: the universities and the public schools preceded wide-scale state education. Similarly, 'A' level preceded and outlived 'O' level, more recently GNVQ Advanced and AVCE awards preceded associated Intermediate and Foundation programmes. Therefore, the National Curriculum launched in 1990 differed little from that offered in the grammar or 'public' school of the late nineteenth century and, not surprisingly, teachers' subject identity remained fixed in just the same way. Thus, we talk not of the *teacher* of geography but of the *geography* teacher. Any attempt at departure, witness the Key Skills and AS elements within the Curriculum 2000 initiative, is presented as an attempt at 'dumbing down'. The newer subjects that have squeezed into the option blocks of the upper secondary timetable present themselves as a GCSE or A level course, whatever the consequence to the subject itself and the proposed teaching and learning involved. The politics of curriculum access require that it is so, homogenising learning and assessment in the process so that doing ten GCSEs, ten variations on a theme, is confused with curriculum breadth, ensuring that success remains with those who are 'good at exams'. Not surprisingly, initial teacher training follows suit with the subject not the pedagogy at the heart of the process, defining the identity of the profession and the *professional* in the process and confirming the school structure and its departmentalised subject tribes. Perhaps we should not be surprised that secondary schools have been so slow to notice or adopt the curriculum flexibility options that characterise the post 2000 National Curriculum, those underlined in the recently published 14-19 Green Paper (DfES 2002).

The argument, therefore, is plain: the foregrounding of the subject deskills teachers and constrains their activity. Further, at secondary level, it atomises an institution already dominated by a single occupational group into a series of subgroups, emphasising a Fordist division of labour, in which GCSE lies at the end of the production line and Ofsted are the visiting 'time and motion' department: scientific management writ large. Fifteen hundred young people on three or four acres with a bell that instructs them to change room on at least an hourly basis, a change necessary because the distinct tribes within *teacherhood*, organised by academic discipline, have convinced themselves that *under no circumstances* can English and mathematics be taught in the same room. Moreover, when the timetable is god, woe betide the community activity, the work experience interview, the careers talk or the learning need that gets in the way. Discipline has to precede learning not simply to clarify teacher-child relations but because blips are bangs in a system of this type.

And as is the case in such settings, change and disturbance, while fun for the inmates, is tough on the warders. Thus is explained a key conundrum of secondary teachers' occupational experience: their feeling, in a supposedly ordered system, is one of constant change and challenge and yet we have the curriculum of a century past. Intriguingly, in the primary sector, where a much weaker subject frame exists, the past five years have seen, with the introduction of the numeracy and literacy strategies, a complete change in two thirds of the curriculum offered and a concurrent, not simply consequential, increase in pupil performance. Meantime, the secondary sector has struggled with the relatively minor aspirations of Curriculum 2000, marginally to broaden the Advanced level curriculum while considering a more skills based approach. The problem would appear to be institutional, structural and systemic, rather than one of personal and collective teacher inertia; the structure of secondary schooling succeeding in maximising the feeling of change while frustrating this change in the process.

Moreover, the institutionalisation that alienates the student demoralises the teacher and disguises, or at best pointlessly contests, the reality of the modern school. For the secondary teacher lives the great pretence of secondary education: the suggestion is order, the reality much messier and the students enjoy the spectacle before them. Although inevitable, in this setting, student 'disaffection' isn't always soul destroying. Sometimes it is just more fun.

For the teacher, no such outlet exists. The secondary teacher's position is, and has always been, one of presiding over a particular kind of chaos and involving the kind of 'incoherence management' to which Barnett (1997) refers. In reality, teachers hold a multi-disciplinary, interdisciplinary occupational identity as managers, social workers, information technology specialists, carers, examiners, counsellors and so forth such that, often, their title as 'teacher' is more a statement of *occupational purpose* than job content. And yet *professionality* has remained central to their work; professionality not simply as teacher but as carer, counsellor, manager and the rest. Whitty's notion of professional literacy (1998) finds application not in terms of a knowledge of some narrow construct called *teaching* but constitutes, instead, a literacy that interprets and draws on a range of occupational identities that traditional professionalism may establish as distinct, separate and mutually exclusive. By comparison, post-professionalism is an amalgam across the structured divides of the modern world; more a plural, less a singular; more a matrix, less a hierarchy.

Here is the foundation from which a post-professional identity might be developed. At the core of any such identity remains professionality, 'a good job well done'. What is lost is the attitudinal extras that characterise so much professionalism: the distancing, the bureaucratisation, the implied consumer dependency and the self imposed isolation that is, at heart, non-collaborative and anti-democratic. As an experienced LEA adviser who has recently moved on from a position in a medium sized suburban education authority to the leadership of an independent educational charity, the implications for my own practice that arise from this analysis are becoming clearer. That my new responsibility is based around support for and promotion of the Education for Citizenship initiative only adds muster, if not a little irony, to the case. Building up the walls of the professional castle is not an option. All that this might involve (closing non-teachers out of the classroom, retreating from youth projects and community schemes, restricting the feed of assessment and appraisal information to those beyond the school) can only undermine the effectiveness and quality, the professionality, of teaching as an enterprise. Opening up networks, access to support services and parental information systems and the like offers a more positive alternative. However, the real challenge is to locate teachers, as the legitimate experts, at the centre of this exercise as facilitators and co-ordinators, celebrating and supporting their *professionalities*, in the process. The purpose of teaching is to develop and share skills and knowledge, usually as lead educators. Doing so is a complex and challenging task. In the school of the 21st century, the principle that underpins teachers' daily practice must surely be the same. It is time to cast aside the professional dream; time, indeed, to view the bigger pictures, those of the teacher and those of the school itself.

The post-professional teacher and the Citizenship School

The image presented here is of a team of creative professionals working in a school setting that is highly institutionalised and personally dis-empowering. Designed in the nineteenth century for *that* century, the structure of the secondary school in particular has become less and less effective in a world where neither students nor parents are deferential to those 'with an education' or the institutions they work in. As more have gained from the benefits of a universal education, they have become less subservient to it and more demanding of it. As teachers have sought to respond to these changes they have become more not less skilled at counselling, guidance, social work and the rest. Nonetheless, the *felt* reality has rarely been one of skills enrichment, of greater professionality. Rather, it has been that of being pulled in all directions, of being consumed by pastoral responsibility, bureaucracy, discipline or whatever while being required to make the school work as an institution. And, in this model, if there is nobody on the corridors at lesson change, on the lunch queue, out on the yard or field at the end of break, it doesn't.

Scientific management in the car plant finally unravelled in the 1970s. It probably began to really struggle in school settings at around the same time but on this we have been in denial. Rather, we have demanded of teachers that they become better at managing an increasingly less manageable set of responsibilities. Moreover, to stimulate them in this process we have rendered their practice open to scrutiny as never before. When there is under-performance in a system there is some merit in this. When that has been eradicated, there is a need to re-engineer aspects of the system itself, to move, as one author puts it, from 'school improvement' to school *transformation* (West-Burnham 2001).

To do otherwise is merely to burn out the engine, the teacher. The recruitment and retention crisis that teaching currently faces is surely evidence of such burn-out. The shortages, which of course are greatest in those schools in the most challenging circumstances, indicate a time to change tack. The challenge is to involve teachers in this change. Given the demonstrable resilience of educational institutions to reform, their ability to magnify the feeling of change amongst the teaching force and the institutionalisation of the profession itself as defender of the school, this is a tall order. However, I want to point to a number of initiatives or developments that might open up opportunities for the involvement of teachers in these transformative processes, processes that themselves lay the foundations for the post professional identity that I have argued here teachers need. In summary, the key dynamics are:

- the growth of in-school mentoring and guidance frameworks, led by non-teachers;

- the increased role played by classroom assistants and non-teaching support staff such as bursars;

- the emergence of 'out of school hours learning' and the role of non-teachers in this;

- the development of learning theory, especially around multiple intelligence frameworks;

- the gradual progress of skills based learning, if not to centre stage, then certainly to ringside;

- the evolution of the 14-19 continuum and the generic shift towards lifelong learning and away from lifetime careers;

- the emergence of Education for Citizenship as a key strand in the school curriculum and beyond.

There is not the space here to unpick each of these in detail but taken together, their impact on teachers, teaching and schooling is likely to be considerable. In terms of mentoring and guidance frameworks, the role of classroom assistants and non-teaching support staff and the emergence of 'out of school hours learning', one key pointer to the world of the post-professional teacher is clear: schools can no longer afford to be single profession sites. The emergence of the Connexions Service with its aspiration that every young person should have a personal adviser, the development, through frameworks like the Excellence in Cities programme and the National Mentoring Network, of learning mentors for particular student cohorts, the maturation of classroom assistants from 'mum's army' to first lieutenant, and the involvement of youth workers, artists in residence and sports coaches in 'out of school hours' learning programmes all point to a world where the teacher remains lead educator, but is no longer lone educator. The traditional professional reaction might be to contest these developments as incursion into the hollowed turf of teaching; the post-professional reaction is to embrace this new cluster that may be paramedics to the teachers' world but are also experts in their own right, their professionality neither subserviant nor in question. At the height of a teacher shortage this may, of course, be to say the unsayable: schools do not have too few teachers; *proportionately*, they have too many. From this standpoint, the 'staffroom' cannot simply be the *teachers'* room anymore. Rather, we need a mix of occupations capable of supporting, within and beyond the classroom, the educational, emotional and social needs of young people in the widest sense and those who teach them. *Non-contact time and class size might slip down the scale of teacher concerns if each teacher had the kind of administrative support that is the norm in the commercial sector.* As one teaching friend, an experienced and skilled head of year, said to me recently, '...just give me some administrative support, a PA for a couple of days a week, and I'll happily get on with the job'.

Recent (or at least for the classroom recently *noticed*) developments in learning theory, especially when coupled with the gradual progression of the skills agenda offer considerable support for the professionality required to underpin a post professional identity for teachers. The first, with its focus on multiple intelligence theory, 'brain based' learning and the need to support individual learning styles and preferences represents the re-assertion of pedagogy, of *learning* and teaching rather than *teaching* and learning. How striking that in the current overburdening of teachers, pedagogy, what teachers are best at, has so often been left to the margins and to chance. The second continues to question positively the purpose of teaching and, in particular, the purpose of atomised subject knowledge. Here, the emergence of 'thinking skills', the introduction of key skills and the policy priority around basic skills, both through the numeracy and literacy strategies at key stages 1 and 2 and 3 and the adult basic skills or 'skills for life' programme all indicate that progress is already underway. In the post professional teaching world, the subject curriculum may not slip gracefully into the past but it is unlikely to be quite so omnipotent. As such, it lays the path for the training of teachers rather than subject teachers, recognising the need to balance the expansion of knowledge with the need to develop the skills to apply that knowledge.

The emergence of the 14-19 continuum and lifelong learning and the decline of lifetime careers, especially when contextualised by the shift towards Education for Citizenship, have further implications for the both initial teacher training and the structure of the school. All three suggest something for the identity of the post-professional teacher. First, the 14-19 continuum; the narrowing of the subject core at this cross-over phase between secondary and further education coupled with the development of multiple assessment points along this continuum move us towards a more individualised curriculum that is not so tightly fixed to mass examination at 16. This opens the way for a less age related, 'just in time', graduation based accreditation structure that lays the foundation for learning in later life. Ultimately, it offers some escape from the dominance of a single examination but schools will need to feel sufficiently confident to make such a move.

Second, the emergence of lifelong learning as a major policy focus; the key point here is that a genuine lifelong learning model (Breslin 2000) requires a repositioning of the role of the school in the biography of individuals and communities. For the individual 'school' and 'education' are no longer synonymous. School is a part of the individual's educational career, not the sum total of it. For the community, the school is one among a set of 'learning centres'. This opens up the opportunity for adult, family and community learning initiatives within the school and the possibility that those young people who do not cope well with the school as a learning setting may access some other community learning setting. Both options produce a fundamentally more dynamic, less didactic relationship between the school and the community and between teachers, students, parents and others who come through the school's gates.

Third, the lifetime career issue; careers teachers and careers officers have long told their students that the 'career for life' model of employment is dead. Those now emerging into the world of work can expect to undertake two, three or four careers. Clearly, the scenario should be no different for those entering teaching. This has two implications; one, there will be more leakage from the teaching profession as younger individuals move onto other pastures; two, there will be more entry into teaching as older workers join the teaching force. Both of these developments should be welcomed. They suggest a more dynamic and mixed teaching force, in which, over a lifetime, a higher percentage of the population participate. In this context, the current practice of bemoaning the numbers leaving teaching as a mortal blow to the profession is misplaced. Rather, the challenge is to ensure that initial teacher training recruitment strategies reach a much wider base than they currently do. Here 'second careerers' emerge as a key target group.

And so to Education for Citizenship. The emergence of Education for Citizenship is well documented. Inspired by a growing democratic deficit, concerns over social inclusion and community cohesion, declining standards of social behaviour and low civic engagement, and the apparent dominance of a selfish, 'me-first' culture, Citizenship has moved to the centre of the educational arena. A National Curriculum subject from September 2002, the view remains prevalent that teaching Citizenship in forty five-minute lessons will, of itself, be insufficient. Thus, over the next five years or so, schools will need to develop a menu of provision – a mix of traditional lessons, special activities, events and cross curricular work – to meet the requirements of Citizenship in the National Curriculum. Here, the objectives are ambitious: to enhance political participation and political literacy, to assert and regenerate the importance of community through civic involvement and to develop a stronger sense of the rights and responsibilities of all. Here my contention is simple but I suggest not simplistic: that Education for Citizenship has the potential to fundamentally change the ethos of the school both *as* a community and *in* the community. As such, the school becomes a different place *to teach and to be a teacher*. One cannot teach community involvement without involving the community; one cannot teach social and moral rights and responsibilities without imparting more of both to the student body; one cannot teach democracy without operationalising it through all that the school does: the staffing structure, the governing body, the student council and so on. None of this sits easily with the traditional managerial hierarchy, disciplinary framework, pastoral system or curricular structure of the secondary school, at least as caricatured earlier. Nor does it sit with a model of teacher professionalism that is, inevitably, so heavily influenced by this institutional setting. Instead, the Citizenship School (Alexander 2001) is remarkable in its complementarity to the post-professional teacher. Thus, the model of schooling is open, inclusive, multi-disciplinary, parent friendly and community focused. The curriculum is open to at least some negotiation, has individual learning needs at its core, is less age related and delivers assessment and accreditation that is 'just in time' rather than 'all at once'. Clearly, such a school is a different place to learn and to teach in. More a set of principles than structures, it offers something, though, that all schools can progress towards, travelling only as far as they and their teachers and students are comfortable.

To seek to rebuild teaching or schooling separately is a folly. To begin to consider what we want each to offer, to each other and to their communities, five, ten, twenty years from now and to develop some models where both evolve together is both achievable and desirable. 'Post-professional' is, of course, an insufficient, even lazy, identity for the teaching force of the future but it does tell us that it is time to move on from where we are now, even if we have only principles for our destination.

From principles to practice: starting points for change

Rather than hard policy proposals, I want to conclude by making a series of tentative observations and pleas around the renewal of teaching and schooling within a 'post-professional' framework. In summary, these are that:

- Schools can no longer afford to be single occupation sites: mentors, advisers, coaches, artists, support staff, administrators need to join what is currently largely a teacher dominated community.

- In a post professional setting, teachers are lead educators but not sole educators and the standard mode of delivery is team rather than individual based.

- The Teacher Training Agency and its delivery partners need to focus on the development of teachers of subjects and skills rather than subject teachers and need to recognise that teaching will not be a lifetime career for all entrants, amending their recruitment strategies in consequence.

- Teaching salaries need to be competitive if the school system is to recruit those numbers that it needs to remain sustainable (Horne 2001) but immediate concerns around teachers' pay must not distract from the longer term objective of improving their working conditions and support structures, for the autonomy, creativity and potential of teachers is unlikely to be harnessed simply by more bucks at the end of the month.

- The emergence of the 14-19 continuum and greater curriculum flexibility, especially at Key Stage 4, should be used as a catalyst to move away from a single critical examination point at 16 and the crude 'league table' systems that derive from this.

- The shift towards a focus around lifelong learning opens up the opportunity for adult, family and community learning initiatives within a range of settings, including the school.

- Schools should be rewarded for using Education for Citizenship frameworks to re-engineer their form as organisations and their relationships with the communities that they serve, such that they become Citizenship Schools (Alexander 2001).

- Ongoing, externally verifiable, self-evaluation models should form the cornerstone of emerging approaches to school inspection and teacher performance.

Of course, the trick is not to impose the above changes but to create or identify settings in which they can be developed and assessed with teacher, learner and community support. While the current crisis around teacher identity and recruitment is not an ideal climate in which to innovate, necessity does require action now. At a time when excellence and diversity are central to the policy agenda, the time is ripe for the identification of a cluster of schools and teachers, from a range of circumstances and settings, that has the confidence and the will to develop complementary and innovatory models of school organisation and teaching practice. From these self selected starting points, we might begin to lay the foundations of schooling and teaching for the century ahead. The task is long overdue.

References

Abercrombie N, Warde A, Soothall K, Urry J and Walby S (1988) *Contemporary British Society* Cambridge: Polity

Alexander T (2001) *Citizenship Schools* Campaign for Learning, London

Apple MW (1997) *The Political Contradictions of Professionalism* Lecture given to students on the University of London's Doctor in Education programme 25 October

Apple MW and Oliver A (1996) 'Becoming Right: Education and the formation of conservative movements' *Teachers College Record* 3.1

Avis J (1991) 'Educational practice, professionalism and social relations' in Avis J, Carspecken P, Clason P, Green A, Hollands B, Johnson R, McEwan D and Vickers A (eds) *Education Limited: Schooling and the and the New Right Since 1979* London: Unwin Hyman

Ball S, Bowe R and Gewirtz S (1995) 'Circuits of Schooling: a sociological choice of school in social class contexts' *Sociological Review* 43.1

Barnett R (1997) *Higher Education: A Critical Business* Buckingham: Open University Press

Barton L, Barrett E, Whitty G, Miles S and Furlong J (1994) 'Teacher Education and teacher professionalism in England: some emerging issues' *Journal of Sociology of Education* 15.4

Bottery M (1996) 'The Challenge to Professionals from the New Public Management: implications for the teaching profession' *Oxford Review of Education* 22.2

Bottery M and Wright N (1996) 'Co-operating in Their Own Deprofessionalisation? On the Need to Recognise the 'Public' and 'Ecological' Roles of the Teaching Profession' British Journal of Educational Studies 44.1

Braverman H (1974) *Labor and Monopoly Capital* New York, Monthly Review Press

Breslin T (2000) 'Local Authorities, Schools and Lifelong Learning' in Lucas B and Greany T (eds) *Schools in the Learning Age* London: Campaign for Learning

Burgess RG (1985) *Education, Schools and Schooling* Basingstoke: Macmillan

Byers S (1997) 'Engine of change in motion' *Times Educational Supplement* 25 July

Davies C (1996) 'The sociology of professions and the profession of gender' *Sociology* 3.1

Department for Education and Skills (2002) *14-19: Extending opportunities, raising standards*

Englund T (1996) 'Are Professional Teachers a Good Thing?' in Goodson IF and Hargreaves A (eds) *Teachers' Professional Lives* London: Falmer Press

Ginsburg MB (1997) Professionalism or politics as a model for educators' engagement with/in communities *Journal of Education Policy* 12.1/2

Gomm R (1986) 'Population and Health' in McNeill P and Townley C (eds) *Fundamentals of Sociology* Cheltenham: Stanley Thornes (Publishers) Limited

Goodson IF and Hargreaves A (1996) 'Teachers' Professionals Lives: Aspirations and Actualities' in Goodson IF and Hargreaves A (eds) *Teachers' Professional Lives* London: Falmer Press

Hargreaves A (1994) *Changing Teachers, Changing Times: Teachers' Work and Culture in the Postmodern Age* London: Cassell

Horne M (2001) *Classroom Assistance* London: Demos

Hoyle E and John PD (1995) *Professional Knowledge and Professional Practice* London: Cassell

Hustler D and McIntyre D (eds) (1996) *Developing Teachers: Approaches to professional competence in teacher education* London: David Fulton

Illich I (1979) *Deschooling Society* London: Pelican

Jenkins E (1997) 'First choice instead of last resort' *Times Educational Supplement* 7 November

Lawn M (1996) *Modern Times? Working, Professionalism and Citizenship in Teaching* London: Falmer Press

Lunt I (1997) 'Values of professional groups dealing with special educational needs' in Lindsay G and Thompson D (eds) *Values into Practice in Special Education* London: David Fulton

Parry N and Parry J (1974) 'The Teachers and Professionalism; the Failure of an Occupational Strategy' in Flude M and Ahier J (eds) *Education, Schooling and Ideology* London: Croon Helm

Popkewitz TS (1994) 'Professionalization in Teaching and Teacher Education: Some Notes on its History, Ideology and Potential' *Teaching and Teacher Education* 10.1

Schon D (1983) *The Reflective Practitioner: How professionals think in action* New York: Basic Books

Shilling C (1991) 'Permanent Supports or Temporary Props? Supply Workers in State Schools and the National Health Service' *Gender and Education* 3.1

Somerville J (1986) Work and Industry in McNeill P and Townley C (eds) *Fundamentals of Sociology* Cheltenham: Stanley Thornes (Publishers) Limited

West-Burnham J (2001) Address to SHA Schools for the 21st Century conference, London, June 2001

Whitty G (1997) 'Marketization, the State, and the Re-formation of the Teaching Profession' in Halsey AH, Lauder H, Brown P, Wells AS (eds) *Education, Culture, Economy, Society* Oxford: Oxford University Press

Whitty G (1998) Lecture to University of London Institute of Education Ed.D students, Contemporary Education Policy Module, London, UK, 21 February

Wilby P (1997) 'Building up the ramparts of the professional castle again' *Times Educational Supplement* 14 November